Globalizing Capital

*

Globalizing Capital

A HISTORY OF THE INTERNATIONAL
MONETARY SYSTEM

*

BARRY EICHENGREEN

PRINCETON UNIVERSITY PRESS

PRINCETON, NEW JERSEY

Copyright © 1996 by Princeton University Press
Published by Princeton University Press, 41 William Street,
Princeton, New Jersey 08540
In the United Kingdom: Princeton University Press, Chichester, West Sussex
All Rights Reserved

Library of Congress Cataloging-in-Publication Data.

Eichengreen, Barry J.
Globalizing Capital : a history of the international monetary
system / Barry Eichengreen.
p. cm.
Includes bibliographical references and index.
ISBN 0-691-02880-X
ISBN 0-691-00245-2 (pbk.)
1. International finance—History.   2. Gold standard—History.
I. Title.
HG3881.E347   1996
332'.042—dc20   96-8084

This book has been composed in Times Roman

Princeton University Press books are printed on acid-free paper
and meet the guidelines for permanence and durability of
the Committee on Production Guidelines for Book Longevity of
the Council on Library Resources

Fourth printing, and first paperback
printing, with an update, 1998

http://pup.princeton.edu

Printed in the United States of America

5   7   9   10   8   6

* Contents *

* Preface *

THIS HISTORY of the international monetary system is short in two senses of the word. First, I concentrate on a short period: the century and a half from 1850 to today. While many of the developments I describe have roots in earlier eras, to draw out their implications I need only consider this relatively short span of time. Second, I have sought to write a short book emphasizing thematic material rather than describing international monetary arrangements in exhaustive detail. Its four main chapters are intended to be digestible in four sittings, as befits their origin as four lectures.

I attempt to speak to several audiences. One is students in economics seeking historical and institutional flesh to place on their textbooks' theoretical bones. They will find references here to concepts and models familiar from the literature of macroeconomics and international economics. A second audience, students in history, will encounter familiar historical concepts and methodologies. General readers interested in monetary reform and conscious that the history of the international monetary system continues to shape its operation and future prospects will, I hope, find this material accessible as well. To facilitate their understanding, a glossary of technical terms follows the text: entries in the glossary are printed in italics in the text the first time they appear.

This manuscript originated as the Gaston Eyskens Lectures at the Catholic University of Leuven. For their kind invitation I thank my friends in the Economics Department at Leuven, especially Erik Buyst, Paul De Grauwe, and Herman van der Wee. The Research Department of the International Monetary Fund and the International Finance Division of the Board of Governors of the Federal Reserve System provided hospitable settings for revisions. It will be clear to even the casual reader that the opinions expressed here are not necessarily those of my institutional hosts.

Progress in economics is said to take place through a cumulative process in which scholars build on the work of their predecessors. In an age when graduate syllabi contain few references to books and articles written as many as ten years ago, this is too infrequently the case. In the present instance, I hope that the footnotes will make clear the extent of my debt to previous scholars. This is not to slight my debt to my contemporaries, to whom I owe, among other things, thanks for comments on previous drafts. For their patience and constructive criticism I am grateful to Michael Bordo, Charles Calomiris, Richard Cooper, Max Corden, Paul De Grauwe, Trevor Dick,

Marc Flandreau, Jeffry Frieden, Giulio Gallarotti, Richard Grossman, Randall Henning, Douglas Irwin, Harold James, Lars Jonung, Peter Kenen, Ian McLean, Jacques Melitz, Allan Meltzer, Martha Olney, Leslie Pressnell, Angela Redish, Peter Solar, Nathan Sussman, Pierre Sicsic, Guiseppe Tattara, Peter Temin, David Vines, and Mira Wilkins. They should be absolved of responsibility for remaining errors, which reflect the obstinacy of the author.

Berkeley, California
February 1996

Globalizing Capital

*

Introduction

THE INTERNATIONAL monetary system is the glue that binds national economies together. Its role is to lend order and stability to foreign exchange markets, to encourage the elimination of balance-of-payments problems, and to provide access to international credits in the event of disruptive shocks. Nations find it difficult to efficiently exploit the gains from trade and foreign lending in the absence of an adequately functioning international monetary mechanism. Whether that mechanism is functioning poorly or well, it is impossible to understand the operation of the international economy without also understanding its monetary system.

Any account of the development of the international monetary system is also necessarily an account of the development of international capital markets. Hence the motivation for organizing this book into four parts, each corresponding to an era in the development of world capital markets. Before World War I, controls on international financial transactions were absent and international capital flows reached high levels. The interwar period saw the collapse of this system, the widespread imposition of *capital controls*, and the decline of international capital movements. The quarter-century following World War II was then marked by the progressive relaxation of controls and the gradual recovery of international financial flows. The latest period, starting with the 1970s, is again one of high capital mobility.

This U-shaped pattern traced over time by the level of international capital mobility is an obvious challenge to the dominant explanation for the post-1971 shift from fixed to flexible *exchange rates*. Pegged rates were viable for the first quarter-century after World War II, the argument goes, because of the limited mobility of financial capital, and the subsequent shift to floating rates was an inevitable consequence of increasing capital flows. Under the Bretton Woods System that prevailed from 1945 through 1971, controls loosened the constraints on policy. They allowed policymakers to pursue domestic goals without destabilizing the exchange rate. They provided the breathing space needed to organize orderly exchange rate changes. But the effectiveness of controls was eroded by the postwar reconstruction of the international economy and the development of new markets and trading technologies. The growth of highly liquid international financial markets in which the scale of transactions dwarfed official international reserves made it all but impossible to carry out orderly adjustments of currency pegs. Not only could discussion before the fact excite the markets and provoke unmanageable capital flows, but the act of devaluation, following obligatory denials, could damage the authorities' reputation for defending the peg. Thus, at the same time that pegged exchange rates became more costly to maintain, they became more difficult to adjust. The shift to floating was the inevitable consequence.

The problem with this story, it will be evident, is that international capital mobility was also high before World War I, yet this did not prevent the successful operation of pegged exchange rates under the classical gold standard. Even a glance back at history reveals that changes in the extent of capital mobility do not by themselves constitute an adequate explanation for the shift from pegged to floating rates.

What was critical for the maintenance of pegged exchange rates, I argue in this book, was protection for governments from pressure to trade exchange rate stability for other goals. Under the nineteenth-century gold standard the source of such protection was insulation from domestic politics. The pressure brought to bear on twentieth-century governments to subordinate currency stability to other objectives was not a feature of the nineteenth-century world. Because the right to vote was limited, the common laborers who suffered most from hard times were poorly positioned to object to increases in central bank interest rates adopted to defend the currency peg. Neither trade unions nor parliamentary labor parties had developed to the point where workers could insist that defense of the exchange rate be tempered by the pursuit of other objectives. The priority attached by *central banks* to defending the pegged exchange rates of the gold standard remained basically unchallenged. Governments were therefore free to take whatever steps were needed to defend their currency pegs.

Come the twentieth century, these circumstances were transformed. It was no longer certain that, when currency stability and full employment clashed, the authorities would opt for the former. Universal male suffrage and the rise of trade unionism and parliamentary labor parties politicized monetary and fiscal policymaking. The rise of the welfare state and the post–World War II commitment to full employment sharpened the trade-off between internal and external balance. This shift from classic liberalism in the nineteenth century to embedded liberalism in the twentieth diminished the credibility of the authorities' resolve to defend the currency peg.[1]

---

[1] The term "embedded liberalism," connoting a commitment to free markets tempered by a broader commitment to social welfare and full employment, is due to John Ruggie (1983).

This is where capital controls came in. They loosened the link between domestic and foreign economic policies, providing governments room to pursue other objectives like the maintenance of full employment. Governments may no longer have been able to take whatever steps were needed to defend a currency peg, but capital controls limited the extremity of the steps that were required. By limiting the resources that the markets could bring to bear against an exchange rate peg, controls limited the steps that governments had to take in its defense. For several decades after World War II, limits on capital mobility substituted for limits on democracy as a source of insulation from market pressures.

Over time, capital controls became more difficult to enforce. With neither limits on capital mobility nor limits on democracy to insulate governments from market pressures, maintaining pegged exchange rates became problematic. In response, some countries moved toward more freely *floating exchange rates*, while others, in Western Europe, sought to stabilize their exchange rates once and for all by establishing a monetary union.

In some respects, this argument is an elaboration of one advanced by Karl Polanyi more than half a century ago.[2] Writing in 1944, the year of the Bretton Woods Conference, Polanyi suggested that the extension of the institutions of the market over the course of the nineteenth century aroused a political reaction in the form of associations and lobbies that ultimately undermined the stability of the market system. He gave the gold standard a place of prominence among the institutions of laissez faire in response to which this reaction had taken place. And he suggested that the politicization of economic relations had contributed to the downfall of that international monetary system. In a sense, this book asks whether Polanyi's thesis stands the test of fifty additional years. Can the international monetary history of the second half of the twentieth century be understood as the further unfolding of Polanyian dynamics, in which democratization again came into conflict with economic liberalization in the form of free capital mobility and fixed exchange rates? Or do recent trends toward floating rates and monetary unification point to ways of reconciling freedom and stability in the two domains?

To portray the evolution of international monetary arrangements as many individual countries responding to a common set of circumstances would be misleading, however. Each national decision was not, in fact, independent of the others. The source of their interdependence was the *network externalities* that characterize international monetary arrangements. When most

---

[2] Polyani 1944.

of your coworkers use IBM PCs, you may choose to do likewise to obtain programming advice and to exchange data, even if there exists a technologically incompatible alternative (call it the Apple Macintosh) that is more efficient when used in isolation. These synergistic effects influence the costs and benefits of the individual's choice of technology. (For example, I wrote this book on a PC rather than a Macintosh because that is the technology used by most of my colleagues.) Similarly, the international monetary arrangement that a country prefers will be influenced by arrangements in other countries. Insofar as the decision of a country at a point in time depends on decisions made by other countries in preceding periods, the former will be influenced by history. The international monetary system will display *path dependence*. Thus, a chance event like Britain's "accidental" adoption of the gold standard in the eighteenth century could place the system on a trajectory where virtually the entire world had adopted that same standard within a century and a half.

Given the network-externality characteristic of international monetary arrangements, reforming them is necessarily a collective endeavor. But the multiplicity of countries creates negotiating costs. Each government will be tempted to free-ride by withholding agreement unless it secures concessions. Those who seek reform must possess political leverage sufficient to discourage such behavior. They are most likely to do so when there exists a nexus of international joint ventures, all of which stand to be jeopardized by noncooperative behavior. Not surprisingly, such encompassing political and economic linkages are rare. This explains the failure of international monetary conferences in the 1870s, 1920s, and 1970s. In each case, inability to reach an agreement to shift the monetary system from one trajectory to another allowed it to continue evolving of its own momentum. The only significant counterexamples are the Western alliance during and after World War II, which developed exceptional political solidarity in the face of Nazi and Soviet threats and was able to establish the Bretton Woods System, and the European Community (now European Union), which made exceptional progress toward economic and political integration and established the European Monetary System.

The implication is that the development of the international monetary system is fundamentally a historical process. The options available to aspiring reformers at any point in time are not independent of international monetary arrangements in the past. And the arrangements of the recent past themselves reflect the influence of earlier events. Neither the current state nor the future prospects of this evolving order can be properly understood without an appreciation of its history.

The Gold Standard

> When we study pre-1914 monetary history, we find ourselves
> frequently reflecting on how similar were the issues of monetary
> policy then at stake to those of our time.
> (Marcello de Cecco, *Money and Empire*)

MANY READERS will imagine that an international monetary system is a set of arrangements negotiated by officials and experts at a summit conference. The Bretton Woods Agreement to manage exchange rates and balances of payments, which emerged from such a meeting at the Mount Washington Hotel at Bretton Woods, New Hampshire, in 1944, might be taken to epitomize the process. In fact, monetary arrangements established by international negotiation are the exception, not the rule. More commonly, such arrangements have arisen spontaneously out of the individual choices of countries constrained by the prior decisions of their neighbors and, more generally, by the inheritance of history.

The emergence of the classical gold standard before World War I reflected such a process. The gold standard evolved out of the variety of commodity-money standards that emerged before the development of paper money and *fractional reserve banking*. Its development was one of the great monetary accidents of modern times. It owed much to Great Britain's accidental adoption of a de facto gold standard in 1717, when Sir Isaac Newton, as master of the mint, set too low a gold price for silver, inadvertently causing all but very worn and clipped silver coin to disappear from circulation. With Britain's industrial revolution and its emergence in the nineteenth century as the world's leading financial and commercial power, Britain's monetary practices became an increasingly logical and attractive alternative to silver-based money for countries seeking to trade with and borrow from the British Isles. Out of these autonomous decisions of national governments an international system of fixed exchange rates was born.

Both the emergence and the operation of this system owed much to specific historical conditions. The system presupposed an intellectual climate in which governments attached priority to currency and exchange rate stability. It presupposed a political setting in which they were shielded from pressure to direct policy to other ends. It presupposed open and flexible markets that linked flows of capital and commodities in ways that insulated economies from shocks to the supply and demand for merchandise and finance.

Already by World War I many of these conditions had been compromised by economic and political modernization. And the rise of fractional reserve banking had exposed the gold standard's Achilles' heel. Banks that could finance loans with deposits were vulnerable to depositor runs in the event of a loss of confidence. This vulnerability endangered the financial system and created an argument for lender-of-last-resort intervention. The dilemma for central banks and governments became whether to provide only as much credit as was consistent with the gold-standard statutes or to supply the additional liquidity expected of a lender of last resort. That this dilemma did not bring the gold-standard edifice tumbling down was attributable to luck and to political conditions that allowed for international solidarity in times of crisis.

PREHISTORY

Coins minted from precious metal have served as money since time immemorial. Even today this characteristic of coins is sometimes evident in their names, which indicate the amount of precious metal they once contained. The English pound and penny derive from the Roman pound and denier, both units of weight. The pound as a unit of weight remains familiar to English speakers, while the penny as a measure of weight survives in the grading of nails.[1]

Silver was the dominant money throughout medieval times and into the modern era. Other metals were too heavy (such as copper) or too light (gold) when cast into coins of a value convenient for transactions.[2] These difficulties did not prevent experimentation: the Swedish government, which was part owner of the largest copper mine in Europe, established a copper standard in 1625. Since the price of copper was one one-hundredth that of silver, full-bodied copper coins weighed one hundred times as much as silver coins of equal value; one large-denomination coin weighed forty-three pounds. This money could not be stolen because it was too heavy for thieves to carry, but wagons were needed for everyday transactions. The Swedish economist Eli Heckscher describes how the country was led to organize its entire transportation system accordingly.[3]

---

[1] An introduction to this topic, which explores it at greater length than is possible here, is Feavearyear 1931.

[2] Still other possibilities were precluded because the metals in question were insufficiently durable or too difficult to work with using existing minting technology.

[3] Heckscher 1954, p. 91.

8

Although gold coins had been used by the Romans, only in medieval times did they come into widespread use in Western Europe, beginning in Italy, the seat of the thirteenth-century commercial revolution, where merchants found them convenient for settling large transactions. Gold florins circulated in Florence, sequins or ducats in Venice. Gold coins were issued in France in 1255 by Louis IX. By the fourteenth century, gold was used for large transactions throughout Europe.[4] But silver continued to dominate everyday use. In *The Merchant of Venice* Shakespeare described silver as "the pale and common drudge 'tween man and man," gold as "gaudy . . . hard food for Midas." Only in the eighteenth and nineteenth centuries did this change.

This melange of gold, silver, and copper coin was the basis for international settlements. When the residents of a country purchased abroad more than they sold, or lent more than they borrowed, they settled the difference with money acceptable to their creditors. This money might take the form of gold, silver, or other precious metals, just as a country today settles a balance-of-payments deficit by transfering U.S. dollars or German marks. Money in circulation rose in the surplus country and fell in the deficit country, working to eliminate the deficit.

Is it meaningful then to suggest, as historians and economists sometimes do, that the modern international monetary system first emerged in the final decades of the nineteenth century? It would be more accurate to say that the gold standard as a basis for international monetary affairs emerged after 1870. Only then did countries settle on gold as the basis for their money supplies. Only then were pegged exchange rates based on the gold standard firmly established.

THE DILEMMAS OF BIMETALLISM

In the nineteenth century, the monetary statutes of many countries permitted the simultaneous minting and circulation of both gold and silver coins. These countries were on what were known as *bimetallic standards*.[5] Only Britain was fully on the gold standard from the start of the century. The German states, the Austro-Hungarian Empire, Scandinavia, Russia, and the Far East operated silver standards.[6] Countries with bimetallic standards provided the link between the gold and silver blocs.

[4] Spooner 1972, chap. 1.

[5] On the origins of the term, see Cernuschi 1887. Bimetallism can involve the circulation of any two metallic currencies, not just those based on gold and silver. Until 1772 Sweden was on a bimetallic silver-copper standard.

[6] Countries were formally on a silver standard when they recognized only silver coin as legal tender and freely coined silver but not gold. In practice, many of these countries were officially

9

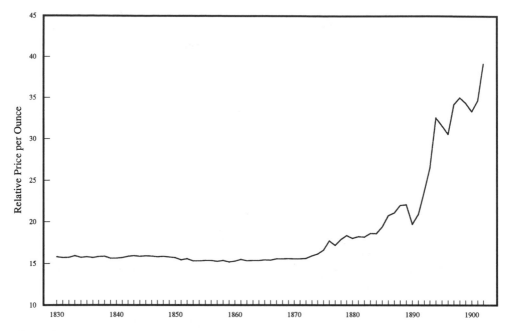

Figure 2.1. Relative Price of Gold to Silver, 1830–1902. *Source*: Warren and Pearson 1933.

The French monetary law of 1803 was representative of their bimetallic statutes: it required the mint to supply coins with legal-tender status to individuals presenting specified qualities of silver or gold. The mint ratio of the two metals was 15½ to 1—one could obtain from the mint coins of equal value containing a certain amount of gold or 15½ times as much silver. Both gold and silver coins could be used to discharge tax obligations and other contractual liabilities.

Maintaining the simultaneous circulation of both gold and silver coin was not easy. Initially, both gold and silver circulated in France because the 15½ to 1 mint ratio was close to the market price—that is, 15½ ounces of silver traded for roughly an ounce of gold in the marketplace. Say, however, that the price of gold on the world market rose more than the price of silver, as it did in the last third of the nineteenth century (see Figure 2.1). Imagine that its price rose to the point where 16 ounces of silver traded for an ounce of gold. This created incentives for arbitrage. The arbitrager could import 15½ ounces of silver and have it coined at the mint. He could exchange that silver coin for one containing an ounce of gold. He could export that gold

bimetallic, but their mint ratios were so out of line with market prices that only silver circulated.

and trade it for 16 ounces of silver on foreign markets (since 16 to 1 was the price prevailing there). Through this act of arbitrage he recouped his investment and obtained in addition an extra half ounce of silver.

As long as the market ratio stayed significantly above the mint ratio, the incentive for arbitrage remained. Arbitragers would import silver and export gold until all the gold coin in the country had been exported. (This can be thought of as the operation of *Gresham's Law*, with the bad money, silver, driving out the good one, gold.) Alternatively, if the market ratio fell below the mint ratio (which could happen, as it did in the 1850s, as a result of gold discoveries), arbitragers would import gold and export silver until the latter had disappeared from circulation. Only if the mint and market ratios remained sufficiently close would both gold and silver circulate.

"Sufficiently close" is a weaker condition than "identical." The simultaneous circulation of gold and silver coin was not threatened by small deviations between the market and mint ratios. One reason was that governments charged a nominal fee, known as *brassage*, to coin bullion. Although the amount varied over time, in France it was typically about one-fifth of 1 percent of the value of the gold involved, and somewhat higher for silver.[7] The difference between the market and mint ratios had to exceed this cost before arbitrage was profitable. Other factors worked in the same direction. Arbitrage took time; the price discrepancy motivating it might disappear before the transaction was complete. There were costs of shipping and insurance: even after the introduction of steamships in the 1820s and rail travel from Le Havre to Paris in the 1840s, transporting bullion between Paris and London could add another ½ percent to the cost. These costs created a corridor around the mint ratio within which there was no incentive for arbitrage.

That the mint in some countries, such as France, stood ready to coin the two metals at a fixed rate of exchange worked to support the simultaneous circulation of both gold and silver. If the world supply of silver increased and its relative price fell, as in the preceding example, silver would be imported into France to be coined, and gold would be exported. The share of silver coin in French circulation would rise. By absorbing silver and releasing gold, the operation of France's bimetallic system reduced the supply of the first metal available to the rest of the world and increased the supply of the second, sustaining the circulation there of both.

Market participants, aware of this feature of bimetallism, factored it into their expectations. When the price of silver fell to the point where arbitrage

---

[7] Brassage was greater for silver than for gold because silver coins were worth only a fraction of what gold coins of the same weight were worth and therefore entailed proportionately more time and effort to mint.

was about to become profitable, traders, realizing that the bimetallic system was about to absorb silver and release gold, bought silver in anticipation. The bottom of the band around the bimetallic ratio thus provided a floor at which the relative price of the abundant metal was supported.[8]

This stabilizing influence was effective only in the face of limited changes in gold and silver supplies, however. Large movements could strip bimetallic countries of the metal that was underpriced at the mint. With no more of that metal to release, their monetary systems no longer provided a floor at which its price was supported.

England is an early example. At the end of the seventeenth century, gold was overvalued at the mint. Brazilian gold was shipped to England to be coined, driving silver out of circulation. To maintain the circulation of both gold and silver coin, English officials had to increase the mint price of silver (equivalently, reducing the silver content of English coins) or reduce the mint price of gold. They chose to lower the price of gold in steps. The last such adjustment, undertaken by Newton in 1717, proved too small to support the continued circulation of silver coin.[9] In the face of continued gold production in Brazil, silver was still undervalued at the mint, and full-bodied silver coins disappeared from circulation. That England had effectively gone onto the gold standard was acknowledged in 1774, when silver's legal-tender status for transactions in excess of £25 was abolished, and in 1821, when its legal-tender status for small transactions was revoked.

In France, bimetallism continued to reign.[10] Napoleon raised the bimetallic ratio from 14⅝ to 15½ in 1803 to encourage the circulation of both gold and silver. Gold initially accounted for about a third of the French money supply. But the market price of gold rose thereafter, and as it became undervalued at the mint it disappeared from circulation. The Netherlands and the United States raised their mint ratios in 1816 and 1834, attracting gold and releasing silver, further depressing the market price of the latter. Scholars disagree about whether gold disappeared from circulation in France, or whether its share of the French money supply declined. The fact that modest amounts of gold were consistently coined by the French mint suggests that

---

[8] The tendency for expectational effects to stabilize an exchange rate within a band is emphasized by Paul Krugman (1991). Versions of the model have been applied to bimetallism by Stefan Oppers (1992) and Marc Flandreau (1993a).

[9] Newton's reputation for brilliance remains untarnished by these events. In his report on the currency he had suggested monitoring the market price of the two metals and, if necessary, lowering the price of gold still further, but he retired before being able to implement his recommendation.

[10] An introduction to French monetary history in this period is Willis 1901, chap. 1.

some continued to circulate. But even those who insist that gold was used as "pocket money for the rich" acknowledge that the French circulation was increasingly silver based.[11]

Gold discoveries in California in 1848 and Australia in 1851 brought about a tenfold increase in world gold production. With the fall in its market price, gold was shipped to France, where the mint stood ready to purchase it at a fixed price. French silver, which was undervalued, flowed to the Far East where the silver standard prevailed. When silver deposits were discovered in Nevada in 1859 and new technologies were developed to extract silver from low-grade ore, the flow reversed direction, with gold moving out of France, silver in. The violence of these oscillations heightened dissatisfaction with the bimetallic standard, leading the French government to undertake a series of monetary inquiries between 1857 and 1868.

In the United States, where many of these shocks to world gold and silver markets originated, maintaining a bimetallic circulation was more difficult still. For the first third of the nineteenth century, the mint ratio was 15 to 1 (a legacy of the Coinage Act of 1792), further from the market ratio than in France, and only silver circulated. When in 1834 it was raised to approximately 16 to 1, silver was displaced by gold.[12]

THE LURE OF BIMETALLISM

Given the difficulty of operating the bimetallic standard, its persistence into the second half of the nineteenth century is perplexing. It is especially so in that none of the popular explanations for the persistence of bimetallism is entirely satisfactory.

One theory, advanced by Angela Redish, is that until the advent of steam power the gold standard was not technically feasible.[13] The smallest gold coin practical for hand-to-hand use was too valuable for everyday transactions. Worth several days' wages, it was hardly serviceable for a laborer. It had to be supplemented by less valuable silver coins, as under a bimetallic standard, or by token coins whose legal-tender value exceeded the value of

[11] M. C. Coquelin 1851, cited in Redish 1992.

[12] The literature on the United States contains the same debate as that on France over whether both metals circulated side by side for any significant period. See Laughlin 1885. Robert Greenfield and Hugh Rockoff 1992 have argued that bimetallism led to alternating monometallism, whereas Arthur Rolnick and Warren Weber 1986 conclude that both metals could and did circulate simultaneously.

[13] See Redish 1990.

their metallic content, as eventually became the practice under the gold standard. But the circulation of token coins created an incentive to take metal whose market value was less than the value of the legal tender made from it and to produce counterfeit coins. Because screw presses powered by men swinging a beam produced a variable imprint, it was difficult to detect counterfeits. The difficulty of preventing counterfeiting is thought to have discouraged the use of tokens and to have delayed the adoption of the gold standard until the second half of the nineteenth century, when steam-powered presses capable of producing coins to high precision were installed in the mints.[14] England, for example, suffered a chronic shortage of small-denomination coins and rampant counterfeiting. In 1816 the British mint was fitted with steam-powered presses, and the abolition of silver's legal-tender status for small transactions followed within five years.[15]

While this theory helps to explain enthusiasm for bimetallism before the 1820s, it cannot account for the subsequent delay in shifting to gold. Portugal's strong trade links with Britain led the country to join Britain on gold in 1854, but other countries waited half a century and more. Of course, experience was required to master new minting techniques; the French mint experimented for years with steam-powered presses before finally installing one in the 1840s.[16] Even so, France clung to bimetallism until the 1870s.

A second explanation is that politics prevented silver's demonetization. Supporting silver's price by creating a monetary use for the metal encouraged its production. This led to the development of a vocal mining interest that lobbied against demonetization. Supplementing gold with subsidiary silver coinage also promised to increase global money supplies relative to those that would prevail if all money were gold based, profiting those with nominally denominated debts. Often this meant the farmer. As David Ricardo observed, the farmer more than any other social class benefited from inflation and suffered from a declining price level because he was liable for mortagage payments and other charges fixed in nominal terms.[17]

But while the secular decline in the economic and political power of Ricardo's agrarian class may account for some weakening of the silver lobby, it does not explain the timing of the shift away from bimetallism in

---

[14] Another alternative was silver monometallism, although the weight of the coins imposed costs on those engaged in large transactions. In addition, contemporaries such as David Ricardo, the English political economist, believed that chemical and mechanical advances were more applicable to mining silver than to mining gold, dooming countries that adopted silver monometallism to inflation. Ricardo 1819, pp. 360–61, cited in Friedman 1990, p. 101.

[15] Feavearyear 1931 describes Britain's failed attempts to introduce token coinage previously.

[16] See Thuillier 1983.

[17] Ricardo 1810, pp. 136–37.

continental Europe. And there is not much evidence that the monetary debate was dominated by conflict between farmers and manufacturers or that either group presented a unified front. Marc Flandreau has surveyed monetary hearings and inquiries undertaken in European countries in the 1860s and 1870s without finding much evidence that farmers uniformly lobbied for the retention of silver or that manufacturers were uniformly opposed.[18] Politicking over the monetary standard there was, but divisions were more complex than urban versus rural or agrarian versus industrial.[19]

If not these factors, what then was responsible for the persistence of bimetallism and for the delay in going onto gold? Bimetallism was held in place by the kind of network externalities described in the preface to this book.[20] There were advantages to maintaining the same international monetary arrangements that other countries had. Doing so simplified trade. This was apparent in the behavior of Sweden, a silver-standard country that established a parallel gold-based system for clearing transactions with Britain. A common monetary standard facilitated foreign borrowing: this was evident in the behavior of Argentina, a debtor country that cleared international payments with gold even though domestic transactions used inconvertible paper. And a common standard minimized confusion caused by the internal circulation of coins minted in neighboring countries.

Hence, the disadvantages of the prevailing system had to be pronounced before there was an incentive to abandon it. As one Dutch diplomat put it, as long as Holland stood between Germany and Britain financially and geographically it had an incentive to conform to their monetary practices.[21] Shocks that splintered the solidarity of the bimetallic bloc were needed for that incentive to be overcome. Eventually such shocks occurred with the spread of the industrial revolution and the international rivalry that culminated in the Franco-Prussian War. Until then, network externalities held bimetallism in place.

THE ADVENT OF THE GOLD STANDARD

The third quarter of the nineteenth century was marked by mounting strains on the bimetallic system. Britain, which had adopted the gold standard

---

[18] See Flandreau 1993b.

[19] Jeffry Frieden (1994) identifies a variety of sectoral cleavages over the monetary standard, emphasizing the distinction between producers of traded and nontraded goods.

[20] In addition, governments that altered their monetary standard by demonetizing silver might not be believed the next time they asserted that they stood behind their legal tender. Reputational considerations thereby lent inertia to the bimetallic standard, as they do to all monetary systems.

[21] Cited in Gallarotti 1993, p. 38.

largely by accident, emerged as the world's leading industrial and commercial power. Portugal, which traded heavily with Britain, adopted the gold standard in 1854. Suddenly there was the prospect that the Western world might splinter into gold and silver or gold and bimetallic blocs.

The European continent, meanwhile, experienced growing difficulties in operating its bimetallic standard. The growth of international transactions, a consequence of the tariff reductions of the 1860s and declining transport costs, led to the increased circulation in many countries of foreign silver coins. Steam power having come to the mint, most of these were tokens. In 1862, following political unification, Italy adopted a monetary reform that provided for the issue of small-denomination silver coins that were 0.835 fine (whose metallic content was only 83.5 percent their legal tender value; see *fineness* in the Glossary). Individuals used Italian coins when possible and hoarded their more valuable French coins (which were 0.9 fine). This practice threatened to flood France with Italian money and drive French money out of circulation. In response, France reduced the fineness of its small-denomination coins from 0.9 to 0.835 in 1864. But Switzerland meanwhile went to 0.8 fineness, and Swiss coins then threatened to drive French, Italian, and Belgian money out of circulation.[22]

Conscious of their interdependence, the countries concerned convened an international conference in 1865 (the first of several such conferences held over the next quarter-century).[23] Belgium provided much of the impetus for the meeting, coin of Belgian issue having all but vanished from domestic circulation. The result was the Latin Monetary Union. The union agreement committed Belgium, France, Italy, and Switzerland (joined subsequently by Greece) to harmonize their silver coinage on a 0.835 basis.[24] Britain was invited to participate but declined. Enabling legislation was introduced into the Congress of the United States, a body with considerable sympathy for silver coinage. But the United States was only beginning to recover from a civil war financed by issues of inconvertible greenbacks and was therefore in no position to act (see *inconvertibility* in the Glossary).

On this fragile position a series of shocks was then superimposed. The outbreak of the Franco-Prussian War forced France, Russia, Italy, and the

---

[22] An introduction to this history is de Cecco 1974.

[23] The authoritative account of these conferences remains Russell 1898.

[24] The other formal monetary agreement of significance was the Scandinavian Monetary Union, established in 1873 in response to Germany's shift from silver to gold. Because they depended on Germany for trade, the members of the Scandinavian Union, Sweden, Denmark, and Norway, sought to follow their larger neighbor. Given that their monies circulated interchangeably (each country recognized the monies of the others as legal tender), the three governments had a strong incentive to coordinate the shift.

Austro-Hungarian Empire to suspend *convertibility*. Britain became an island of monetary stability. Suddenly it was no longer clear what form the postwar monetary system would take.

Germany tipped the balance. Since inconvertible paper currency rather than silver circulated in Austria-Hungary and Russia, the silver standard was of no advantage in Germany's trade with the east. In any case, the British market, organized around gold, and not that of Eastern Europe, had expanded most rapidly in the first two-thirds of the nineteenth century. A significant portion of Germany's trade was financed in London by credits denominated in sterling and hence stable in terms of gold. The establishment of the German Empire diminished the relevance of reputational considerations; the old monetary system could be dismissed as an artifact of the previous regime, allowing the government to abolish the unlimited coinage of silver without damaging its reputation.

The indemnity received by Germany from France as a result of the latter's defeat in the Franco-Prussian War provided the basis for Germany's new gold-based currency unit, the mark.[25] The peace treaty of Frankfurt, concluded in 1871, committed France to pay an indemnity of 5 billion francs. Germany used the proceeds to accumulate gold, coining the specie it obtained. Meanwhile, Germany sold silver for gold on world markets.[26]

This first step toward the creation of an international gold standard lent further momentum to the process. Germany was the leading industrial power of continental Europe. Berlin had come to rival Paris as the continent's leading financial center. With this one shift in standard, the attractions of gold were considerably enhanced.

Historians usually explain the subsequent move to the gold standard by citing silver discoveries in Nevada and elsewhere in the 1850s and Germany's liquidation of the metal.[27] These events glutted the world silver market, it is said, creating difficulties for countries seeking to operate bimetallic standards. Coming on the heels of the discovery of new deposits, Germany's decision supposedly provoked a chain reaction: its liquidation of silver further depressed the metal's market price, forcing other countries to submit to inflationary silver imports or to abandon bimetallism for gold.

Difficulties there may have been, but their magnitude should not be exag-

[25] Initially, silver coins could still be struck at a gold-to-silver ratio of 15½ to 1. Only gold could be coined on demand, however, and starting in 1873 the coinage of silver was limited by the imperial government.

[26] Germany moderated the pace at which it converted its stock of silver into gold in order to avoid driving down the price of the metal it was in the process of liquidating. See Eichengreen and Flandreau 1996.

[27] See, for example, the references cited by Gallarotti 1993.

gerated. Considerable quantities of silver could have been absorbed by France and the other bimetallic countries without destabilizing their bimetallic standards. The composition of the circulation in bimetallic countries could have simply shifted toward a higher ratio of silver to gold. Stefan Oppers calculates that, as a result of Germany's demonetization of silver, the share of gold in the money supplies of the countries of the Latin Monetary Union would have declined from 57 percent in 1873 to 48 percent in 1879 but that the 15½ to 1 mint ratio would not have been threatened.[28]

Why, then, did a procession of European countries pick the 1870s to adopt the gold standard? At one level the answer is the industrial revolution. Its symbol, the steam engine, removed the technical obstacle. Industrialization rendered the one country already on gold, Great Britain, the world's leading economic power and the main source of foreign finance. This encouraged other countries seeking to trade with and import capital from Britain to follow its example. When Germany, Europe's second-leading industrial power, did so in 1871, their incentive was reinforced. The network externalities that had once held bimetallism in place pulled countries toward gold. A chain reaction, unleashed not by Germany's liquidation of silver but by the incentive for each country to adopt the monetary standard shared by its commercial and financial neighbors, was under way.

The transformation was swift, as the model of network externalities would predict. Denmark, Holland, Norway, Sweden, and the countries of the Latin Monetary Union were among the first to join the gold standard. They shared proximity to Germany; they traded with it, and Germany's decision strongly affected their economic self-interest. Other countries followed. By the end of the nineteenth century, Spain was the only European country still on inconvertible paper. Although neither Austria-Hungary nor Italy officially instituted gold convertibility—aside from an interlude in the 1880s when Italy did so—from the end of the nineteenth century they pegged their currencies to those of gold-standard countries. The United States omitted reference to silver in the Coinage Act of 1873; when the greenback rose to par and convertibility was restored in 1879, the United States was effectively on gold. The system reached into Asia in the final years of the nineteenth century, when Russia and Japan adopted gold standards. India, long a silver-standard country, pegged the rupee to the pound and thereby to gold in 1898, as did Ceylon and Siam shortly thereafter. Even in Latin America, where silver-mining interests were strong, Argentina, Mexico, Peru, and Uruguay instituted gold convertibility. Silver remained the monetary standard only in China and a few Central American countries.

[28] Oppers 1994, p. 3. Flandreau 1993 reaches similar conclusions.

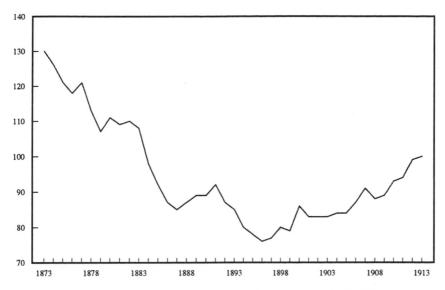

Figure 2.2. British Wholesale Prices, 1873–1913. *Source*: Mitchell 1978.

Milton Friedman and others have argued that international bimetallism would have delivered a more stable price level than that produced by the gold standard.[29] The British price level fell by 18 percent between 1873 and 1879 and by an additional 19 percent by 1886, as silver was demonetized and less money chased more goods (see Figure 2.2). Alfred Marshall, writing in 1898, complained that "the precious metals cannot afford a good standard of value."[30] Had free silver coinage been maintained in the United States and Europe, more money would have chased the same quantity of goods, and this deflation could have been avoided.

We should ask whether nineteenth-century governments can be expected to have understood that the gold standard was a force for deflation. It is reasonable to expect them to have understood the nature but not the extent of the problem. Post-1850 silver discoveries focused attention on the association between silver coinage and inflation. But there was no basis for forecasting the magnitude of the price-level decline that began in the 1870s. Only in the 1880s, after a decade of deflation, was this understood and reflected in populist unrest in the United States and elsewhere.[31]

[29] See also Drake 1985, Flandreau 1993b, and Oppers 1994.

[30] Marshall 1925, p. 192.

[31] Robert Barsky and J. Bradford DeLong's analysis of price-level movements in this period is consistent with this view. It suggests that the deflation was predictable, at least in part, but that an accumulation of evidence from the 1870s and 1880s was required before this became the case. See Barsky and DeLong 1991.

Why did countries not restore international bimetallism in the late 1870s or early 1880s when gold's deflationary bias had become apparent? A large part of the answer is that network externalities created coordination problems for countries that would have wished to undertake such a shift. The move was in no one country's interest unless other countries moved simultaneously. No one country's return to bimetallism would significantly increase the world money supply and price level. The smaller the country, the greater the danger that the resumption of free silver coinage would exhaust its gold reserves, placing it on a silver standard and causing its exchange rate to fluctuate against the gold-standard world. The wider the exchange rate fluctuations, the greater the disruption to its international finance and trade.

The United States, where silver-mining interests were strong and farmers opposing deflation were influential, convened an international monetary conference in 1878 in the hope of coordinating a shift to bimetallism. Germany, only recently having gone over to the gold standard, declined to attend. Its government may not have wished to have its policy of continued silver sales subjected to international scrutiny. Britain, fully committed to gold, attended mainly in order to block proposals for a monetary role for silver. Given the reluctance of these large countries to cooperate, smaller ones were unwilling to move first.

SHADES OF GOLD

By the beginning of the twentieth century there had finally emerged a truly international system based on gold. Even then, however, not all national monetary arrangements were alike. They differed prominently along two dimensions (see Figure 2.3).[32] Only four countries—England, Germany, France, and the United States—maintained pure gold standards in the sense that money circulating internally took the form of gold coin; and to the extent that paper currency and subsidiary coin also circulated, they kept additional gold in the vaults of their central banks or national treasuries into which those media could be converted. And even in those four countries, adherence to the gold standard was tempered. France was on a "limping" gold standard: silver remained legal tender although it was no longer freely coined. Bank of France notes were convertible into gold or silver coin by residents and foreigners at the option of the authorities. In Belgium,

---

[32] The basic reference for readers seeking more detail on the issues discussed here is Bloomfield 1959.

Domestic Circulation in the Form of:

		Largely Gold Coin	Gold, Silver, Token Coinage, and Paper
	Gold	England Germany France United States	Belgium Switzerland
Reserves in the Form of:	Largely Foreign Exchange	Russia Australia South Africa Egypt	Austria-Hungary Japan Netherlands Scandinavia Other British Dominions
	Entirely Foreign Exchange		Philippines India Latin American Countries

Figure 2.3. Structure of the Post-1880 International Gold Standard.

Switzerland, and the Netherlands, convertibility by residents was also at the authorities' discretion. Other instruments for encouraging gold inflows and discouraging outflows were the so-called *gold devices*. Central banks extended interest-free loans to gold importers to encourage inflows. Those with multiple branches, like the Bank of France and the German Reichsbank, could obtain gold by purchasing it at branches near the border or at a port, reducing transit time and transportation costs. They could discourage gold exports by redeeming their notes only at the central office. They could raise the buying and selling price for gold bars or redeem notes only for worn and clipped gold coin.

In the United States, the gold standard was qualified until 1900 by statutes requiring the Treasury to purchase silver. The Bland-Allison Act of 1878 and the Sherman Act of 1890 passed to placate silver-mining interests seething over "the crime of '73" (as the decision not to resume the free coinage of silver had come to be known) required the Treasury to purchase silver and mint it into coins exchangeable for gold at the old ratio of 16 to 1 (or to issue silver certificates entitling the holder to a commensurate amount of gold).[33] The 1878 act had been passed over President Hayes's veto, when the

---

[33] These were but two of a series of gestures that spanned much of the nineteenth century by hard-money groups seeking to keep inflationists at bay. See Gallarotti 1995, p. 156 and passim.

admission of western states dominated by free-silver men tipped the balance in Congress. The 1890 act was a quid pro quo for their conceding eastern industrialists' desire for the McKinley tariff, one of the most protectionist tariffs in U.S. history, adopted that same year.

The obligation to coin silver was limited. Under the Sherman Act the secretary of the Treasury was to purchase 4.5 million ounces of silver bullion each month and to issue a corresponding quantity of legal-tender Treasury notes. Because purchases were undertaken at the market price rather than the mint ratio, this was not bimetallism in the strict sense. Still, it raised questions about the credibility of the U.S. commitment to gold. Only in 1900 was that commitment solidified by the Gold Standard Act, which defined the dollar as 25.8 grains of 0.9 fine gold and made no provision for silver purchases or coinage.

In other countries, money in circulation took the form mainly of paper, silver, and token coin. Those countries were on the gold standard in that their governments stood ready to convert their monies into gold at a fixed price on demand. The central or national bank kept a reserve of gold to be paid out in the event that its liabilities were presented for conversion. Such central banks were usually privately owned institutions (the Swedish Riksbank, the Bank of Finland, and the Russian State Bank being exceptions) that, in return for a monopoly of the right to issue bank notes, provided services to the government (holding a portion of the public debt, advancing cash to the national treasury, watching over the operation of the financial system).[34] They engaged in business with the public, which created scope for conflict between their public responsibilities and private interests. The Bank Charter Act (Peel's Act), under which the Bank of England operated from 1844, acknowledged the coexistence of banking and monetary functions by creating separate Issue and Banking Departments.[35] Other countries, in this and in other respects, followed the British example. But, as we shall see, attempts to segment these responsibilities were not completely successful.

The composition of *international reserves* and the statutes governing their utilization also differed from country to country. In India, the Philippines,

---

[34] The extent to which such banks allowed their actions to be dictated by these responsibilities varied from country to country and over time. The Bank of Italy is an example of an institution that acknowledged its central banking functions relatively late. And their monopoly of note issue was not necessarily complete: in England, Finland, Germany, Italy, Japan, and Sweden other banks retained the right to issue currency, albeit at levels that were low and that declined over time.

[35] For details on Peel's Act, see Clapham 1945.

and much of Latin America, reserves took the form of financial claims on countries whose currencies were convertible into gold. In Russia, Japan, Austria-Hungary, Holland, Scandinavia, and the British Dominions, some but not all international reserves were held in this form. Such countries might maintain a portion of their reserves in British Treasury bills or bank deposits in London. If their liabilities were presented for conversion into gold, the central bank or government could convert an equivalent quantity of sterling into gold at the Bank of England. Japan, Russia, and India were the largest countries to engage in this practice; together they held nearly two-thirds of all foreign-exchange reserves.

The share of foreign balances increased from perhaps 10 percent of total reserves in 1880 to 20 percent on the eve of World War I.[36] The pound sterling was the preeminent reserve currency, accounting for perhaps 40 percent of all exchange reserves at the end of the period (see Table 2.1). French francs and German marks together accounted for another 40 percent. The remainder was made up of Belgian, Swiss, and French francs, Dutch kroner, and U.S. dollars, the last of which were important mainly for Canada and the Philippines.

Exchange reserves were attractive because they bore interest. They were held because governments borrowing in London, Paris, or Berlin were required by the lenders to keep a portion of the proceeds on deposit in that financial center. Even when this was not requested, the borrowing country might choose to maintain such deposits as a sign of its creditworthiness.

National statutes differed in the quantity of reserves the central bank was required to hold. Britain, Norway, Finland, Russia, and Japan operated *fiduciary systems*: the central bank was permitted to issue a limited amount of currency (the "fiduciary issue") not backed by gold reserves. Typically this portion of the circulation was collateralized by government bonds. Any further addition to the money supply had to be backed pound for pound or ruble for ruble with gold. In contrast, many countries of the European continent (Belgium, the Netherlands, Switzerland, and for a time, Denmark) operated *proportional systems*: subject to qualifications, their gold and foreign exchange reserves could not fall below some proportion (typically 35 or 40 percent) of money in circulation. Some systems (those of Germany, Austria-Hungary, Sweden, and for a period, Italy) were hybrids of these two forms.

Some monetary statutes included provisions permitting reserves to fall below the legal minimum upon the authorization of the finance minister (as in Belgium) or if the central bank paid a tax (as in Austria-Hungary, Ger-

---

[36] The definitive study of these questions is Lindert 1969.

23

TABLE 2.1
Growth and Composition of Foreign-Exchange Assets, 1900–13
(in millions of dollars)[a]

	End of 1899	End of 1913	Change	1913 Index (1899 = 100)
Official institutions	246.60	1,124.7	878.1	456
Known sterling	105.1	425.4	320.3	405
Known francs	27.2	275.1	247.9	1,010
Known marks	24.2	136.9	112.7	566
Other currencies	9.4	55.3	45.9	590
Unallocated	80.7	232.0	151.2	287
Private institutions	157.6	479.8	340.2	316
Known sterling	15.9	16.0	0.1	100
Known francs	—	—	—	—
Known marks	—	—	—	—
Other currencies	62.0	156.7	94.7	253
Unallocated	79.7	325.1	245.4	408
All institutions	404.2	1,622.5	1,218.3	401
Known sterling	121.0	441.4	320.4	408
Known francs	27.2	275.1	247.4	1,010
Known marks	24.2	136.9	112.7	566
Other currencies	71.4	212.0	140.6	297
Unallocated	160.4	557.1	396.7	347
Sum of sterling, francs, marks, and unallocated holdings				
All institutions	332.8	1,410.5	1,077.7	424
Official institutions	237.2	1,069.4	832.2	451
Private institutions	95.6	341.1	245.5	357

Source: Lindert 1969, p. 22.
[a]Details may not add up to totals because of rounding.
—. = not applicable.

many, Italy, Japan, and Norway). There was elasticity in the relationship between the money supply and gold and foreign-exchange reserves for other reasons as well. Statutes governing the operation of fiduciary and proportional systems specified only minimum levels for reserves. Nothing prevented central banks from holding more.[37] For example, the Banking Department of the Bank of England might hold as a cash reserve some of the £14

---

[37] Except, that is, the desire to minimize holdings of assets that bore no interest.

million in fiduciary currency emitted by the Issue Department. This would allow it to discount or buy bonds and inject currency into circulation without acquiring gold or violating the gold-standard statute. In countries with proportional systems, central banks might hold reserves in excess of the 35 or 40 percent of eligible liabilities required by statute and increase the money supply by buying bonds for cash even when there was no addition to their gold reserves. This lent flexibility to the operation of their gold standards. If currency was presented to the central bank for conversion into gold that was then exported, it no longer followed that the money supply had to decline by the amount of the gold losses, as it would under a textbook gold standard.[38]

This is not to deny that the process had limits. These were the essence of the gold standard, as we now shall see.

How the Gold Standard Worked

The most influential formalization of the gold-standard mechanism is the *price-specie flow model* of David Hume.[39] Perhaps the most remarkable feature of this model is its durability: developed in the eighteenth century, it remains the dominant approach to thinking about the gold standard today.

As with any powerful model, simplifying assumptions are key. Hume considered a world in which only gold coin circulated and the role of banks was negligible. Each time merchandise was exported, the exporter received payment in gold, which he took to the mint to have coined. Each time an importer purchased merchandise abroad, he made payment by exporting gold.

For a country with a trade deficit, the second set of transactions exceeded the first. It experienced a gold outflow, which set in motion a self-correcting chain of events. With less money (gold coin) circulating internally, prices fell in the deficit country. With more money (gold coin) circulating abroad, prices rose in the surplus country. The specie flow thereby produced a change in relative prices (hence the name "price-specie flow model").

Imported goods having become more expensive, domestic residents would reduce their purchases of them. Foreigners, for whom imported goods had

---

[38] To be precise, only if a country were sufficiently large to affect world interest rates or if domestic and foreign interest-bearing assets were imperfect substitutes for each other could central bank management alter the demand for money. Otherwise, any attempt by the central bank to prevent the money supply from declining by increasing its domestic credit component would simply lead to corresponding reserve losses that left the money stock unchanged. See Dick and Floyd 1992.

[39] See Hume 1752.

become less expensive, would be inclined to purchase more. The deficit country's exports would rise, and its imports fall, until the trade imbalance was eliminated.

The strength of this formulation—one of the first general equilibrium models in economics—was its elegance and simplicity. It was a parsimonious description of the balance-of-payments adjustment mechanism of the mid-eighteenth century. But as time passed and financial markets and institutions continued to develop, Hume's model came to be an increasingly partial characterization of how the gold standard worked.

Accuracy required extending Hume's model to incorporate two features of the late-nineteenth century world. One was international capital flows. Net capital movements due to foreign lending were larger, often substantially, than the balance of commodity trade. Hume had said nothing about the determinants of these flows—of factors such as the level of interest rates and the activities of commercial and central banks. The other feature was the absence of international gold shipments on the scale predicted by the model. Leaving aside flows of newly mined gold from South Africa and elsewhere to the London gold market, these were but a fraction of countries' trade deficits and surpluses.

Extending Hume's model to admit a role for capital flows, interest rates, and central banks was feasible. But not until the end of World War I in the report of the Cunliffe Committee (a British government committee established to consider postwar monetary problems) was this version of the model properly elaborated.[40] The Cunliffe version worked as follows. Consider a world in which paper rather than gold coin circulated or, as in Britain, paper circulated alongside gold. The central bank stood ready to convert currency into gold. When one country, say Britain, ran a trade deficit against another, say France, importing more merchandise than it exported, it paid for the excess with sterling notes, which ended up in the hands of French merchants. Having no use for British currency, these merchants (or their bankers in London) presented it to the Bank of England for conversion into gold. They then presented that gold to the Bank of France for conversion into francs. The money supply fell in the deficit country, Britain, and rose in the surplus country, France. In other words, nothing essential differed from the version of the price-specie flow model elaborated by Hume. Money supplies having moved in opposite directions in the two countries, relative prices would adjust as before, eliminating the trade imbalance. The only difference was that the money supply that initiated the process took the form

---

[40] See Committee on Currency and Foreign Exchanges after the War 1919. Hints of a price-specie flow model incorporating capital flows can, however, be found in, inter alia, Cairnes 1874.

of paper currency. Gold, rather than moving from circulation in the deficit country to circulation in the surplus country, moved from one central bank to the other.

But the Cunliffe version continued to predict, at odds with reality, substantial transactions in gold. To eliminate this discrepancy it was necessary to introduce other actions by central banks. When a country ran a payments deficit and began losing gold, its central bank could intervene to speed up the adjustment of the money supply. By reducing the money supply, central bank intervention put downward pressure on prices and enhanced the competitiveness of domestic goods, eliminating the external deficit as effectively as a gold outflow. Extending the model to include a central bank that intervened to reinforce the impact of incipient gold flows on the domestic money supply thus could explain how external adjustment took place in the absence of substantial gold movements.

Typically, the instrument used was the discount rate.[41] Banks and other financial intermediaries (known as *discount houses*) lent money to merchants for sixty or ninety days. The central bank could advance the bank that money immediately, in return for possession of the bill signed by the merchant and the payment of interest. Advancing the money was known as discounting the bill; the interest charged was the discount rate. Often, central banks offered to discount however many eligible bills were presented at the prevailing rate (where eligibility depended on the number and quality of the signatures the bill carried, the conditions under which it had been drawn,

---

[41] Another instrument for doing this was open-market operations, in which the central bank sold bonds from its portfolio. The cash it obtained was withdrawn from circulation, reducing the money supply in the same way that a gold outflow did but without requiring the gold shipment to take place. But open-market operations were relatively rare under the classical gold standard. They required a bond market sufficiently deep for the central bank to intervene anonymously. For most of the nineteenth century, only London qualified. Starting in the 1840s, the Bank of England occasionally sold government bonds (*consols*) to drain liquidity from the market. (It did so in conjunction with repurchase agreements, contracting to buy back the consols the next month, a practice known as "borrowing on consols," or "borrowing on contango.") From the end of the century, with the growth of the Berlin market, the German Reichsbank also engaged in the practice. In contrast, few other central banks employed open-market operations before 1913. In addition, central banks could intervene in the foreign-exchange market or have a correspondent bank do so in London or New York, purchasing domestic currency with sterling or dollars when the exchange rate weakened. Like a contractionary open-market operation, this reduced the money supply without requiring an actual flow of gold. The Austro-Hungarian Bank utilized the technique extensively. It was also employed by the central banks of Belgium, Germany, Holland, Sweden, and Switzerland. Countries with extensive foreign-exchange reserves but underdeveloped financial markets, like India, the Philippines, Ceylon, and Siam, utilized this device to the exclusion of others. See Bloomfield 1959.

and its term to maturity). If the bank raised the the rate and made discounting more expensive, fewer financial intermediaries would be inclined to present bills for discount and to obtain cash from the central bank. By manipulating its discount rate, the central bank could thereby affect the volume of domestic credit.[42] It could increase or reduce the availability of credit to restore balance-of-payments equilibrium without requiring gold flows to take place.[43] When a central bank anticipating gold losses raised its discount rate, reducing its holdings of domestic interest-bearing assets, cash was drained from the market. The money supply declined and external balance was restored without requiring actual gold outflows.[44]

This behavior on the part of central banks came to be known as playing by the rules of the game. There existed no rule book prescribing such behavior, of course. "The rules of the game" was a phrase coined in 1925 by the English economist John Maynard Keynes, when the prewar gold standard was but a memory.[45] That the term was introduced at that late date should make us suspicious that central banks were guided, even implicitly, by a rigid code of conduct.

In fact, they were not so guided, although this discovery was made only indirectly. In an influential treatise published in 1944 whose purpose was to explain why the international monetary system had functioned so poorly in the 1920s and 1930s, Ragnar Nurkse tabulated by country and year the number of times between 1922 and 1938 that the domestic and foreign assets of central banks moved together, as if the authorities had adhered to "the rules of the game," and the number of times they did not.[46] Finding that domestic

[42] In addition, it could alter the terms of discounting (broadening or limiting the eligibility of different classes of bills) or announce the rationing of discounts (as the Bank of England did in 1795–96).

[43] Thus, even if the money supply were exogenous (see Dick and Floyd 1992), central bank intervention could still affect the volume of gold flows needed for the restoration of payments equilibrium by altering the share of the money stock backed by international reserves.

[44] Along with providing a place for central banks in the operation of the gold standard, this mechanism introduces a role for capital flows in adjustment. When a central bank losing gold raised its discount rate, it made that market more attractive for investors seeking remunerative short-term investments, assuming that domestic and foreign assets were imperfect substitutes, which allowed for some slippage between on- and off-shore interest rates. Higher interest rates rendered the domestic market more attractive for investors seeking remunerative short-term investments and attracted capital from abroad. Thus, discount rate increases worked to stem gold losses not only by damping the demand for imports but also by attracting capital.

[45] His first use of the phrase may have been in *The Economic Consequences of Mr. Churchill* (1925, reprinted in Keynes 1932, p. 259).

[46] Imagine that gold begins to flow out and that the central bank responds by selling bonds from its portfolio for cash, reducing currency in circulation and thereby stemming the gold

and foreign assets moved in opposite directions in the majority of years, Nurkse attributed the instability of the interwar gold standard to widespread violations of the rules and, by implication, the stability of the classical gold standard to their preservation. But when in 1959 Arthur Bloomfield replicated Nurkse's exercise using prewar data, he found to his surprise that violations of the rules were equally prevalent before 1913.

Clearly, then, factors other than the balance of payments influenced central banks' decisions about where to set the discount rate. Profitability was one of these, given that many central banks were privately owned. If the central bank set the discount rate above market interest rates, it might find itself without business. This was a problem for the Bank of England beginning in the 1870s. The growth of private banking after mid-century had reduced the Bank's market share. Previously, it had been "so strong that it could have absorbed all the other London banks, their capitals and their reserves, and yet its own capital would not have been exhausted."[47] When the Bank's discounts were reduced to only a fraction of those of its competitors, a rise in its discount rate (*Bank rate*) had less impact on market rates. Raising Bank rate widened the gap between it and market rates, depriving the Bank of England of business. If the gap grew too large, Bank rate might cease to be "effective"—it might lose its influence over market rates. Only with time did the Bank of England learn how to restore Bank rate's effectiveness by selling bills (in conjunction with repurchase agreements) in order to drive down their price, pushing market rates up toward Bank rate.[48]

Another consideration was that raising interest rates to stem gold outflows might depress the economy. Interest-rate hikes increased the cost of financing investment and discouraged the accumulation of inventories, although central banks were largely insulated from the political fallout.

Finally, central banks hesitated to raise interest rates because doing so increased the cost to the government of servicing its debt. Even central banks that were private institutions were not immune from pressure to protect the government from this burden. The Bank of France, though privately owned, was headed by a civil servant appointed by the minister of finance. Three of the twelve members of the Bank's Council of Regents were appointed by the government. Most employees of the German Reichsbank were civil

---

outflow. Its foreign and domestic assets will both have declined; hence, this positive correlation is what we should expect had the monetary authorities been playing by the rules.

[47] In the words of Walter Bagehot, long-time editor of the *Economist* magazine. Bagehot 1874, p. 152.

[48] Another means of achieving the same end was for the central bank to borrow from the commercial banks, discount houses, and other large lenders.

servants. Although the Reichsbank directorate decided most policy questions by majority vote, in the case of conflict with the government it was required to follow the German chancellor's instructions.[49]

Any simple notion of "rules of the game" would therefore be misleading—increasingly so over time. Central banks had some discretion over the policies they set. They were well shielded from political pressures, but insulation was never complete. Still, their capacity to defend gold convertibility in the face of domestic and foreign disturbances rested on limits on the political pressure that could be brought to bear on the central bank to pursue other objectives incompatible with the defense of gold convertibility. Among those in a position to influence policy, there was a broad-based consensus that the maintenance of convertibility should be a priority. As we shall now see, the stronger that consensus and the policy credibility it provided, the more scope central banks possessed to deviate from the "rules" without threatening the stability of the gold standard.

THE GOLD STANDARD AS A HISTORICALLY SPECIFIC INSTITUTION

If not through strict fidelity to the rules of the game, how then was balance-of-payments adjustment achieved in the absence of significant gold flows? This question is the key to understanding how the gold standard worked. Answering it requires understanding that this international monetary system was more than the set of equations set out in textbooks in the section headed "gold standard." It was a socially constructed institution whose viability hinged on the context in which it operated.

The cornerstone of the prewar gold standard was the priority attached by governments to maintaining convertibility. In the countries at the center of the system—Britain, France, and Germany—there was no doubt that officials would ultimately do what was necessary to defend the central bank's gold reserve and maintain the convertibility of the currency. "In the case of each central bank," concluded the English economist P. B. Whale from his study of the nineteenth-century monetary system, "the primary task was to maintain its gold reserve at a figure which safeguarded the attachment of its currency to the gold standard."[50] Other considerations might influence at most the timing of the actions taken by the authorities. As long as there was no articulated theory of the relationship between central bank policy and the economy, observers could disagree over whether the level of interest rates

[49] On the politics of monetary policy in France and Germany, see Plessis 1985 and Holtfrerich 1988.

[50] Whale 1939, p. 41.

was aggravating unemployment.[51] The pressure twentieth-century governments experienced to subordinate currency stability to other objectives was not a feature of the nineteenth-century world. The credibility of the government's commitment to convertibility was enhanced by the fact that the workers who suffered most from hard times were ill positioned to make their objections felt. In most countries, the right to vote was still limited to men of property (women being denied the vote virtually everywhere). Labor parties representing working men remained in their formative years. The worker susceptible to unemployment when the central bank raised the discount rate had little opportunity to voice his objections, much less to expel from office the government and central bankers responsible for the policy. The fact that wages and prices were relatively flexible meant that a shock to the balance of payments that required a reduction in domestic spending could be accommodated by a fall in prices and costs rather than a rise in unemployment, further diminishing the pressure on the authorities to respond to employment conditions. For all these reasons the priority that central banks attached to maintaining currency convertibility was rarely challenged.

Investors were aware of these priorities. Machlup notes that there was little discussion among investors of the possibility of devaluation before 1914.[52] Foreign investment was rarely hedged against currency risk because currency risk was regarded as minimal.[53] When currency fluctuations did occur, investors reacted in stabilizing ways. Say the exchange rate fell toward the gold export point (where domestic currency was sufficiently cheap that it was profitable to convert currency into gold, to export that gold, and to use it to obtain foreign currency). The central bank would begin losing reserves. But funds would flow in from abroad in anticipation of the profits that would be reaped by investors in domestic assets once the central bank took steps to strengthen the exchange rate. Because there was no question about the authorities' commitment to the parity, capital flowed in quickly and in significant quantities. The exchange rate strengthened of its own accord, minimizing the need for central bank intervention.[54] It may be too strong to assert, as the Swedish economist Bertil Ohlin did, that capital

[51] The absence of a theory of the relationship between central bank policy and aggregate fluctuations is striking, for example, in the writings of Bagehot, the leading English financial journalist of the day. Frank Fetter (1965, p. 7 and passim) notes how underdeveloped banking theory was in the late-nineteenth century.

[52] Machlup 1964, p. 294. We will want to distinguish between countries at the center of the international system, with which Machlup was mainly concerned, and those at the periphery of the gold standard, both in southern Europe and in South America.

[53] Bloomfield 1963, p. 42.

[54] Econometric evidence documenting these relationships is supplied by Olivier Jeanne (1995).

movements of a "disturbing sort" practically did not exist before 1913, but it is undoubtedly true that destabilizing flows "were of relatively much less importance then than they were thereafter."[55]

Hence, central banks could delay intervening as ordained by the rules of the game without suffering alarming reserve losses. They could even intervene in the opposite direction for a time, offsetting rather than reinforcing the impact of reserve losses on the money supply. Doing so neutralized the impact of reserve flows on domestic markets and minimized their impact on output and employment.[56]

Central banks could deviate from the rules of the game because their commitment to the maintenance of gold convertibility was credible. Although it was possible to find repeated violations of the rules over periods as short as a year, over longer intervals central banks' domestic and foreign assets moved together. Central banks possessed the capacity to violate the rules of the game in the short run because there was no question about obeying them in the long run.[57] Knowing that the authorities would ultimately take whatever steps were needed to defend convertibility, investors shifted capital toward weak-currency countries, financing their deficits even when their central banks temporarily violated the rules of the game.[58]

INTERNATIONAL SOLIDARITY

An increase in one country's discount rate, which attracted financial capital and gold reserves, weakened the balances of payments of the countries from which the capital and gold were drawn. One central bank's discount-rate increase might therefore set off a round of such increases. "So long as the Bank of England and the Bank of France were both short of gold, any measure adopted by either to attract gold would be sure to evoke a counter-

[55] The first quotation in this sentence is from Ohlin 1936, p. 34; the second is from Bloomfield 1959, p. 83.

[56] The practice was known, for obvious reasons, as *sterilization* (*neutralisation* in France). It was impossible, of course, in the extreme case in which perfect international capital mobility and asset substitutability tightly linked domestic and foreign interest rates.

[57] This is John Pippinger's (1984) characterization of Bank of England discount policy in this period, for which he provides econometric evidence.

[58] Again, the analogy with the recent literature on exchange rate *target zones* is direct (see Krugman 1991). When reserves flowed out and the exchange rate weakened, capital flowed in because investors expected the authorities to adopt policies which would lead to currency appreciation, providing capital gains, subsequently. In other words, violations of the rules of the game in the short run still delivered stabilizing capital flows because of market confidence that the authorities would follow the rules in the long run.

acting measure from the other," was the way the English economist Ralph Hawtrey put it.[59] Similarly, a discount-rate reduction by one central bank might permit reductions all around. Bloomfield documented the tendency for discount rates to rise and fall together during the twenty years preceding World War I.[60]

Ideally, someone would assume responsibility for the common level of discount rates, which should be high when economies threatened to overheat but low when global recession loomed. When credit conditions were overly restrictive and a loosening was required, for example, adjustment had to be undertaken simultaneously by several central banks. The need for adjustment was signaled by rising reserve ratios, since gold coin moved from circulation to the coffers of the central bank and reserves rose relative to deposits and other liabilities with the decline in economic activity. Alternatively, the need for adjustment could be signaled by the level of interest rates (high when the economy was booming, low when it was depressed). Central banks therefore "followed the market," adjusting Bank rate to track market interest rates.

A limitation of this approach was its inability to anticipate and moderate predictable cycles in activity. For this, central bank rates had to lead market rates rather than follow them. This the Bank of England began to do in the 1870s, coincident with the advent of the international gold standard.[61] Such practices highlighted the need for coordination: if one bank reduced its discount rate but the others did not follow, the former would suffer reserve losses and the convertibility of its currency might be threatened. Hence, a follow-the-leader convention developed. The Bank of England, the most influential central bank of its day, signaled the need to act, its discount rate providing a focal point for the harmonization of policies. The Bank "called the tune"; in a famous passage, Keynes dubbed it "the conductor of the international orchestra."[62] By following its lead, the central banks of different countries coordinated adjustments in global credit conditions.[63]

[59] Hawtrey 1938, p. 44.

[60] Bloomfield 1959, p.36 and *passim*. See also Triffin 1964.

[61] The Bank had attempted to lead interest rates in the 1830s and 1840s. The 1857 financial crisis led, however, to the "1858 rule" of limiting assistance to the money market so as to encourage self reliance among financial institutions. Thus, attempts to lead the market starting in 1873 can be seen as a return to previous practice. See King 1936, pp. 284–287. The extent of this practice should not be exaggerated, however. There were limits, as discussed above, on how far the Bank could deviate from market rates without starving itself of or flooding itself with business.

[62] Keynes 1930, vol. 2, pp. 306–307.

[63] There is debate over exactly how much influence the Bank of England's discount rate exercised over those of other central banks, as well as over the extent of reciprocal influence. See Eichengreen 1987 and Giovannini 1989.

The harmonization of policies was more difficult in turbulent times. Containing a financial crisis might require the discount rates of different central banks to move in opposite directions. A country experiencing a crisis and suffering a loss of reserves might be forced to raise its discount rate in order to attract gold and capital from abroad. Cooperation would require that other countries allow gold to flow to the central bank in need rather than responding in kind. The follow-the-leader approach did not suffice. Indeed, a serious financial crisis might require foreign central banks to take exceptional steps to support the one in distress. They might have to discount bills on behalf of the affected country and lend gold to its monetary authorities. In effect, the resources on which any one country could draw when its gold parity was under attack extended beyond its own reserves to those that could be borrowed from other gold-standard countries.

An illustration is the Baring crisis in 1890, when the Bank of England was faced with the insolvency of a major British merchant bank, Baring Brothers, which had extended bad loans to the government of Argentina. The Bank of England borrowed £3 million of gold from the Bank of France and obtained a pledge of £1.5 million of gold coin from Russia. The action was not unprecedented. The Bank of England had borrowed gold from the Bank of France before, in 1839. It had returned the favor in 1847. The Swedish Riksbank had borrowed several million kroner from the Danish National Bank in 1882. But 1890 was the first time such action was needed to buttress the stability of the international gold standard and its key currency, sterling. "The assistance thus given by foreign central banks [in 1890] marks an epoch" was the way Hawtrey put it.[64]

The crisis had been precipitated by doubts about whether the Bank of England possessed the resources to defend the sterling parity. Investors questioned whether the Bank had the capacity to both act as lender of last resort and defend the pound. Foreign deposits were liquidated, and the Bank began to lose gold despite having raised the discount rate. Britain, it appeared, might be forced to choose between its banking system and the convertibility of its currency into gold. The dilemma was averted by the assistance of the Bank of France and the Russian State Bank. The Bank of England's gold reserves having been replenished, it could provide liquidity to the London market and, with the help of other London banks, contribute to a guarantee fund for Baring Brothers without depleting the reserves needed to make good on its pledge to convert sterling into gold. Investors were reassured, and the crisis was surmounted.

[64] Hawtrey 1938, p. 108.

This episode having illustrated the need for solidarity to support the gold standard in times of crisis, regime-preserving cooperation became increasingly prevalent. In 1893 a consortium of European banks, with the encouragement of their governments, contributed to the U.S. Treasury's defense of the gold standard. In 1898 the Reichsbank and German commercial banks obtained assistance from the Bank of England and the Bank of France. In 1906 and 1907 the Bank of England, faced with another financial crisis, again obtained support from the Bank of France and the German Reichsbank. The Russian State Bank in turn shipped gold to Berlin to replenish the Reichsbank's reserves. Also in 1907, the Canadian government took steps to increase the stock of unbacked Dominion currency notes partly to free up reserves for a U.S. financial system experiencing an exceptional credit squeeze.[65] In 1909 and 1910 the Bank of France again discounted English bills, making gold available to London. Smaller European countries such as Belgium, Norway, and Sweden borrowed reserves from foreign central banks and governments.

This kind of international cooperation, while not an everyday event, was critical in times of crisis. It belies the notion that the gold standard was an atomistic system. Rather, its survival depended on collaboration among central banks and governments.

THE GOLD STANDARD AND THE LENDER OF LAST RESORT

The operation of the gold-standard system rested, as we have seen, on the overriding commitment of central banks to the maintenance of external convertibility. As long as there did not exist a fully articulated theory linking discount policy and interest rates generally to the business cycle, there was, at most, limited pressure for the monetary authorities to direct their instruments toward other targets. The rise of fractional reserve banking, in which banks took deposits but kept only a fraction of their assets in the form of cash and liquid securities, challenged this state of affairs. It raised the possibility that a run by depositors could force the failure of an illiquid but fundamentally solvent bank. Some worried further that a bank run could shatter confidence and spread contagiously to other institutions, threatening the stability of the entire financial system. Contagion might operate through psychological channels if the failure of one bank undermined confidence in others, or through liquidity effects as the creditors of the bank in distress were forced to liquidate their deposits at other banks in order to raise cash.

[65] For details on Canadian policy in the 1907 crisis, see Rich 1989.

35

Either scenario created an argument for lender-of-last resort intervention to prevent the crisis from spreading.

Although it is hard to date the dawning of this awareness on the part of central banks, in England the Overend and Gurney crisis of 1866 was a turning point. Overend and Gurney was a long-established firm that had just been incorporated as a limited-liability company in 1865. The failure in 1866 of the Liverpool railroad-contracting company of Watson, Overend, and the subsequent collapse of the Spanish merchant firm Pinto, Perez, to which Overend and Gurney was known to be committed, forced the firm to close. Panic spread through the banking system. Banks sought liquidity by discounting bills with the Bank of England. Several complained that the Bank failed to extend adequate assistance. Concerned about the level of its own reserve, the Bank had refused to meet the demand for discounts. At the height of the panic it had failed to grant advances against government securities.[66] The panic was severe.

Partly as a result of this experience, the Bank of England had gained greater awareness of its lender-of-last-resort responsibilities by the time of the Baring crisis in 1890. The problem was that its desire to act as a lender of last resort might clash with its responsibilities as steward of the gold standard. Say that a British merchant bank was subjected to a run, as its creditors converted their deposits into cash and then into gold, draining reserves from the Bank of England. To support the bank in distress, the Bank of England might provide liquidity, but this would violate the rules of the gold-standard game. At the same time that its gold reserves were declining, the central bank was increasing the provision of credit to the market. As the central bank's reserves declined toward the lower limit mandated by the gold-standard statute, its commitment to maintaining gold convertibility might be called into question. Once worries arose that the central bank might suspend gold convertibility and allow the exchange rate to depreciate rather than permitting the domestic banking crisis to spread, the shift out of deposits and currency and into gold could accelerate, as investors sought to avoid the capital losses that holders of domestic-currency-denominated assets would suffer in the event of currency depreciation. The faster liquidity was injected into the banking system, therefore, the faster it leaked back out. Lender-of-last-resort intervention was not only difficult; it could be counterproductive.

In the 1930s the authorities were impaled on the horns of this dilemma, as we shall see in Chapter 3. Before World War I the predicament was still one

[66] These criticisms are recounted in articles in the *Bankers' Magazine*, as described by Grossman 1988.

that most of them managed to dodge. In part, the idea that central banks had lender-of-last-resort responsibilities developed only gradually; indeed, in countries like the United States there was still no central bank to assume this obligation. Many central banks and governments first accepted significant responsibility for the stability of their banking systems in the 1920s as part of the general expansion of government's role in the regulation of the economy. In addition, the credibility of central banks' and governments' overriding commitment to maintaining the gold standard parity reassured investors that any violation of the gold-standard "rules" for lender-of-last-resort reasons would be temporary. As it would in other contexts, therefore, foreign capital would flow in stabilizing directions. If the exchange rate weakened as the central bank injected liquidity into the financial system, capital flowed in from abroad as investors anticipated the currency's subsequent recovery (and the capital gains they would enjoy in the event). The trade-off between the gold standard and domestic financial stability was blunted. If investors required additional incentive, the central bank could increase interest rates to raise the rate of return. This was known as Bagehot's rule: to discount freely in response to an "internal drain" (a shift out of deposits and currency into gold) and to raise interest rates in response to an "external drain" (in order to contain the balance-of-payments consequences).

Further enhancing the central bank's room for maneuver were *escape-clause* provisions that could be invoked in exceptional circumstances. If a crisis were grave, the central bank might allow its reserves to decline below the statutory minimum and permit the currency to fall below the gold export point. As mentioned above, this was permitted in some countries upon the approval of the finance minister or with the payment of a tax. Even in Britain, where the gold-standard statute made no provision for such an action, the government could ask Parliament to authorize an exceptional increase in the fiduciary issue. Because this escape clause was invoked in response to circumstances that were both independently verifiable and clearly not of the authorities' own making, it was possible to suspend convertibility under exceptional conditions without undermining the credibility of the authorities' commitment to maintaining it in normal times.[67] In this way the gold-standard constraint on lender-of-last-resort intervention could be relaxed temporarily.

A further escape clause was invoked by the banking system itself. The

[67] This escape clause provision of the classical gold standard is emphasized by Michael Bordo and Finn Kydland (1994) and Barry Eichengreen (1994). Matthew Canzoneri (1985) and Maurice Obstfeld (1993a) demonstrate that a viable escape clause requires that the contingencies in response to which it is invoked are both independently verifiable and clearly not of the authorities' own making.

banks could meet a run on one of their number by allowing it to suspend operations and by collectively taking control of its assets and liabilities in return for an injection of liquidity. Through such "life-boat operations" they could in effect privatize the lender-of-last-resort function. In the case of a generalized run on the system, they might agree to simultaneously suspend the convertibility of deposits into currency. This last practice was resorted to in countries like the United States that lacked a lender of last resort. Because the banks all restricted access to their deposits simultaneously, they avoided deflecting the demand for liquidity from one to another. Because the restriction limited the liquidity of commercial bank liabilities, it led to a premium on currency (a situation in which a dollar of currency was worth more than a dollar of bank deposits). The demand for currency having been stimulated, gold might actually flow into the country, notwithstanding the banking crisis, as it did, for example, during the U.S. financial crisis in 1893.[68] Again, the potential for a conflict between domestic and international financial stability was averted.

INSTABILITY AT THE PERIPHERY

Experience was less happy beyond the gold standard's European center.[69] Some of the problems experienced by countries at the periphery are attributable to the fact that cooperation rarely extended that far. That the Bank of England was the recipient of foreign support in 1890 and again in 1907 was no coincidence. The stability of the system hinged on the participation of the British; the Bank of England then had leverage when the time came to enlist foreign support. Elsewhere the situation was different. The leading central banks acknowledged the danger that financial instability might spread contagiously, and countries like France and Germany could expect their support. But problems at the periphery did not threaten systemic stability, leaving Europe's central banks less inclined to come to the aid of a country in, say, Latin America.

Indeed, many countries outside Europe lacked central banks with which

[68] Another way to understand the response of gold flows is that investors realized that with a dollar's worth of gold they could acquire claims against banks that would be worth more than a dollar once the temporary suspension had ended; gold flowed in as investors sought to take advantage of this opportunity. Victoria Miller (1995) describes how this mechanism operated in the United States during the 1893 crisis.

[69] Analyses of gold-standard adjustment at the periphery include Ford 1962, de Cecco 1974, and Triffin 1947 and 1964.

such cooperative ventures might be arranged. In the United States, a central bank, the Federal Reserve System, was first established in 1913. Many countries in Latin America and other parts of the world did not establish central banks along American lines until the 1920s. Banking systems at the periphery were fragile and vulnerable to disturbances that could bring a country's foreign as well as domestic financial arrangements crashing down, all the more so in the absence of a lender of last resort. A loss of gold and foreign-exchange reserves led to a matching decline in the money supply, since there was no central bank to sterilize the outflow or even a bond or discount market on which to conduct sterilization operations.

Additional factors contributed to the special difficulties of operating the gold standard outside north-central Europe. Primary-producing countries were subject to exceptionally large goods-market shocks. Many specialized in the production and export of a narrow range of commodities, exposing them to volatile fluctuations in the *terms of trade*. Countries at the periphery also experienced destabilizing shifts in international capital flows. In the case of Britain, and to a lesser extent other European creditors, an increase in foreign lending might provoke an offsetting shift in the balance of merchandise trade. Increasingly after 1870—coincident with the advent of the international gold standard—British lending financed overseas investment spending.[70] Borrowing by Canada or Australia to finance railway construction created a demand for steel rail and locomotives. Borrowing to finance port construction engendered a demand for ships and cranes. The fact that Britain was a leading source of capital goods imports to the countries it lent money to thus helped to stabilize its balance of payments.[71] A decline in the volume of capital flows toward primary-producing regions, in contrast, gave rise to no stabilizing increase in demand for their commodity exports elsewhere in the world. And similarly, a decline in commodity export receipts would render a capital-importing country a less attractive market in which to invest. Financial inflows dried up as doubts arose about the adequacy of export revenues for servicing foreign debts. And as capital inflows dried up, exports suffered from the scarcity of credit. Shocks to the current and capital accounts thus reinforced each other.

Finally, the special constellation of social and political factors that supported the operation of the gold standard in Europe functioned less powerfully elsewhere. U.S. experience illustrates the point. Doubts about the

[70] Cairncross 1953, p. 188. See also Feis 1930 and Fishlow 1985.

[71] Other countries had weaker commercial ties with the markets to which they lent; their foreign lending did not stimulate exports of capital goods to the same extent. This point is documented for France, for example, by Harry Dexter White (1933).

depth of the United States' commitment to the prevailing dollar price of gold were pervasive until the turn of the century. Universal male suffrage enhanced the political influence of the small farmer critical of deflation. Each U.S. state, including those of the sparsely settled agricultural and mining West, had two senators in the upper house of the Congress. Silver mining was an important industry and political lobby. Unlike European farmers who competed with imports and whose opposition to the gold standard could be bought off with tariff protection, export-oriented American agriculture did not benefit from tariffs. And the fact that silver-mining interests and indebted farmers were concentrated in the same regions of the United States facilitated the formation of coalitions.

By the 1890s, the U.S. price level had been declining for twenty years. Deflation meant lower product prices but not a commensurate fall in the burden of mortgage debt. At the root of this deflation, the leaders of the Populist movement surmised, was the fact that output worldwide was growing faster than the global gold stock. To stem the fall in the price level, they concluded, the government must issue more money, ideally in the form of silver coin. The 1890 Sherman Silver Purchase Act was designed to achieve this.

When the Treasury purchased silver in exchange for legal tender notes, prices stopped falling, as predicted. Silver replaced gold in circulation. But as spending rose, the U.S. balance of payments moved into deficit, draining gold from the Treasury. It was feared that there might come a time when the Treasury would lack the specie required to convert dollars into gold. In 1891 a poor European harvest boosted U.S. exports, deferring the inevitable. But the victory of S. Grover Cleveland in the 1892 presidential election heightened fears; market participants worried that the newly installed Democrat would compromise with the powerful soft-money wing of his party. The collapse of another international monetary conference in December 1892, its participants having failed to reach agreement on an international bimetallic system, heightened this sense of unease. By April 1893, the Treasury's gold reserve had dipped below $100 million, the minimum regarded as compatible with safety, and public apprehension about currency stability became "acute."[72] Investors shifted capital into European currencies to avoid the losses they would

[72] Taus 1943, p. 91. Recall that the interregnum between the election and inauguration of a president stretched from early November to early March. The uncertainty that could arise as a result of such a long delay again figured importantly in the dollar crisis of early 1933, as I describe in Chapter 3.

suffer on dollar-denominated assets if convertibility were suspended and the dollar depreciated.[73]

In the autumn of 1893 Cleveland declared himself for hard money. The Sherman Act was repealed on November 1 on the president's insistence, saving the dollar for another day. But the underlying conflict had not been removed. It resurfaced during the next presidential campaign and was resolved only when the electorate rejected William Jennings Bryan, the candidate of the Democrats and Populists, in favor of the Republican, William McKinley. Bryan had campaigned for unlimited silver coinage, imploring the electorate not to crucify the American farmer and worker on a "cross of gold." The possibility of free silver coinage and dollar depreciation had prompted capital to take flight and interest rates to rise. Only with the victory of McKinley, himself a recent convert to the cause of gold and monetary orthodoxy, did tranquillity (and the flight capital) return.

That by 1896 prices worldwide had begun to rise improved McKinley's electoral prospects. Gold discoveries in western Australia, South Africa, and Alaska and the development of the cyanide process to extract gold from impure ore stimulated the growth of money supplies. Deposit money was increasingly pyramided on top of monetary gold as a result of the development of fractional reserve banking. The association of the gold standard with deflation dissolved. The dollar's position was solidified by passage of the Gold Standard Act of 1900.

Elsewhere, pressures for currency depreciation were not dispatched so easily. "Latin" countries in southern Europe and South America were repeatedly forced to suspend gold convertibility and to allow their currencies to depreciate. This was true of Argentina, Brazil, Chile, Italy, and Portugal.[74] Often, the explanation for their inability to defend convertibility was the political influence of groups that favored inflation and depreciation. In Latin America as in the United States, depreciation was welcomed by landowners with fixed mortgages and by exporters who wished to enhance their international competitiveness. And the two groups were often one and the same. Their ranks were swelled by mining interests that welcomed the coinage of silver. Latin American countries, particularly small ones, continued to coin silver long after the principal European countries had gone onto gold. Their gold losses and problems of maintaining the convertibility of currency into

[73] See Calomiris 1993.

[74] National experiences differed in that not all suspensions led to rapid depreciation and inflation. In particular, several European countries that were forced to suspend convertibility continued to follow policies of relative stability.

gold were predictable. Over much of the world, the absence of the special political and social factors that lent the gold standard its credibility at the system's European core rendered its operation problematic.

THE STABILITY OF THE SYSTEM

Open an international economics textbook and you will likely read that the gold standard was the normal way of organizing international monetary affairs before 1913. But as this chapter has shown, the gold standard became the basis for Western Europe's international monetary affairs only in the 1870s. It did not spread to the greater part of the world until the end of the nineteenth century. The exchange rate stability and mechanical monetary policies that were its hallmarks were exceptions rather than norms.

Least normal of all, perhaps, were the economic and political circumstances that allowed the gold standard to flourish. Britain's singular position in the world economy protected her balance of payments from shocks and allowed sterling to anchor the international system. Links between British lending on the one hand and capital-goods exports on the other stabilized her external accounts and relieved pressure on the Bank of England. The same was true, to an extent, of other countries at the gold standard's European core. In this sense, that the late-nineteenth century was a period of expanding and increasingly multilateral trade was not simply a consequence of the stability of exchange rates under the gold standard. The openness of markets and buoyancy of trade themselves supported the operation of the gold-standard adjustment mechanism. That overseas markets for British exports of capital goods were unobstructed allowed British merchandise exports to chase British capital exports, stabilizing the balance of payments of the country at the center of the system. That Britain and other industrial countries freely accepted the commodity exports of primary-producing regions helped the latter to service their external debts and adjust to balance-of-payments shocks. The operation of the gold standard both rested on and supported this trading system.

On the political side, the insulation enjoyed by the monetary authorities allowed them to commit to the maintenance of gold convertibility. The effects were self-reinforcing: the market's confidence in the authorities' commitment caused traders to purchase a currency when its exchange rate weakened, minimizing the need for intervention and the discomfort caused by steps taken to stabilize the rate. That the period from 1871 to 1913 was an exceptional interlude of peace in Europe facilitated the international cooperation that supported the system when its existence was threatened.

There are reasons to doubt that this equilibrium would have remained stable for many more years. By the turn of the century Britain's role was being undermined by the more rapid pace of economic growth and financial development in other countries. A smaller share of the country's capital exports was automatically offset by increases in its capital-goods exports. Less of its lending automatically returned to London in the form of foreign deposits.

As the gold discoveries of the 1890s receded, concern resurfaced about the adequacy of gold supplies to meet the needs of the expanding world economy. It was not clear that supplementing gold with foreign exchange provided a stable basis for the international monetary order. The growth of exchange reserves heightened the danger that shocks to confidence leading to the liquidation of foreign reserves would at some point cause the liquidation of the system. The growth of the United States, a leading source of shocks to global financial markets, raised the risk that crises might become more prevalent still. The United States, while still heavily agricultural, was by the end of the nineteenth century the largest economy in the world. The still heavily agricultural orientation of the economy, along with its relatively rudimentary rural banking system, meant that the demand for currency and coin—and along with it, the level of interest rates and the demand for gold—rose sharply each planting and harvest season. Much of this gold was drawn from London. With some regularity, U.S. banks that had run down their reserves in response to the demand for credit experienced serious difficulties. Fearing for the solvency of the banks, American investors fled to the safety of gold, drawing it from countries such as Britain and Canada and straining their financial systems. The ability of the Bank of England to draw gold "from the moon," in the famous words of English financial journalist Walter Bagehot, was put to the test.

Political developments were not propitious either. The extension of the franchise and the emergence of political parties representing the working classes raised the possibility of challenges to the single-minded priority the monetary authorities attached to convertibility. Rising consciousness of unemployment and of trade-offs between internal and external balance politicized monetary policy. The growth of political and military tensions between Germany, France, and Britain after the scramble for Africa eroded the solidarity upon which financial cooperation had been based.

The question of whether these developments seriously threatened the stability of the gold standard or whether the system would have evolved to accommodate them was rendered moot by World War I. But for those interested in speculating about the answer, there is no better place to look than to attempts to reconstruct the international monetary system in the 1920s.

Interwar Instability

The term 'The Gold Standard' embodies a fallacy, one of
the most expensive fallacies which has deluded the world. It is
the fallacy that there is one particular gold standard, and one only.
The assumption that the widely divergent standards of
currency masquerading under the name of the gold
standard are identical has recently brought
the world to the verge of ruin.
(Sir Charles Morgan-Webb, *The Rise and Fall
of the Gold Standard*)

IN THE previous chapter we saw how the prewar gold standard was supported by a particular set of economic and political circumstances specific to that time and place. Interwar experience makes the same point by counterexample. Sterling, which had provided a focal point for the harmonization of policies, no longer enjoyed a favored position in the world economy. Britain's industrial and commercial preeminence was past, the nation having been forced to sell off many of its foreign assets during World War I. Complementarities between British foreign investment and exports of capital goods no longer prevailed to the extent that they had before 1913. Countries like Germany that had been international creditors were reduced to debtor status and became dependent on capital imports from the United States for the maintenance of external balance.

With the spread of unionism and the bureaucratization of labor markets, wages no longer responded to disturbances with their traditional speed.[1] Negative disturbances gave rise to unemployment, intensifying the pressure on governments to react in ways that might jeopardize the monetary standard.[2] Postwar governments were rendered more susceptible to this pressure

---

[1] By the "bureaucratization" of labor markets, a term that follows the title of Sanford Jacoby's 1985 book, I mean the rise of personnel departments and other formal structures to manage labor relations in large enterprises.

[2] Using data from a sample of six industrial countries, Tamim Bayoumi and I (1996) found that there was a flattening of the average slope of the aggregate supply curve, consistent with the view that nominal flexibility declined between the prewar and interwar periods. Robert Gordon (1982) shows that this increase in nominal rigidity was greater in the United States than

by the extension of the franchise, the development of parliamentary labor parties, and the growth of social spending. None of the factors that had supported the prewar gold standard was to be taken for granted anymore.

The interwar gold standard, resurrected in the second half of the 1920s, consequently shared few of the merits of its prewar predecessor. With labor and commodity markets lacking their traditional flexibility, the new system could not easily accommodate shocks. With governments lacking insulation from pressure to stimulate growth and employment, the new regime lacked credibility. When the system was disturbed, financial capital that had once flowed in stabilizing directions took flight, transforming a limited disturbance into an economic and political crisis. The 1929 downturn that became the Great Depression reflected just such a process. Ultimately, the casualties included the gold standard itself.

A lesson drawn was the futility of attempting to turn the clock back. Bureaucratized labor relations, politicized monetary policymaking, and the other distinctive features of the twentieth-century environment were finally acknowledged as permanent. When the next effort was made, in the 1940s, to reconstruct the international monetary system, the new design featured greater exchange rate flexibility to accommodate shocks and restrictions on international capital flows to contain destabilizing speculation.

Chronology

If the essence of the prewar system was a commitment by governments to convert domestic currency into fixed quantities of gold and freedom for individuals to export and import gold obtained from official and other sources, then World War I terminated it abruptly. Precious metal became an essential resource for purchasing abroad the supplies needed to fuel the war machine. Governments passed laws and imposed regulations prohibiting gold exports except upon the issuance of licenses that they were rarely prepared to grant. With gold market arbitrage disrupted, exchange rates began to float. Their fluctuation was limited by the application of controls that prohibited most transactions in foreign currency.

To mobilize resources for the war, the authorities imposed new taxes and issued government bonds. When the resources so mobilized proved inadequate, they suspended the statutes requiring them to back currency with gold or foreign exchange. They issued *fiat money* (unbacked paper) to pay soldiers and

---

in the United Kingdom or Japan, consistent with its attribution to the bureaucratization of labor markets, given that personnel departments and internal labor markets developed and diffused first in the United States.

purchase war matériel at home. Different rates of fiat-money creation in different countries caused exchange rates to vary widely.

Consequently, part of the reconstruction following the war was monetary. By extending advances to their governments, the United States had helped its French and British allies to peg their currencies against the dollar at somewhat depreciated rates. The end of the war meant the end of this support. Inflation in Britain and elsewhere in Europe having outstripped that in the United States, the British government realized that the end of U.S. support would expose it to extensive gold losses if it attempted to maintain its overvalued pound, and it suspended convertibility. Of the major currencies, only the dollar remained convertible into gold. Although controls were dismantled quickly, years would pass before convertibility was restored.

A notable feature of postwar international monetary arrangements was the freedom of the float. As a rule, central banks did not intervene in the foreign-exchange market. The first half of the 1920s thus provides a relatively clean example of a floating exchange rate regime.

Among the first countries to reestablish gold convertibility were those that had endured *hyperinflation*: Austria, Germany, Hungary, and Poland. Their inflations had been fueled by the paper money used to finance government budget deficits. Eventually, the problem bred its own solution. Opposition to tax increases and spending cuts was overshadowed by the trauma of uncontrolled inflation and the breakdown of the monetary economy. Austria stabilized its exchange rate in 1923, Germany and Poland in 1924, Hungary in 1925. They issued new currencies whose supplies were governed by the provisions of gold-standard laws. Reserves were replenished by loans endorsed by the League of Nations (and in Germany's case by the Reparations Commission established to oversee compensatory transfers to the Allies). As a condition of this foreign assistance, the independence of central banks was fortified.

Countries that had experienced moderate inflation stabilized their currencies and restored gold convertibility without German-style *currency reform*. Belgium stabilized in 1925, France in 1926, Italy in 1927.[3] Each had endured inflation and currency depreciation during the period of floating. By the end of 1926 the French franc, for instance, purchased only one-fifth as many dollars as it had before the war. Since reversing more than a fraction of this inflation threatened to disrupt the economy, France and other countries in its position chose instead to stabilize their exchange rates around prevailing levels.

Countries in which inflation had been contained at an early date could

---

[3] In the French case, this refers to de facto stabilization of the franc. De jure stabilization followed in June 1928.

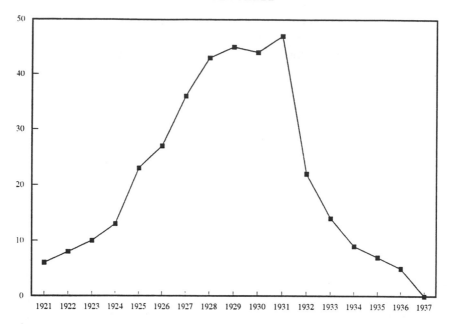

Figure 3.1. Number of Countries on the Gold Standard, 1921–37. *Source*: Palyi 1972, table IV-1.

restore the prewar price of gold and the traditional dollar exchange rate. Sweden did so in 1924. Britain's restoration of the prewar parity in 1925 prompted Australia, the Netherlands, Switzerland, and South Africa to follow. A critical mass of countries having restored the gold standard, the network-externality characteristic of the system drew the remaining countries into the fold. Canada, Chile, Czechoslovakia, and Finland stabilized in 1926. France followed at the end of the year. Figure 3.1 depicts the number of countries on the gold standard by year.

If France's stabilization in 1926 is taken to mark the reestablishment of the gold standard and Britain's devaluation of sterling in 1931 its demise, then the interwar gold standard functioned as a global system for less than five years. Even before this sad end, its operation was regarded as unsatisfactory. The *adjustment mechanism* was inadequate: weak-currency countries like Britain were saddled with chronic balance-of-payments deficits and hemorrhaged gold and exchange reserves, while strong-currency countries like France remained in persistent surplus. The adjustments in asset and commodity markets needed to restore balance to the external accounts did not seem to operate. The global supply of reserves was inadequate: it declined precipitously in 1931 as central banks scrambled to convert foreign exchange into gold.

Before World War I, as we saw in Chapter 2, the gold standard had never been firmly established outside the industrial countries, a failure that was blamed on the absence of the requisite institutions. Following the example of the United States, which sought to redress the shortcomings of its financial system by creating the Federal Reserve System in 1913, countries in Latin America and elsewhere established central banks in the 1920s. Money doctors, such as Edwin Kemmerer of Princeton University, roamed the world, preaching the gospel of the gold standard and central bank independence. But the mere existence of a central bank was no guarantee of stability. In keeping with the prewar pattern, the onset of the Great Depression in 1929 caused the gold standard to crumble at the periphery. Primary-producing nations were hit by simultaneous declines in capital imports and revenues from commodity exports. As their reserves declined, central banks were forced to acquiesce to the contraction of money supplies. Politics then came into play. Deepening deflation strengthened the hand of those who argued for relaxing the gold-standard constraints in order to halt the downward spiral. Responding to their calls, the governments of Argentina and Uruguay limited gold convertibility at the end of 1929. Canada introduced an embargo on gold exports tantamount to devaluation. Brazil, Chile, Paraguay, Peru, Venezuela, Australia, and New Zealand abridged their gold standards by making gold difficult to obtain, allowing their currencies to slip below their official parities.

In the summer of 1931, instability spread to the system's industrial core. Austria and Germany suffered banking crises and runs on their international reserves. The more aid they extended to their banking systems, the faster their central banks hemorrhaged gold. They were driven to suspend convertibility and impose *exchange controls*. Britain's balance of payments, already weakened by the decline in earnings on overseas investments caused by the Depression, was further unsettled by the Central European banking crisis. The British government suspended convertibility in September 1931 after pressure on the Bank of England's reserves. Within weeks, a score of other countries followed. Many traded heavily with Britain and relied on the London market for finance: for them it made sense to peg to the pound and hold their exchange reserves as sterling balances in London.

By 1932 the international monetary system had splintered into three blocs: the residual gold-standard countries, led by the United States; the *sterling area* (Britain and countries that pegged to the pound sterling); and the Central and Eastern European countries, led by Germany, where exchange control prevailed. A few countries adhered to no group: Canada, with ties to both the United States and the United Kingdom, followed Britain off the gold standard but did not allow its currency to depreciate as dramatically as sterling in order to avoid disrupting financial relations with the United States. Japan, which competed with Lancashire in world textile markets, followed Britain off gold but did not join the sterling area. The network externalities that had drawn countries to a common monetary standard under the integrated world economy of the late-nineteenth century operated less powerfully in the fragmented economic world of the 1930s.

And this tripolar international monetary system was not particularly stable either. Currency depreciation by Britain and its partners in the sterling area, together with the imposition of exchange control by Germany and its Eastern European neighbors, eroded the payments position of countries still on gold. The latter were forced to apply restrictive monetary and fiscal measures to defend their reserves, which further depressed their economies. Political pressure mounted to relax these policies of austerity. Traders began to sell gold-backed currencies in anticipation of an impending policy shift. As central banks suffered reserve losses, they were forced to ratchet up interest rates, aggravating unemployment and intensifying the pressure for devaluation, which was the source of *capital flight*. Ultimately, every member of the *gold bloc* was forced to suspend convertibility and depreciate its currency. Franklin Delano Roosevelt's defeat of Herbert Hoover in the 1932 U.S. presidential election was due in no small part to the macroeconomic consequences of Hoover's determination to defend the gold standard. One of the new president's first actions was to take the United States off gold in an effort to halt the descent of prices. Each day, Roosevelt raised the dollar price at which the *Reconstruction Finance Corporation* purchased gold, in the succeeding nine months pushing the currency down by 40 percent against those of the gold-standard countries. While the dollar's devaluation helped to contain the crisis in the American banking system and to launch the United States on the road to recovery, it was felt by other countries as a deterioration in their competitive positions. Pressure on the remaining members of the gold bloc intensified accordingly. Czechoslovakia devalued in 1934, Belgium in 1935, France, the Netherlands, and Switzerland in 1936. Through this chaotic process the gold standard gave way once more to floating rates.

This time, however, in contrast to the episode of freely flexible exchange rates in the first half of the 1920s, governments intervened in the foreign-exchange market. *Exchange Equalization Accounts* were established to carry out this function. Typically, they "leaned against the wind," buying a currency when its exchange rate weakened, selling it when it strengthened. Sometimes they sold domestic assets with the goal of pushing down the exchange rate and securing a competitive advantage for producers.

EXPERIENCE WITH FLOATING: THE CONTROVERSIAL
CASE OF THE FRANC

As the first twentieth-century period when exchange rates were allowed to float freely, the 1920s had a profound impact on perceptions of monetary arrangements. Floating rates were indicted for their volatility and their susceptibility to destabilizing speculation—that is, for their tendency to be perturbed by speculative sales and purchases ("hot money flows," as they were called) unrelated to economic fundamentals.

Dismayed by this experience, policymakers sought to avoid its repetition. When floating resumed after the collapse of the interwar gold standard, governments intervened to limit currency fluctuations. Floating in the 1930s was managed precisely because of dissatisfaction with its performance a decade earlier. And when after World War II it came time to reconstruct the international monetary system, there was no hesitancy about applying controls to international capital flows. Clearly, the 1920s cast a long shadow.

The definitive account of interwar experience was a League of Nations study by the economist Ragnar Nurkse, publication of which coincided with the Bretton Woods negotiations over the design of the post–World War II international monetary order.[4] Nurkse issued a blanket indictment of floating rates. His prototypical example was the French franc, of which he wrote:

> The post-war history of the French franc up to the end of 1926 affords an instructive example of completely free and uncontrolled exchange rate variations. . . . The dangers of . . . cumulative and self-aggravating movements under a regime of freely fluctuating exchanges are clearly demonstrated by the French experience. . . . Self-aggravating movements, instead of promoting adjustment in the balance of payments, are apt to intensify any initial disequilibrium and to produce what may be termed "explosive" conditions of instability. . . . We may recall in particular the example of the French franc during the years 1924–26.

It is hard to imagine a more damning indictment. But as interwar traumas receded, revisionists disputed Nurkse's view. The most prominent was Milton Friedman, who observed that Nurkse's critique of floating rates rested almost entirely on the behavior of this one currency, the franc, and questioned whether even it supported Nurkse's interpretation. "The evi-

---

[4] Nurkse 1944. This is the influential study cited in Chapter 2 that calculated violations by interwar central banks of the rules of the game.

dence given by Nurkse does not justify any firm conclusion," Friedman wrote. "Indeed, so far as it goes, it seems to me clearly less favorable to the conclusion Nurkse draws, that speculation was destabilizing, than to the opposite conclusion, that speculation was stabilizing."[5]

Neither Friedman nor his followers objected to Nurkse's characterization of the franc exchange rate as volatile, but they argued that its volatility was simply a reflection of the volatility of monetary and fiscal policies. The exchange rate had been unstable because policy had been unstable. For them, the history of the franc provides no grounds for doubting that floating rates can function satisfactorily when monetary and fiscal policies are sensibly and consistently set.

Nurkse, however, had offered a specific diagnosis of the problem with floating rates—that they were subject to "cumulative and self-aggravating movements" that tended to "intensify any initial disequilibrium." There was no disagreement, then, about the instability of policy. Dispute centered on Nurkse's argument that policy instability was itself induced or at least aggravated by exchange rate fluctuations; his critics contended that policy instability was a given and exchange rate instability its consequence. In their view, the exchange rate responded to policy, whereas Nurkse saw causality running also in the other direction.

Friedman et al. have little trouble explaining events as they unfolded through 1924.[6] French inflation and currency depreciation in this period are explicable in terms of large budget deficits run to finance the costs of reconstruction and underwritten by Bank of France purchases of government debt. Depreciation accelerated each time new information became available about the size of prospective budget deficits and how they would be financed.

For more than half a decade, those deficits persisted. New social programs were demanded by the men and women who had defended the French nation. The high cost of repairing the roads, railways, mines, factories, and housing destroyed in the ten *départements* of the northeast, where the most destructive battles had been waged, placed additional burdens on the fiscal authorities. Meanwhile, revenues were depressed by the slow pace of recovery. Disagreement over whose social programs should be cut and whose taxes should be raised resulted in an extended fiscal deadlock. The parties of the Left demanded increased taxes on capital and wealth, those of the Right reductions in social spending. As long as agreement remained elusive, inflation and currency depreciation persisted.

---

[5] Friedman 1953, p. 176. Leland Yeager (1966, p. 284) similarly suggested that "the historical details . . . undermine [Nurkse's] conclusions."

[6] The most complete account and analysis of the behavior of the franc in the 1920s remains Dulles 1929.

The French government was obliged by a law of 1920 to repay all out-standing advances from the central bank at a rate of 2 billion francs a year. Since doing so required budget surpluses, this legislation stabilized expectations of fiscal policy and bolstered confidence in the currency. But it was easier to mandate repayments than to effect them. The government repeatedly missed the deadline for its annual installment, and even when it satisfied the letter of the law it violated its spirit by financing its payment to the central bank by borrowing from private banks to which the central bank lent. By 1922 this pattern of deception had become apparent, and the currency's depreciation accelerated.

Compounding the dispute over taxes was the conflict over Germany's contribution to the reconstruction of the French economy. Raising taxes would have undermined the argument that the defeated enemy should finance France's reconstruction costs. The French position was that the nation had suffered so heavily from the war that it lacked the resources to finance reconstruction. Budget deficits were evidence of this fact. The larger the deficits and the more rapid the inflation and currency depreciation they provoked, the stronger France's negotiating position.

Through 1924 the franc's fluctuations were shaped by the course of those negotiations. Each time it appeared that substantial reparations would be made, observers revised downward their forecasts of French budget deficits and their expectations of inflation and currency depreciation. The franc strengthened in 1921, for example, when the Allies agreed to impose a $31 billion charge on Germany. It fell in June 1922 when a committee of experts submitted to the Reparations Commission a pessimistic assessment of Germany's capacity to pay (see Figure 3.2).

About then it became clear that the new French prime minister, Raymond Poincaré, rather than being willing to compromise, was prepared to extract reparations by force. To make good on this threat, in January 1923 the French and Belgian armies invaded the Ruhr region of Germany. The Ruhr produced 70 percent of Germany's coal, iron, and steel, making it an obvious source of reparations in kind. In the first months of the occupation, the franc strengthened, reflecting expectations that the occupation would solve France's budgetary problem. As it became evident that Germany's passive resistance was frustrating the effort to forcibly secure the transfer, the ground that had been made up was lost. German workers refused to cooperate with the occupying armies, and their government printed astronomical numbers of currency notes (on occasion only on one side to save time and printing capacity) to pay their salaries. As the expedition bogged down, the franc resumed its descent, this time—with the added expense of running an army of occupation—faster than before.

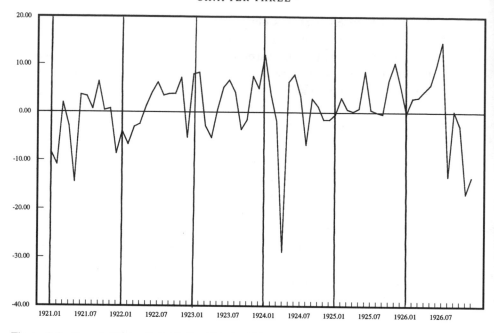

Figure 3.2. French Franc–U.S. Dollar Nominal Exchange Rate, 1921–26 (monthly percentage change). *Source*: Federal Reserve Board 1943. *Note*: The exchange rate is defined so that an increase indicates a depreciation of the French franc. Vertical lines drawn at January of each year.

When the possibility of a settlement surfaced at the end of 1923, the franc stabilized. A committee was appointed under the chairmanship of Charles Dawes, an American banker, to mediate a compromise. Once it became evident that the Dawes Committee was prepared to recommend the postponement of most reparations transfers, the franc's depreciation resumed. For the second year running, the government requested that Parliament pass a special act exempting it from the requirement to repay 2 billion francs in central bank advances, demoralizing the market.

Eventually, a reparations compromise—the Dawes Plan—was reached. Germany was to make annual payments amounting to approximately 1 percent of its national income. The absolute value of the transfer would rise with the expansion of the German economy. Besides supplementing the French government's other revenue sources, the settlement clarified the international situation sufficiently for the French authorities to address their fiscal problems without undermining their international position. It removed the incentive to delay negotiating a domestic settlement in order to strengthen the country's hand in its dealings with Germany. The *Bloc Na-*

tional, a coalition of Center-Right parties, succeeded in raising turnover taxes and excise duties by some 20 percent. Budget balance was restored. Borrowing by the state fell from 3.8 billion prewar francs in 1923 to 1.4 billion in 1924 and 0.8 billion in 1925. This permitted the government to borrow $100 million through the investment bankers J. P. Morgan and Co. in New York and more than $20 million through Lazard Frères in London. The exchange rate improved abruptly.[7]

Had this been the end of the story, Nurkse's critics would be on firm ground in arguing that the franc's instability simply reflected the instability of French policy. But despite the restoration of budget balance and the removal of the most serious sources of reparations uncertainty, the franc's depreciation resumed in 1925. From nineteen to the dollar at the beginning of the year, it fell to twenty-eight at the end of 1925 and to forty-one in July 1926. Traders sold francs in anticipation of further decline, producing the very depreciation they feared. The further the exchange rate diverged from its prewar parity, the less likely it became that the government would be prepared to impose the radical deflation required to restore the prewar price level and rate of exchange; those contemplating the prospects for depreciation were effectively offered a one-way bet. As wage and price setters came to regard the depreciation as permanent, the transmission of currency depreciation into inflation picked up speed. Only after losing more than half of its remaining value was the franc finally stabilized a year and a half later, having apparently suffered precisely the "cumulative and self-aggravating movement" of which Nurkse warned.[8]

Unfortunately for those who believe this episode supports the hypothesis of destabilizing speculation, a second interpretation is equally consistent with the facts. While there is no evidence of instability in current policies in the statistics on the budget or the rate of money creation, there may have been reason to anticipate renewed instability in the future.[9] The Dawes Plan had settled the reparations dispute between France and Germany, but it had not ended the domestic struggle over taxation. The increases in indirect taxes imposed in 1924 by Poincaré's Center-Right government were resented

---

[7] This is evident in the downward spike shown in Figure 3.2. There are two interpretations of this turn of events. One is that the government used these resources to intervene in the foreign-exchange market, purchasing francs and thereby teaching a painful lesson to speculators who had sold them short in anticipation of further depreciation. The other is that the fundamentals had been transformed: budget balance, a reparations settlement, and a loan providing hard currency sufficient to defend the exchange rate provided sound reasons for the change in market sentiment.

[8] This is the conclusion of Pierre Sicsic (1992) in his study of the episode.

[9] This has been argued in Prati 1991 and Eichengreen 1992b.

by the Left. Poincaré's coalition was brought down in elections later that year and replaced by a Center-Left government led by Edouard Herriot, who was better known for his biography of Beethoven than for any competence on economic matters. Investors feared that the new government would substitute wealth and income taxes—specifically a 10 percent *capital levy* on all wealth, payable over ten years—for Poincaré's indirect impost. The Senate, dominated by monied interests elected by local councils, brought down Herriot's government with a vote of no confidence in the spring of 1925. Five ineffectual minority governments followed over the next fourteen months. All the while, the possibility of a capital levy lingered. Reporting in May 1926 on his European trip, Benjamin Strong of the Federal Reserve Bank of New York noted rumors that the government would be dissolved in favor of yet another Herriot government, "which of course would have the backing of the Blum [Socialist] element, who stand so strongly for a capital levy. If they should have such a government, the situation would no doubt become much worse. The French people would be frightened and I fear the flight from the franc would get much worse than it is now."[10]

To shelter themselves, wealth holders spirited their assets out of the country. They exchanged Treasury bonds and other franc-denominated assets for sterling- and dollar-denominated securities and bank deposits in London and New York. The shift into sterling and dollars caused the franc to plummet. And the more investors transferred their assets out of the country, the stronger became the incentive for others to follow. Capital flight reduced the base to which a capital levy could be applied, implying higher taxes on assets left behind. Like a run on deposits ignited by the formation of a line outside a bank, flight from the franc, once under way, fed on itself.

In the end, the Left lacked the parliamentary majority to force through the levy. But not until the summer of 1926 did this become evident. In the final stages of the crisis, between October 1925 and July 1926, a new finance minister took office every five weeks, on average. The consequences for confidence were predictable. "All France to-day is seething with anxiety" was the way one newspaper put it.[11]

"The crisis of the franc" was finally resolved in July 1926 by a polity that had grown weary of financial chaos. Ten years of inflation had reconciled the Frenchman in the street to compromise. Poincaré returned to power at the head of a government of national union. Serving as his own finance minister and granted plenary powers to make economic policy, he decreed a

[10] Cited in Eichengreen 1992c, p. 93. Thomas Sargent (1983) similarly emphasizes continued fear of a capital levy as motivation for capital flight.

[11] Cited in Eichengreen 1992a, p. 182.

symbolic increase in indirect taxes and cuts in public spending. More important, political consolidation banished the capital levy from the fiscal agenda once and for all. The franc's recovery was immediate. Funds that had fled abroad were repatriated, and the currency stabilized.

Where does this leave the debate over destabilizing speculation? There is no question that the franc's depreciation in 1925–26 reflected currency traders' expectations of future policy imbalances (the reemergence of government budget deficits and Bank of France monetization). The question is whether the reappearance of deficits was itself a function of, and therefore contingent upon, speculative sales of francs, which caused inflation to accelerate and the real value of tax collections to fall relative to public spending (as Nurkse's destabilizing speculation theory suggests), or whether those budget deficits and inflation reflected the absence of a resolution to the distributional conflict and would have resurfaced even in the absence of the speculative attack. At some level, it is inevitable that this debate remains unresolved, given the impossibility of actually observing the expectations of currency traders.

Thus, both proponents and critics of floating exchange rates could draw support from the first half of the 1920s. The question is why the negative view dominated. One might argue that recent history always tends to be the most influential—that fears of instability under floating rates dominated fears of the fragility of pegged rates because the first experience was more immediate. More fundamentally, observers failed to realize that the unprecedented political circumstances that introduced the scope for instability under floating posed an equally serious threat to the pegged exchange rates of the gold standard. Simply restoring the gold standard did not remove the political pressures that had prompted speculative capital flows. Disputes over the incidence of taxation and the unemployment costs of central bank policy, which had grown more heated since the war, could not be made to disappear by pegging the currency. The lesson that *should* have been drawn from the experience with floating was that the new gold standard would inevitably lack the credibility and durability of its prewar predecessor.

RECONSTRUCTING THE GOLD STANDARD

In the event, the experience of the first half of the 1920s reinforced the desire to resurrect the gold standard of prewar years. Those who believed that floating rates had been destabilized by speculation hankered for the gold standard to deny currency traders this opportunity. Those who blamed erratic policy saw the restoration of gold convertibility as a way of imposing discipline on governments. Wicker's description of the United States in the 1920s is applicable more broadly: "A 'sound' currency and domestic gold convertibility were indistinguishable and formed the basis of public opinion regarding currency matters."[12]

The key step was Britain's resumption of convertibility. What Britain succeeded in restoring in 1925 was convertibility at the prewar price: £3.17s.9d per ounce of 11/12 fine gold. Since the United States had not altered the dollar price of gold, the prewar parity implied the prewar rate of exchange between the dollar and the pound sterling ($4.86 per pound). In order to make that rate defensible, British prices had to be lowered, if not to the prewar level, then at least to the somewhat higher level that U.S. prices had scaled.

The transition was undertaken gradually to avoid the dislocations of rapid deflation. British prices had fallen sharply in 1920–21, when government spending had been curtailed to prevent the postwar boom from eluding control; at the same time, the Bank of England had increased its discount rate to prevent sterling from falling further against the dollar. The rise in interest rates and fall in prices were recessionary; within a year, the percentage of the insured labor force recorded as unemployed had risen from 2.0 to 11.3 percent. The lesson drawn was the desirability of completing the transition gradually rather than at once.

There remained a considerable distance to go. The United States had curtailed public spending after the armistice and raised interest rates to rein in the boom. Benjamin Strong, the governor of the recently established Federal Reserve Bank of New York, thought it advisable to move the U.S. price level back toward that of 1913. In the summer of 1920, at the height of the boom, the Federal Reserve System ran low on gold; the cover ratio fell perilously close to the statutory 40 percent floor. The Fed adopted harsh deflationary policies in order to raise its reserve.

This move heightened the burden on the Bank of England. Reducing the British price level relative to that prevailing in the United States was that much more difficult when U.S. prices were falling. The Bank was forced to pursue even more restrictive policies to push up sterling against the dollar, given the more restrictive policies being pursued by the Federal Reserve.

Once the U.S. price level stopped falling in 1922, Britain's prospects brightened. The Bank of England made slow but steady progress for a couple of years. But the act of Parliament suspending Britain's gold standard

[12] Wicker 1966, p. 19.

expired at the end of 1925. The Conservative government would be embarrassed if, fully seven years after the war, it had not succeeded in restoring convertibility. A number of Britain's traditional allies, including Australia and South Africa, signaled their intention to restore convertibility whether or not Britain did so; their breaking rank would further embarrass London.

In 1924 the Federal Reserve Bank of New York reduced its discount rate at the behest of Benjamin Strong in order to help Britain back onto gold.[13] As funds flowed from New York to London in search of higher yields, sterling strengthened. Realizing that the Conservatives would be forced to act by the expiration at the end of 1925 of the Gold and Silver (Export Control) Act, the markets bid up the currency in anticipation.[14] Sterling was hovering around its prewar parity by the beginning of 1925, and the government announced the resumption of gold payments on April 25. But the relationship between British and foreign prices had not been restored. The fact that the exchange rate had moved before the price level meant that British prices were too high, causing competitive difficulties for the textile exporters of Lancashire and for import-competing chemical firms. Sterling's *overvaluation* depressed the demand for British goods, aggravating unemployment. It drained gold from the Bank of England, forcing it to raise interest rates even at the cost of depressing the economy. The slow growth and double-digit unemployment that plagued the British economy for the rest of the decade are commonly laid on the doorstep of the decision to restore the prewar parity.

Keynes estimated that sterling was overvalued by 10 to 15 percent. In *The Economic Consequences of Mr. Churchill* (1925) he lamented the decision. The particulars of Keynes's calculations were challenged subsequently. From an assortment of U.S. price indexes, he had just happened to choose the one for the state of Massachusetts indicating the largest difference in national price levels.[15] But even though more representative indexes suggested a somewhat smaller overvaluation—on the order of 5 or 10, not 15, percent—the qualitative conclusion stood.

Why was the government prepared to overlook these facts? Sir James Grigg, private secretary to Winston Churchill, the chancellor of the Exche-

---

[13] See Howson 1975, chap. 3.

[14] This is the view of the episode modeled by Marcus Miller and Alan Sutherland (1994).

[15] On the debate and the different price indexes available to contemporaries, see Moggridge 1969. Modern writers have refined these calculations, comparing British prices not with U.S. prices alone but with a trade-weighted average of the price levels prevailing in the different countries with which British producers competed. See Redmond 1984.

quer, tells of a dinner at which proponents and opponents of the return to gold sought to sway the chancellor.[16] Keynes and Reginald McKenna, a former chancellor himself and subsequently chairman of Midland Bank, argued that overvaluation would price British goods out of international markets and that the wage reductions required in response would provoke labor unrest. Churchill may have chosen to proceed nonetheless, Grigg suggests, because Keynes was not in top form and did not argue convincingly. Personality conflict between the strong-willed Churchill and Keynes may have caused the chancellor to dismiss the don's recommendations. And Churchill may have feared that returning to gold at a devalued rate would rob the policy of its benefits. For Britain's commitment to gold to be credible, this argument ran, convertibility had to be restored at the prewar parity. To tamper with the parity once would signal that the authorities might be prepared to do so again. Foreign governments, central banks, firms, and investors held sterling deposits in London and conducted international financial business there. To devalue the pound, even under exceptional circumstances, would prompt them to reconsider their investment strategy. Loss of international financial business would damage Britain and its financial interests. Special-interest politics, which reflected the triumph of financial interests over a stagnating industrial sector, may have thereby played a role in the politicians' decision.

Resumption by Britain was the signal for other countries to follow. Australia, New Zealand, Hungary, and Danzig did so immediately. Where prices had risen dramatically as a result of wartime and postwar inflation, reducing them to prewar levels would have involved massive redistribution from debtors to creditors and was therefore ruled out. Hence, when Italy, Belgium, Denmark, and Portugal returned to the gold standard, they, like France, did so at devalued rates (higher domestic currency prices of gold). Their subsequent experience, in comparison with Britain's, can be used to test the proposition that restoring the prewar parity enhanced credibility.

By 1926 the gold standard was operating in thirty-nine countries.[17] By 1927 its reconstruction was essentially complete. France had not made legal the December 1926 decision to stabilize the franc at the prevailing rate, a step finally taken in June 1928. And countries at the fringes of Europe, in the Baltics and the Balkans, had yet to restore convertibility. Spain never would. Neither China nor the Soviet Union wished to join the gold-standard club. But, notwithstanding these exceptions, the gold standard again spanned much of the world.

[16] Grigg 1948, pp. 182–84.
[17] See Brown 1940, Vol. 1, p. 395.

THE NEW GOLD STANDARD

Gold coin had all but disappeared from circulation during World War I. Only in the United States did a significant share of money in circulation—8 percent—take the form of gold. Postwar governments hoped that the world's scarce gold supplies would stretch further if concentrated in the vaults of central banks. To ensure that gold did not circulate, governments provided it only to those with enough currency to purchase substantial quantities. Obtaining the minimum of 400 fine ounces required by the Bank of England required an investment of about £1,730 ($8,300). Other countries imposed similar restrictions.

Another device to stretch the available gold reserves further (providing traditional levels of backing for an expanded money supply) was to extend the prewar practice of augmenting gold with foreign exchange—to transform the gold standard into a *gold-exchange standard*. Belgium, Bulgaria, Finland, Italy, and Russia were the only European countries that had not limited the use of foreign-exchange reserves in 1914.[18] Countries that stabilized with League of Nations assistance (and as a condition for obtaining League-sponsored loans buttressed the independence of their central banks) included in their central bank statutes a provision entitling that institution to hold its entire reserve in the form of interest-bearing foreign assets. Other countries authorized their central banks to hold some fixed fraction of their reserves in foreign exchange.

The desire to concentrate gold in central banks and to supplement it with foreign exchange reflected fears of a global gold shortage. The demand for currency and deposits had been augmented by the rise in prices and the growth of the world economy. Gold supplies, meanwhile, had increased only modestly. Policymakers worried that this "gold shortage" prevented the further expansion of money supplies and that financial stringency depressed the rate of economic growth.

If gold were scarce and obtaining it costly, could central banks not individually increase their use of exchange reserves? Contemporaries were skeptical that this action would be viable. A country that unilaterally adopted the practice might fall prey to speculators who would sell its currency for one backed solely by gold. Only if all countries agreed to hold a portion of their reserves in the form of foreign exchange

---

[18] Austria, Denmark, Greece, Norway, Portugal, Romania, Spain, and Sweden had permitted their central banks and governments to hold foreign exchange as reserves but limited the practice.

would they be protected from this threat. The existence of a coordination problem thereby precluded the shift.

Coordination problems are solved through communication and cooperation. The 1920s saw a series of international conferences at which this was attempted. The most important was a 1922 conference in Genoa.[19] It assembled all of the major gold-standard countries but the United States, whose isolationist Congress viewed the meeting as a source of international entanglements akin to the League of Nations, participation in which it had already vetoed. Under the leadership of the British delegation, a subcommittee on financial questions drafted a report recommending that countries negotiate an international convention authorizing their central banks to hold unlimited foreign-exchange reserves.

The other theme of the Genoa Conference was international cooperation. Central banks were instructed to formulate policy "not only with a view to maintaining currencies at par with one another, but also with a view to preventing undue fluctuations in the purchasing power of gold."[20] ("The purchasing power of gold" was a phrase used to denote the price level. Since central banks pegged the domestic-currency price of gold, the metal's purchasing power rose as the price level fell.) If central banks engaged in a noncooperative struggle for the world's scarce gold reserves, each raising interest rates in an effort to attract gold from the others, none would succeed (since their interest-rate increases would be mutually offsetting), but prices and production would be depressed. If they harmonized their discount rates at more appropriate levels, the same international distribution of reserves could be achieved without provoking a disastrous deflation.

Keynes and Ralph Hawtrey (the latter then director of financial enquiries at the Treasury) played significant roles in drafting the Genoa resolutions, which therefore reflected a British perspective on international monetary relations. British dependencies like India had long maintained foreign-exchange reserves; London consequently saw the practice as a natural solution to the world's monetary problems. The Bank of England had been party to most prewar episodes of central bank cooperation and was in regular contact with the banks of the Commonwealth and the Dominions; it viewed such cooperation as both desirable and practical. The Genoa resolutions reflected British self-interest: a further decline in world prices due to inadequate international reserves would complicate its effort to restore sterling's prewar parity. London, with its highly developed financial structure, was sure to be a leading repository of exchange reserves, as it had been in the nineteenth

---

[19] For a history of the Genoa Conference, see Fink 1984.

[20] *Federal Reserve Bulletin* (June 1922): 678–80.

century. Revitalizing its role would bring much-needed international banking business to the City (as its financial district was known). It would help to reconstruct the balance-of-payments adjustment mechanism that had functioned so admirably before the war.

The subcommittee that drafted the Genoa resolutions on finance recommended convening a meeting of central banks to settle the details. That meeting was never held, however, owing to lack of American support. Although the United States had declined to participate in the Genoa Conference, Federal Reserve officials resented the decision to make the Bank of England responsible for organizing the summit of central banks. U.S. observers questioned the efficacy of the gold-exchange standard and the need for central bank cooperation. During World War I, the United States had exported agricultural commodities and manufactures in return for gold and foreign exchange. Its gold reserves had risen from $1.3 billion in 1913 to $4 billion in 1923. The United States did not need to deflate in order to restore convertibility. In addition, officials of the newly established Federal Reserve System may have harbored a false impression of the gold standard's automaticity. Not having contributed to its prewar management, they failed to appreciate the role played by exchange reserves and central bank cooperation.[21]

Thus, the proposed meeting of central banks was never held. Efforts to encourage central bank cooperation and the use of foreign-exchange reserves were left to proceed on an ad hoc basis. Attempts to reconstruct the international monetary system out of whole cloth proved unavailing. Like the prewar system, the interwar gold standard evolved incrementally. Its structure was the sum of national monetary arrangements, none of which had been selected for its implications for the operation of the system as a whole. As Nurkse lamented, "The piecemeal and haphazard manner of international monetary reconstruction sowed the seeds of subsequent disintegration."[22]

Problems of the New Gold Standard

By the second half of the 1920s, currencies were again convertible into gold at fixed domestic prices, and most significant restrictions on international transactions in capital and gold had been removed. These two elements combined, as before World War I, to stabilize exchange rates between national

---

[21] In particular, Benjamin Strong, governor of the Federal Reserve Bank of New York and the leading figure in U.S. international monetary relations in the 1920s, became an increasingly sharp critic of the gold-exchange standard.

[22] See Nurkse 1944, p. 117.

monies and to make international gold movements the ultimate means of balance-of-payments settlement.

The years 1924 to 1929 were a period of economic growth and strong demand for money and credit worldwide. Once the gold standard was restored, the additional liquidity required by the expanding world economy had to be based on an increase in the stock of international reserves. Yet the world supply of monetary gold had grown only slowly over the course of World War I and in the first half of the 1920s, despite the concentration of gold stocks in the vaults of central banks. The ratio of central bank gold reserves to notes and sight (or demand) deposits dropped from 48 percent in 1913 to 40 percent in 1927.[23] Central banks were forced to pyramid an ever-growing superstructure of liabilities on a limited base of monetary gold.

Particularly disconcerting was the fact that two countries, France and Germany, absorbed nearly all of the increase in global monetary reserves in the second half of the 1920s (see Table 3.1). The Bank of France's gold reserves more than doubled between 1926 and 1929. By the end of 1930 they had tripled. By the end of 1931 they had quadrupled. France became the world's leading repository of monetary gold after the United States. This gold avalanche pointed to an undervaluation of the franc Poincaré (as the currency was known in honor of the prime minister who had presided over its stabilization). So much gold would not have flooded into the coffers of the Bank of France if the rate at which the French authorities had chosen to stabilize had not conferred on domestic producers an undue competitive advantage. Had they allowed market forces to operate instead of intervening to prevent the currency's appreciation at the end of 1926, a stronger franc would have eliminated this artificial competitive advantage and neutralized the balance-of-payments consequences. A stronger franc would have reduced the price level, at the same time increasing the real value of notes and deposits in circulation and obviating the need for gold imports. France would not have been a sump for the world's gold, relieving the pressure on the international system.

Why did the Bank of France pursue such perverse policies? In reaction against the abuse of credit facilities by earlier French governments, the Parliament adopted statutes prohibiting the central bank from extending credit to the government or otherwise expanding the domestic-credit component of the *monetary base*. The 1928 law that placed France on the gold standard not only required it to hold gold equal to at least 35 percent of its notes and deposits but also restricted its use of open-market operations. Another cen-

---

[23] League of Nations 1930, p. 94.

TABLE 3.1

Gold Reserves of Central Banks and Governments, 1913–35

(percent of total)

Country	1913	1918	1923	1924	1925	1926	1927	1928	1929	1930	1931	1932	1933	1934	1935
United States	26.6	39.0	44.4	45.7	44.4	44.3	41.6	37.4	37.8	38.7	35.9	34.0	33.6	37.8	45.1
England	3.4	7.7	8.6	8.3	7.8	7.9	7.7	7.5	6.9	6.6	5.2	4.9	7.8	7.3	7.3
France	14.0	9.8	8.2	7.9	7.9	7.7	10.0	12.5	15.8	19.2	23.9	27.3	25.3	25.0	19.6
Germany	5.7	7.9	1.3	2.0	3.2	4.7	4.7	6.5	5.3	4.8	2.1	1.6	0.8	0.1	0.1
Argentina	5.3	4.5	5.4	4.9	5.0	4.9	5.5	6.0	4.2	3.8	2.2	2.1	2.0	1.9	2.0
Australia	0.5	1.5	1.5	1.5	1.8	1.2	1.1	1.1	0.9	0.7	0.5	0.4	a	a	a
Belgium	1.0	0.7	0.6	0.6	0.6	0.9	1.0	1.3	1.6	1.7	3.1	3.0	3.2	2.7	2.7
Brazil	1.9	0.4	0.6	0.6	0.6	0.6	1.1	1.5	1.5	0.1	n.a.	n.a.	0.1[b]	0.1[b]	0.1
Canada	2.4	1.9	1.5	1.7	1.7	1.7	1.6	1.1	0.8	1.0	0.7	0.7	0.6	0.6	0.8
India	2.5	0.9	1.3	1.2	1.2	1.2	1.2	1.2	1.2	1.2	1.4	1.4	1.4	1.3	1.2
Italy	5.5	3.0	2.5	2.5	2.5	2.4	2.5	2.7	2.7	2.6	2.6	2.6	3.1	2.4	1.6
Japan	1.3	3.3	7.0	6.5	6.4	6.1	5.7	5.4	5.3	3.8	2.1	1.8	1.8	1.8	1.9
Netherlands	1.2	4.2	2.7	2.3	2.0	1.8	1.7	1.7	1.7	1.6	3.2	3.5	3.1	2.6	2.0
Russia-USSR	16.2	—	0.5	0.8	1.0	0.9	1.0	0.9	1.4	2.3	2.9	3.1	3.5	3.4	3.7
Spain	1.9	6.3	5.6	5.5	5.5	5.4	5.2	4.9	4.8	4.3	3.8	3.6	3.6	3.4	3.3
Switzerland	0.7	1.2	1.2	1.1	1.0	1.0	1.0	1.0	1.1	1.3	4.0	4.0	3.2	2.9	2.0
All other	9.9	7.8	7.1	6.9	7.4	7.3	7.4	7.3	7.0	6.3	6.4	6.0	6.9	6.7	6.6
Total	100.0	100.0	100.0	100.0	100.0	100.0	100.0	100.0	100.0	100.0	100.0	100.0	100.0	100.0	100.0

Source: Hardy 1936, p. 93.

a. Less than 0.05 of 1 percent.

b. Bolivia, Brazil, Ecuador, and Guatemala.

tral bank with a statute requiring 35 percent backing could have used expansionary open-market operations to increase the currency circulation by nearly three francs each time it acquired a franc's worth of gold. But the Bank of France was prohibited from doing so by the stabilization law. France was not one of those countries in which *open-market operations* were widely used before 1913, as we saw in the previous chapter. Again, perceptions of the appropriate structure and operation of the interwar system were strongly—too strongly—conditioned by prewar experience.

The French central bank retained other instruments that it might have used to expand domestic credit and stem the gold inflow. It could have encouraged banks to rediscount their bills by lowering the discount rate. It could have sold francs on the foreign-exchange market. But the Paris market for discounts was narrow, limiting the effectiveness of discount policy. And French officials felt uncomfortable about holding foreign exchange. Indeed, in 1927 the Bank of France began to liquidate its foreign currency reserves. To limit the franc's appreciation, it had acquired $750 million in foreign exchange in the second half of the previous year, nearly matching its gold reserves. French officials recalled that the Bank of France had held large amounts of gold and little foreign exchange before World War I. They viewed the Genoa proposals to institutionalize the gold-exchange standard as a British ploy to fortify London's position as a financial center at the expense of Paris.

The problems posed by the tightness of French monetary policy were exacerbated when, in 1927, Emile Moreau, the stubborn provincial gentleman who then headed the Bank of France, began converting his bank's foreign exchange into gold. When Moreau presented 20 percent of what he had acquired in the previous six months for conversion at the Bank of England, the latter warned that such demands might force Britain to suspend convertibility. For French officials who saw the gold standard as a bulwark of financial stability, this threat was serious; Moreau moderated his demands.[24]

That Germany was the other country that enjoyed large increases in gold reserves in the latter half of the 1920s is surprising at first blush. Germany still had to cope with the difficulties created by reparations transfers, but it was the leading destination of U.S. foreign investment. To reassure citizens made skittish by the hyperinflation, the Reichsbank maintained higher interest rates than other gold-standard countries, which made Germany an attrac-

---

[24] As explained below, French efforts to convert the Bank of France's foreign exchange into gold resumed in 1931, at what turned out to be the worst possible time for the global system.

tive destination for funds. As a result of capital inflows, the Reichsbank's gold reserves more than tripled between 1924 and 1928.[25]

Its Brooklyn-born president, Hjalmar Horace Greeley Schacht, shared Moreau's skepticism about the gold-exchange standard (appropriately, it might be added, since the nineteenth-century American politician and journalist after whom Schacht was named had himself been a strong believer in gold). The German hyperinflation had reinforced Schacht's belief in the desirability of a rigid gold standard to insulate central banks from political pressures. But Schacht had inherited significant quantities of foreign exchange via the Dawes Plan, under whose provisions Germany received a foreign currency loan. As long as European currencies, like sterling, appreciated in anticipation of Britain's return to gold, it made sense for Germany to retain the sterling proceeds of the Dawes loan and reap the capital gains. Starting in 1926, however, Schacht began converting his exchange reserves into gold.[26] To encourage gold imports, he announced that the Reichsbank would accept gold in Bremen as well as Berlin, saving arbitragers the cost of shipping it to an inland city.

The absorption of gold by France and Germany intensified the pressure on other central banks. The Bank of England was described by its interwar governor, Montagu Norman, as continuously "under the harrow."[27] As gold flowed toward France and Germany, other central banks were forced to raise interest rates and tighten credit to defend their increasingly precarious reserves.

The largest holder of monetary gold, the United States, was no help. In 1926 the United States possessed nearly 45 percent of the world's supply (see Table 3.1). Fully a quarter was *free gold*—that is, it exceeded the 40 percent backing required by the country's gold standard law.[28] Reducing Reserve Bank discount rates or undertaking expansionary open-market operations would have encouraged capital outflows and redistributed this gold to the rest of the world. 1927 saw modest efforts in this di-

[25] See Lüke 1958.

[26] See Schacht 1927, p. 208.

[27] In his testimony to the Macmillan Committee, cited in Sayers 1976, Vol. 1, p. 211.

[28] The precise legal provisions were more complicated. Until 1932, Federal Reserve monetary liabilities not backed by gold had to be collateralized by the Fed's holdings of "eligible securities," where eligible collateral included commercial paper but not Treasury bonds. Thus, the central bank's free gold was limited to that portion over and above the 40 percent minimum not also required to back liabilities acquired through purchases of Treasury bonds and the like. A debate over whether this constraint was binding before its elimination in 1932 revolves around whether the Fed could acquire additional eligible securities whenever it wished. See Friedman and Schwartz 1963 and Wicker 1966.

rection, notably when the New York Fed reduced its discount rate and undertook open-market purchases to assist Britain through a payments crisis. U.S. policy subsequently took a contractionary turn. The rate of growth of the U.S. money supply declined. Yields on U.S. government bonds stopped falling. Short-term rates began to rise. These events further discomfited foreign central banks.

What was on the minds of Federal Reserve officials is no mystery. They had become increasingly preoccupied over the course of 1927 by the Wall Street boom, which they saw as diverting resources from more productive uses. To discourage stock market speculation, the Federal Reserve Bank of New York raised its discount rate from 3½ to 5 percent in the first half of 1928. In addition, the Fed was concerned by the decline in its gold cover ratio. The late-1920s boom having augmented stocks of money and credit more dramatically than U.S. gold reserves, the Fed raised interest rates in what it saw as the reponsibility of any central bank.[29]

Its actions were felt both at home and abroad. Tighter money slowed the expansion of the U.S. economy.[30] Higher interest rates kept American capital from flowing abroad. The Fed's failure to release gold heightened the strains on other countries, which were forced to respond with discount-rate increases of their own.

THE PATTERN OF INTERNATIONAL PAYMENTS

It did not take long for the architects of the new gold standard to conclude that it was not operating as planned. Some countries lapsed into persistent balance-of-payments deficit, depleting their gold and foreign-exchange reserves. Aside from a small surplus in 1928, Britain was in overall payments deficit every year between 1927 and 1931. Other countries enjoyed persistent surpluses and reserve inflows. The French balance of payments, as mentioned earlier, was in surplus every year between 1927 and 1931. The United States ran payments surpluses for most of the 1920s. The adjustment mechanism that was supposed to eliminate surpluses and deficits and restore balance to the international accounts seemed to function inadequately. And the stabilizing capital flows that had financed the *current-account* deficits of industrial countries in times past could no longer be relied upon.

[29] Wicker (1966) and Wheelock (1991) stress the role of gold reserves in the conduct of Federal Reserve monetary policy in this period.

[30] There now is widespread consensus on this point. See Field 1984 and Hamilton 1987.

These inadequacies were dramatized by changes in the pattern of international settlements that strained the system's adjustment capacity. When European merchandise exports to Latin America had been curtailed in 1914, U.S. producers leapt to fill the void. The marketing and distribution networks they had set up during the war proved hard to dislodge after 1918. For example, the United States' share in Argentina's imports rose from 15 percent in 1913 to 25 percent in 1927, while that of the United Kingdom fell from 31 to 19 percent. Wartime disruptions also provided Japan the opportunity to penetrate Asian markets long dominated by European producers. The consequence was a deterioration in Europe's competitive position.

War debts and reparations compounded Europe's difficulties. Between 1924 and 1929 the victorious powers received nearly $2 billion in reparations payments from Germany. They passed a portion on to the United States as principal and interest on debts incurred during the war. About $1 billion in war-debt-related transfers to the United States were completed between mid-1926 and mid-1931.

These transactions augmented the flow of gold and foreign exchange toward the United States. They strengthened the balance of payments of the United States and weakened that of other countries. The logical response to these shifts was the one predicted by the price-specie flow model: a rise in U.S. prices and costs relative to those prevailing in the rest of the world. But little such adjustment took place. Instead, the United States lent much of its surplus back to Europe and other parts of the world. As long as U.S. capital exports persisted, they could finance Europe's current-account deficits, obviating the need for substantial changes in relative prices. And U.S. lending reached high levels in the second half of the 1920s. The war had transformed the country from an international debtor into the world's leading creditor.[31] European investors had been forced to liquidate their holdings of U.S. securities and to incur new foreign debts. Wartime devastation left Europe capital-scarce, whereas the United States emerged from the war unscathed. Capital scarcity meant high rates of return, providing an incentive for American capital to flow across the Atlantic.

Except in 1923, the year of the Ruhr invasion, the United States lent large amounts overseas (see Figure 3.3). New security issues for foreign borrowers, which peaked in 1927–28, were the leading component of this flow. Issuing dollar-denominated bonds on behalf of foreign governments and corporations was a new undertaking for American investment banks. Indeed,

---

[31] The standard introduction to this transformation is Lewis 1938.

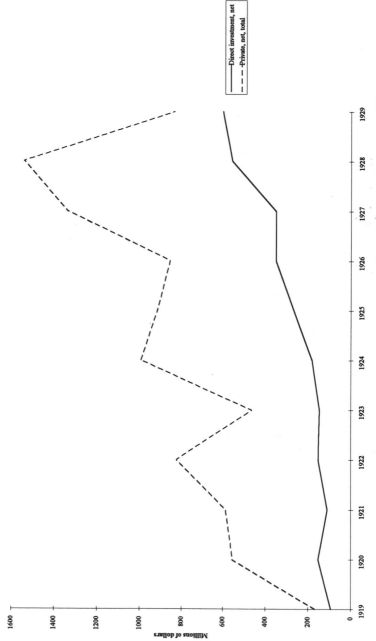

Figure 3.3. Private, Net, Total U.S. Capital Outflow, 1919–29. *Source:* Office of Business Economics 1954.

the very scale of the bond business was new: as late as 1914, no more than 200,000 Americans invested in bonds; that number quintupled by 1929.[32] National banks, which had become involved in the wartime campaign to distribute Liberty bonds, sought to retain their newly acquired customers by interesting them in foreign securities. To ensure a steady supply of foreign bonds, they began originating them, a practice that provided further pressure to market them. The banks opened storefronts from which their bond departments could attract walk-in customers and hired traveling salesmen to peddle foreign bonds to farmers and widows.

Given the dependence of other countries on capital imports from the United States, the collapse of the recycling process in 1928 was a difficult blow. The interest-rate increases initiated by the Fed to slow the Wall Street boom and stem the decline in the gold cover ratio increased the attractiveness of investing in U.S. fixed-interest securities. Higher interest rates also damaged the creditworthiness of heavily indebted countries suddenly saddled with higher interest charges. U.S. foreign lending, which had been running at high levels in the first half of 1928, fell to zero in the second half of the year.

Once capital stopped flowing in, demand in the debtor countries was curtailed. The consequent fall in the relative prices of the goods they produced was the mechanism by which they boosted their exports and compressed their imports to bridge the gap created by the evaporation of capital inflows. In other words, the price-specie flow mechanism finally began to operate. But with the onset of the Great Depression in 1929, export markets were dealt a further blow, which made the earlier changes in relative prices wholly inadequate.

There were two obvious ways of attenuating the impact of the decline in U.S. lending and the shock to balances of payments posed by the onset of the Great Depression. First, war debts and reparations could be abolished. Eliminating unrequited transfers from Germany to France and Britain and from France and Britain to the United States would have strengthened Europe's balance of payments and reduced its dependence on U.S. capital. But a moratorium on war debts and reparations proved impossible to negotiate over the relevant time frame. Second, a further reduction in prices and costs, along the lines of the price-specie flow model, could have priced European and Latin American goods back into international markets. But there were limits to how far prices could be pushed down without setting in motion a deflationary spiral. Because foreign debts were denominated in nominal

---

[32] These estimates are drawn from Stoddard 1932 and Cleveland and Huertas 1985.

terms, reductions in the price level increased the real resource cost of servicing them, aggravating the problem of external balance. Because the debts of farmers and firms were denominated in nominal terms, price-level reductions, which cut into sales receipts, aggravated problems of default and foreclosure. If, as a result, the volume of nonperforming loans grew large enough, the stability of the banking system could be jeopardized.[33] For all these reasons, there were limits on the efficacy of the standard deflationary medicine.

RESPONSES TO THE GREAT DEPRESSION

Those familiar with gold-standard history will find nothing surprising about these simultaneous capital- and commodity-market shocks; primary-producing countries had experienced them repeatedly before the war. As in that earlier era, the developing countries had few options. They could use their remaining foreign-exchange earnings to keep current the service on their external obligations, or they could husband their central bank reserves and defend the convertibility of their currencies. To default on the debt would cause the creditors to revoke their capital-market access, but to fail to maintain adequate central bank reserves would raise grave questions about financial stability. Concluding that compromises of their gold-standard statutes could be more readily reversed, Argentina, Australia, Brazil, and Canada modified the rules of convertibility and allowed their currencies to depreciate in the second half of 1929 and the first half of 1930. Others followed.

While it was not unprecedented for countries experiencing shocks to suspend gold convertibility, earlier suspensions had been limited in scope; at no time between 1880 and 1913 had virtually all the countries of the periphery abandoned the gold standard simultaneously. Suspensions had been provoked by harvest failures, military conflicts, and economic mismanagement in individual countries, events that had caused exports to fall and capital inflows to dry up. In 1929 the suspensions resulted from a global economic crisis and were correspondingly more damaging to the international system.

The gold standard's disintegration at the periphery undermined its stability at the center. Contemporaries were not unaware of this danger; the report of Britain's Macmillan Committee (established to probe the connections between finance and industry), drafted in the summer of 1931, warned: "Credi-

---

[33] The technical term for this process, "debt deflation," was coined by Irving Fisher (1933).

tor countries must, unless they are ready to upset the economic conditions, first of the debtor countries and then of themselves, be prepared to lend back their surplus, instead of taking it in gold."[34] This proved easier said than done.

This fragile financial situation was superimposed on a more fundamental problem: the collapse of industrial production. The industrial world had seen recessions before, but not like that which began in 1929. U.S. industrial production fell by a staggering 48 percent between 1929 and 1932, German industrial production by 39 percent. Recorded unemployment peaked at 25 percent of the labor force in the United States; in Germany unemployment in industry reached 44 percent.[35]

Governments naturally wished to stimulate their moribund economies. But injecting credit and bringing down interest rates to encourage consumption and investment was inconsistent with maintenance of the gold standard. Additional credit meant additional demands for merchandise imports. Lower interest rates encouraged foreign investment. The reserve losses they produced raised fears of currency depreciation, prompting capital flight. Governments tempted to use policy to halt the downward spiral of economic activity were confronted by the incompatibility of expansionary initiatives and gold convertibility.

At this point the changed political circumstances of the 1920s came into play. Before the war it had been clear that the governments of countries at the gold standard's industrial core were prepared to defend the system. When a country's exchange rate weakened, capital flowed in, supporting rather than undermining the central bank's efforts to defend convertibility, since currency traders were confident of the official commitment to hold the exchange rate within the *gold points* and therefore expected the currency's weakness to be reversed. In this new policy environment, it was no longer obvious that a currency's weakness was temporary. "The most significant development of the period," as Robert Triffin put it, "was the growing importance of domestic factors as the final determinant of monetary policies."[36] In this more politicized environment, it was uncertain how the authorities would react if forced to choose between defense of the gold standard and measures to reduce unemployment.

As soon as speculators had reason to think that a government might expand domestic credit, even if doing so implied allowing the exchange rate to depreciate, they began selling its currency to avoid the capital losses that

[34] Committee on Finance and Industry 1931, para. 184.
[35] See Galenson and Zellner 1957.
[36] Triffin 1947, p. 57.

depreciation would entail. The losses they would suffer if the weak currency recovered were dwarfed by the gains they would reap if convertibility were suspended and the currency allowed to depreciate. In contrast to the situation before World War I, capital movements "of a disturbing sort" (to invoke the phrase of Bertil Ohlin cited in Chapter 2) became widespread.

With the growth of fears for the stability of exchange rates, questions arose about key currencies like sterling and the dollar. A prudent central banker would hesitate to hold deposits in London or New York if there were a risk that sterling or the dollar would be devalued. The British resorted to moral suasion to discourage the liquidation of other countries' London balances. When their promise to defend sterling proved empty, central banks suffered substantial losses and became even more averse to holding exchange reserves. One country after another replaced its exchange reserves with gold, driving up the relative price of the latter. In countries whose central banks still pegged the nominal price of gold, this meant a further decline in commodity prices. The liquidation of foreign exchange reduced the volume of international reserves (gold plus foreign exchange): the reserves of twenty-four leading countries declined by about $100 million over the course of 1931.[37] With this further decline in the availability of reserves, central banks were forced to ratchet up their discount rates to ensure reserve adequacy and convertibility.

The intensity of speculation against a currency depended on the credibility of the government's commitment to the maintenance of its gold standard peg. Where credibility was greatest, capital still flowed in stabilizing directions, blunting the trade-off between internal and external balance. Where credibility was questionable, destabilizing speculation aggravated the pressure brought to bear on a government seeking to balance conflicting interests. One might think that credibility derived from past performance—that is, from whether a country had defended its gold standard parity in the face of past crises and, when forced to suspend gold convertibility, had restored it subsequently at the initial rate. The belief that credibility could be obtained by cultivating such a record had provided one of the motivations for the British decision to return to gold at the prewar parity. It now transpired that the governments of countries that had maintained the prewar parity, the United Kingdom and the United States among them, enjoyed the least credibility, while financial market participants invested the greatest confidence in the governments of countries that had returned to gold at a depreciated rate, as France and Belgium had done.

[37] Nurkse 1944, p. 235.

This inversion reflected two facts. First, a searing experience with inflation that prevented the restoration of convertibility at the prewar parity often rendered a government singularly committed to defending its new parity in order to prevent a recurrence of the financial and social turmoil of the previous decade. This was the case in France, Belgium, and Italy, for example. In other words, current policy priorities mattered more than past performance. Second, current economic conditions mattered as much as if not more than past performance for the sustainability of gold-standard commitments. Where the downturn was severe, as it was in the United States, doubts about the political sustainability of the harsh deflationary measures needed to defend the gold-standard peg might be more prevalent than where the initial decline was relatively mild, as it was in France. Credibility was the casualty.

BANKING CRISES AND THEIR MANAGEMENT

These dilemmas were most painful in countries with weak banking systems. The falling prices associated with the Depression made it difficult for bank borrowers to repay. By eroding the value of collateral, they left banks hesitant to roll over existing loans or to extend new ones. Small firms unable to obtain working capital were forced to curtail operations. Enterprises with profitable investments found themselves starved of the financing needed to undertake them.

Central banks, as lenders of last resort to the banking system, were not unaware of these problems. But they were discouraged from intervening on behalf of the banking system by the priority they attached to the fixed rates of the gold standard. Injecting liquidity into financial markets might have violated the statutes requiring them to hold a minimum ratio of gold to foreign liabilities. It would have reinforced doubts about the depth of their commitment to defending the gold-standard parity. Indeed, the fear that central banks might be prepared to bail out the banking system, even if doing so would require allowing the currency to depreciate, provoked the further liquidation of deposits as investors sought to avoid the capital losses consequent on depreciation. As a result, the faster central banks injected liquidity into the financial system, the faster it leaked back out via capital flight. In these circumstances, lender-of-last-resort intervention might be not only difficult but also counterproductive.[38]

[38] The United States is the one country for which it has been argued that the central bank possessed sufficient gold to address its banking and monetary problems without jeopardizing

These difficulties were compounded by the fact that many of the mechanisms that had been utilized for managing banking crises before the war could not be invoked. When the entire banking system was in distress, it was impossible to arrange collective support operations in which strong banks supported weak ones. For countries like the United States, life-boat operations like that which had been arranged by the Bank of England in 1890 in response to the Baring crisis did not provide a way out. Generalized suspensions of the convertibility of deposits into currency like that which had occurred in 1893 did not take place until four years into the Depression, when a new president, Franklin Roosevelt, took office and declared a nationwide bank holiday. One explanation is that the consortia of banks in New York and other financial centers, which had jointly suspended operations in 1893 and on other occasions, neglected their collective responsibilities in the belief that the newly created Federal Reserve System would ride to the rescue. If so, their confidence was misplaced.

Moreover, temporary departures from the gold standard, which had allowed nineteenth-century governments and central banks to relax the gold-standard constraints, were not resorted to in the 1930s.[39] As discussed in Chapter 2, only if strict conditions were met could this "escape clause" be invoked without damaging the credibility of the government's commitment to defend its gold-standard parity. It had to be clear that the internal or external drain in response to which convertibility was being temporarily suspended resulted from circumstances that were not of the authorities' own making. Because there had been no question before World War I of the overriding priority attached by central banks to the defense of convertibility, there was no reason to believe that excessively expansionary policies of the central bank were themselves responsible for the crisis in response to which the temporary suspension occurred.

After World War I, priorities were different, and central banks and governments were subjected to strong pressure to cut interest rates and undertake expansionary open-market operations in response to deteriorating domestic economic conditions. It was no longer clear, in other words, that the external drain arose for circumstances not of the government's own making. Suspending convertibility and depreciating the currency might be seen as validation of this fact and severely damage policy credibility. With the credibility of their commitment to convertibility already in doubt, central banks

---

gold convertibility. This is the view of Milton Friedman and Anna Schwartz (1963). Dissenting opinions include those of Barrie Wigmore (1984) and Barry Eichengreen (1992b).

[39] As we shall see below, most countries that suspended gold convertibility did so permanently. Those few that restored it subsequently, such as the United States, did so only after depreciating their currencies.

had no choice but to reassure the markets by defending the gold parity to the bitter end. Hence, the gold standard posed a binding constraint on intervention in support of the banking system.

The way out of this bind was international cooperation. If other countries supported the exchange rate of the nation in distress, it no longer followed that, when its central bank provided liquidity to the financial system, an exchange rate crisis necessarily ensued. Similarly, had expansionary monetary and fiscal initiatives been coordinated internationally, the external constraint would have been relaxed. Expansion at home might still weaken the balance of payments, but expansion abroad would strengthen it. Coordinating domestic and foreign economic policies would have made it possible to neutralize the balance-of-payments consequences. The worldwide shortage of liquidity produced by the collapse of financial intermediation would have been averted.

Unfortunately, differences of interpretation impeded efforts to coordinate reflation internationally. In Britain the slump was attributed to the inadequate provision of money and credit by the Bank of England. This view was articulated in 1931 by Keynes in his private testimony to the Macmillan Committee and by other critics of Churchill's 1925 decision to restore the prewar parity. In France, in contrast, monetary expansion was regarded as the problem rather than the solution. Given the double-digit inflation through which the nation had suffered in the first half of the 1920s, the French associated monetary expansion with financial and political chaos. They viewed the Depression as the consequence of excessive credit creation by central banks that had failed to adhere to the gold standard's rules. Cheap credit, they believed, had fueled excessive speculation, setting the stage for the 1929 crash. For central banks to again intervene when prices had only begun to fall threatened to provoke another round of speculative excesses and, ultimately, another depression. It would be healthier to purge such excesses by liquidating overextended enterprises. A similar liquidationist view informed U.S. policy until Franklin Roosevelt took office in 1933.

Given these incompatible outlooks, international cooperation was hopeless. And unilateral policy initiatives to stabilize the economy were precluded by the constraints of the gold standard.

DISINTEGRATION OF THE GOLD STANDARD

Against this backdrop it is possible to understand the gold standard's collapse. Austria was the first European country to experience banking and balance of payments crises. That it was first to be so affected was far from random. Austria's short-term foreign indebtedness exceeded $150 million, a considerable sum for a small country. Much of this debt took the form of liquid deposits in Viennese banks. And the banks were already weakened by extensive loans to an industrial sector that suffered disproportionately from the slump.

Austria's largest deposit bank, the Credit Anstalt, was in particularly dire straits. The too-big-to-fail principle applied with a vengeance: the Credit Anstalt's liabilities were larger than the Austrian government budget.[40] For its deposits to be frozen for any period would have had devastating economic effects. Hence, the authorities did not hesitate to bail out the bank when its directors revealed in May 1931 that bad loans had wiped out its capital.

Although the government moved quickly to replenish the Credit Anstalt's capital, its intervention did not reassure the depositors. There were rumors, ultimately confirmed, that the bank's losses were greater than those announced. There was the revelation that Austria and Germany had discussed the establishment of a customs union in violation of the Versailles Treaty, a fact that hardly enhanced prospects for French and British assistance. Above all, the government's provision of liquidity to the banking system was potentially incompatible with its maintenance of the gold standard. The central bank increased its note circulation by more than 25 percent in the last three weeks of May as a result of purchasing Credit Anstalt shares and providing other support to distressed financial institutions, this during a period when its international reserves were falling, not rising. The budget had already lapsed into deficit because of the slump in economic activity. That the government had shouldered what was effectively an unlimited state guarantee for the liabilities of the Credit Anstalt only augured additional deficits.[41] While the central bank was prohibited by law from providing direct finance for those deficits, it had violated its charter before by rediscounting finance bills.[42] None of this reassured the markets. Fearing devaluation or the imposition of exchange controls, savers liquidated their deposits as a first step toward transferring funds out of the country.

Aiding the banking system without jeopardizing the gold standard (and, for that matter, defending gold convertibility without destabilizing the banking system) required a foreign loan. Negotiations commenced at the Bank

---

[40] See Schubert 1990, pp. 14–15. The Credit Anstalt's difficulties had been compounded by bad loans inherited as a result of its absorption of another bank, the Bodenkreditanstalt, in 1929. That merger had been imposed on a reluctant Credit Anstalt by a government wishing to protect the national bank from losses on rediscounts it had extended to the Bodenkreditanstalt. This gave the Credit Anstalt a special claim to assistance in 1931.

[41] This linkage is emphasized by Harold James (1992, p. 600 and passim).

[42] Schubert 1991, pp. 59–61.

for International Settlements (BIS), the bankers' bank in Basel that was the logical agent to coordinate financial cooperation. They dragged on inconclusively. That the BIS had been created to manage the transfer of German reparations lent its deliberations a political cast. The French insisted that Austria first renounce the customs union proposal as a condition of receiving support. And the loan it finally obtained was a drop in the bucket given the rate at which funds were flowing out of the country.

Unable to avoid choosing between defending its banking system and defending its gold standard, Austria opted for the first alternative. But with memories of hyperinflation under floating rates still fresh, the government chose to impose exchange controls rather than allowing its currency to depreciate. Initially, controls were administered informally by the banking system. As the price of government support, the major Viennese banks agreed not to transfer capital or gold abroad or to provide funds to their customers for such purposes. Although these restraints worked surprisingly well, there remained an incentive for individual banks to renege on the agreement. In September, therefore, exchange controls were made official. The Austrian schilling fell to a 10–15 percent discount in Viennese coffee houses, the only place where foreign exchange was still traded.[43]

From Austria the crisis spread to Hungary and Germany. The Credit Anstalt possessed a controlling interest in Hungary's largest bank. When panic broke out in Vienna, foreign investors therefore began withdrawing their funds from Budapest's banks. Hungary was also burdened by reparations obligations and as an agricultural exporter had suffered significant terms-of-trade losses. The central bank had few resources at its disposal. A bank holiday was declared in July. The government froze foreign deposits and imposed exchange controls. The convertibility of domestic currency into gold and the right to export specie were suspended. As in Austria, the gold standard became a hollow shell.

Although the Credit Anstalt's investments in Germany were insignificant and German deposits in Vienna were limited, the Austrian and German banking systems resembled each other in important respects. German banks, like their Austrian counterparts, were heavily committed to industry and suffered extensive losses as a result of the Depression. The Credit Anstalt crisis therefore alerted observers to their vulnerability.[44] In Germany, as in Austria, the external accounts were only tenuously balanced, German payments stability hinging on capital inflows. The German *balance of trade* remained in modest surplus (Germany, as an exporter of industrial goods,

---

[43] See Ellis 1941, p. 30.

[44] Harold James 1984 and Peter Temin 1994a question the interdependence of the Austrian and German crises, downplaying these informational channels.

having experienced terms-of-trade gains rather than losses), but that surplus sufficed only to finance reparations, not also to service commercial debts.

Both domestic and foreign depositors withdrew their money from German banks after the outbreak of the Austrian crisis.[45] Initially, the Reichsbank provided liquidity to the banking system. But with Germany's short-term liabilities to foreigners three times the Reichsbank's reserves, the central bank had little room for maneuver. As recently as the end of May, Germany's monetary gold stock had been the fourth largest in the world and its ratio of gold to notes and sight liabilities was more than 50 percent. By June 21, the ratio had fallen to 40 percent, the statutory minimum. Episodes like this afforded "ample evidence," in the words of one observer, "that no gold supply can ever be adequate if adequacy is tested by the ability of a country to meet gold drains based on loss of confidence in the country's credit structure."[46]

Germany, like Austria, sought a foreign loan and a reparations moratorium. But Clement Moret, the governor of the Bank of France, echoing his country's position in its negotiations with Austria, demanded that the German government first reaffirm its pledge to provide reparations. George Harrison of the Federal Reserve Bank of New York insisted, perversely, that Germany agree to limit the provision of credit to the banking system. Harrison was willing to loan money to the Reichsbank only if the latter promised not to use it!

Meanwhile, the Reichsbank did what it could to defend the gold standard, limiting credit to the banking system in an effort to defend its reserves. The result of this stringency was, predictably, a banking crisis. The precipitating event was the failure of a textile firm, Nordwolle, that was a client of one of the large Berlin banks. On July 13 the government was forced to declare a bank holiday. It then imposed exchange controls. Germany, the largest industrial country in Europe and the world's second-leading industrial power, was no longer a member of the gold-standard club.

STERLING'S CRISIS

Because British banks had only loose connections with industry, they were insulated relatively well from the slump in industrial production.[47] But the

---

[45] Much as Swedish officials complained in 1992 that foreign investors caught unaware by the Finnish crisis were unable to distinguish one Nordic country from another, German politicians complained that foreigners failed to distinguish Berlin from Vienna and Budapest. See Chapter 5.

[46] Hardy 1936, p. 101.

[47] In addition, by U.S. standards, British banking was concentrated, providing an extra cush-

standstill agreements in Central Europe created difficulties for several of the merchant banks; Lazard Frères, for example, was on the brink of closure in July and was sustained only by extensive support from the Bank of England. Rumors were rife that other houses were in similar difficulties.[48]

In addition, the Bank of England had been battling reserve losses ever since the return to gold in 1925. For support the Bank had relied on the nation's "invisible earnings": interest and dividends on foreign investments, income from tourism, and receipts from shipping, insurance, and financial services rendered to foreigners (see *invisibles account* in the Glossary). Starting in 1930, other countries imposed tariffs to protect slump-ridden industries from foreign competition, and world trade collapsed, cutting into Britain's earnings from shipping and insurance. Larger still was the decline in interest, dividends, and profits on foreign investments. In 1930 this reflected the general deterioration of business conditions. In 1931 it was reinforced by debt default in Latin America and prohibitions on interest transfers by Austria, Hungary, and Germany. Between 1929 and 1931 the United Kingdom's trade balance deteriorated by £60 million, but its invisible balance worsened by more than twice that amount, making it increasingly difficult for the Bank of England to hold sterling within the gold points.[49] Gold losses accelerated in the second half of 1930, causing the Bank of France and the Federal Reserve Bank of New York to intervene in sterling's support. The exchange rate fell from $4.86¼ to $4.85½ in January 1931 before recovering (see Figs. 3.4–3.7).

Historians have emphasized these balance-of-payments trends.[50] The worsening current account, they observe, drained gold from the Bank of England and set the stage for the attack on sterling. The problem with this story is that the Bank possessed a powerful instrument, the discount rate, with which to defend itself. Utilizing it did not threaten the banking system, unlike the situation in Austria and Germany. The Bank raised its rate by a full point on July 23 and by another point a week later. If historical experience is any guide, these increases should have sufficed to attract capital in amounts that more than offset the deterioration in the current account.[51]

The question, then, is why capital kept flowing out. It may be that the markets viewed the Bank's discount-rate increases as unsustainable. Higher interest rates exacerbated unemployment and weakened support for a Labour

---

ion of profits, and widely branched, insulating it from region-specific shocks. An analysis of the implications for financial stability is Grossman 1994.

[48] See Sayers 1976, Vol. 2, pp. 530–31; James 1992, p. 602.

[49] Sayers 1976, Vol. 3, pp. 312–13.

[50] See, for example, Moggridge 1970.

[51] This is the conclusion drawn by Cairncross and Eichengreen (1983, pp. 81–82) on the basis of simulations of a small model of the British balance of payments.

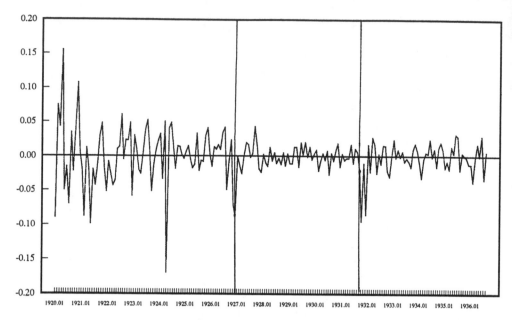

Figure 3.4. Franc-Sterling Real Exchange Rate, Janurary 1920–August 1936 (monthly change in relative wholesale prices). *Sources*: Nominal exchange rates from Federal Reserve Board 1943; wholesale prices from International Conference of Economic Services 1938.

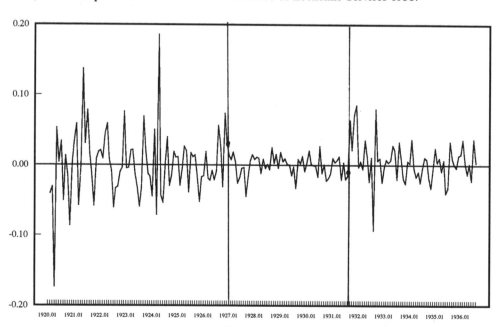

Figure 3.5. Swedish Krona–French Franc Real Exchange Rate, January 1920–August 1936 (monthly change in relative wholesale prices). *Sources*: Nominal exchange rates from Federal Reserve Board 1943; wholesale prices from International Conference of Economic Services 1938.

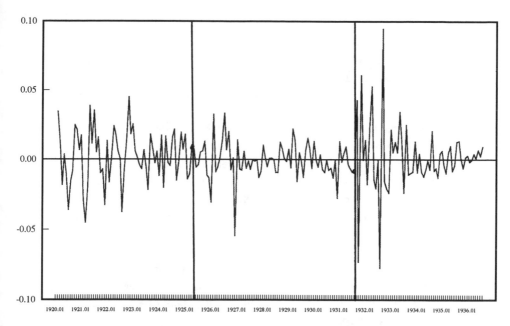

Figure 3.6. Swedish Krona–Sterling Real Exchange Rate, January 1920–August 1936 (monthly change in relative wholesale prices). *Sources*: Nominal exchange rates from Federal Reserve Board 1943; wholesale prices from International Conference of Economic Services 1938.

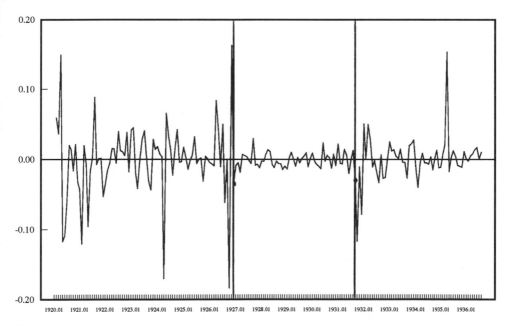

Figure 3.7. Belgian Franc–Sterling Real Exchange Rate, January 1920–August 1936 (monthly change in relative wholesale prices). *Sources*: Nominal exchange rates from Federal Reserve Board 1943; wholesale prices from International Conference of Economic Services 1938.

government that possessed only a parliamentary minority.[52] They aggravated the problem of nonperforming loans, weakening the position of banks whose earnings had already been devastated by the Central European standstill. High interest rates increased the cost of servicing the public debt and further undermined the fiscal position. Government debt was dominated by the huge mass of liquid bonds known as "war debt," and interest charges absorbed a third of government expenditure. The budget, having been in surplus in the late 1920s, lapsed into deficit in 1930–31.[53] If conditions failed to improve and unemployment continued to rise, pressure on the Bank to abandon its policies of austerity might prove irresistible.[54] The German crisis, which boded ill for European economic recovery, increased the likelihood that this would ultimately come to pass. The report of the Macmillan Committee had already called for measures to halt "the violent downturn of prices, the effects of which upon political and social stability have already been very great."[55] Anticipating that the government and the Bank of England might be forced to reverse course, speculators sold sterling.[56]

The Bank was prepared to maintain its discount rate at 2.5 percent, the July 16 level, or 3.5 percent, the July 23 level, notwithstanding unemployment of 20 percent. In the absence of an attack, the sterling parity was sustainable with a discount rate at that level. What was not sustainable for political reasons were additional increases in interest rates, or even the current level of rates, as the slump continued to worsen. Realizing that there were limits on how far the Bank of England was prepared to go, and that the Bank and the government were likely to reduce interest rates and switch to a

[52] In the words of Sidney Pollard (1969, p. 226), "It was, in part, the depth of the slump and the level of unemployment which inhibited the raising of the bank rate to panic heights." According to Diane Kunz (1987, p. 184), "With business already very depressed, neither management nor labour nor their representatives in Parliament were willing to pay the price which such a high Bank rate would exact."

[53] The Committee on National Expenditure, under Sir George May, called attention to these problems in a report published in July.

[54] These dynamics are modeled formally by Ozkan and Sutherland (1994).

[55] Committee on Finance and Industry 1931, p. 92.

[56] The timing of events supports this interpretation: on July 15, two days after the Darmstaedter und Nationalbank, one of Germany's largest financial institutions, failed to open its doors, sterling dropped by a cent and a half, passing through the lower gold point against other major currencies. When the seven-power conference on German reparations deadlocked, making it apparent that the German crisis would not be resolved quickly, sterling fell again. The government's £56 million in proposed spending cuts and the Bank of England's success in obtaining credits from the Bank of France and the Federal Reserve Bank of New York delayed the collapse until September, but none of these expedients reduced unemployment or eliminated the problem it created for defense of the sterling parity.

policy of "cheap money" once their investment in the gold standard was lost, the markets forced the issue. The German crisis provided a focal point for concerted action by currency traders. By selling sterling in sufficient quantities to force interest-rate increases of a magnitude that no democratically elected government facing 20 percent unemployment could support, they precipitated the abandonment of a parity that would otherwise have remained viable. Borrowing limited amounts of hard currency in New York and London, as the government did in early September, only put off the day of reckoning; although it placed additional resources at the government's command, it also increased the country's foreign indebtedness, reinforcing the skepticism of speculators about its long-term prospects and encouraging them to redouble their efforts.[57] Once launched, the attack on sterling was impossible to contain.

Britain's suspension of convertibility on September 19, 1931, more than any other event, symbolized the interwar gold standard's disintegration. Sterling had been at the center of the prewar system. It had been one of the dual anchors of its interwar successor. Then it lost a third of its value against gold in three months. This decline undermined confidence in other currencies. Foreign central banks shifted out of dollar reserves and into gold for fear that they might suffer capital losses on their dollar balances. The markets, suddenly willing to think the unthinkable—that the dollar might be devalued—sold off the currency, forcing the Federal Reserve to jack up interest rates.

The shift from dollars to gold compressed the reserve base of the global monetary system. By the beginning of 1932, some two dozen countries responded to the pressure by abandoning convertibility and depreciating their currencies. As a global system, the gold standard was history.

THE DOLLAR FOLLOWS

Gold convertibility was then limited to Western Europe (where France, Belgium, Switzerland, Holland, Czechoslovakia, Poland, and Romania continued to adhere), to the United States and the Latin American countries in its sphere of influence, and to those nations' overseas dependencies (the Netherlands East Indies and the Philippines, for example). A second group of countries in Central and Eastern Europe supported their currencies by applying exchange controls. Although their exchange rates remained nomi-

---

[57] Buiter (1987) analyzes a model in which borrowing abroad to defend the exchange rate can only intensify a crisis.

nally unchanged, international financial flows were controlled and supplies of foreign currency were rationed, leading to the emergence of black-market discounts. A third group was made up of countries that followed the Bank of England off gold and pegged to sterling. They enjoyed many of the benefits of exchange rate stability by linking their currencies to the pound and, like Britain, reduced interest rates to stimulate recovery from the Depression.

In countries that abandoned the gold standard and depreciated their currencies, expenditure shifted away from the products of the gold bloc, which had become more expensive. The exchange controls of Germany and its Eastern European neighbors had the same effect. Members of the gold bloc saw their competitive positions worsen and their balances of payments deteriorate. Demand weakened in the gold-standard world, deepening the Depression and intensifying the pressure to reverse policies of austerity. With the writing on the wall, investors began to question the stability of the remaining gold-based currencies.

First to go was the dollar, which was devalued in 1933. Until FDR assumed office in March, output continued to fall and unemployment worsened. Banks failed at an alarming rate. The Hoover administration had few options, for the gold standard precluded reflationary initiatives. Late in 1931, the Bank of France, which had suffered a 35 percent loss on its sterling exchange as a result of Britain's devaluation, resumed the liquidation of its foreign balances, including its dollars. The Federal Reserve, which possessed little free gold, was forced to permit these reserve losses to further deplete the U.S. money supply.

In March of 1932, a Congress looking forward to an election campaign began pressing the Fed to initiate expansionary open-market operations. It passed the Glass-Steagall Act, removing the free-gold constraint that had previously inhibited expansionary initiatives (although the 40 percent gold cover requirement remained).[58] The Open-Market Committee acceded to congressional pressure, expanding domestic credit by purchasing bonds. Predictably, reserves flowed out, and the dollar's gold parity was threatened. In the nick of time, Congress adjourned for the reelection campaign, permitting the Fed to curtail its intervention. While the Fed's about-face succeeded in supporting the dollar's gold parity, the episode revealed the breadth of support for reflationary action. It heightened skepticism in currency markets about the commitment of elected officals, especially Democratic ones, to the maintenance of the gold standard.[59]

[58] For details on the operation of the free-gold constraint, see footnote 28 above.

[59] A review of these political developments and their impact on the markets is provided by Epstein and Ferguson 1984.

Roosevelt's victory confirmed their fears. Observers, conscious of FDR's penchant for experimentation, were aware of the pressure he would feel from the variety of proposals wending their way through Congress to force the Treasury and the Federal Reserve System to reflate the economy. Echoing the Populist Alliance of the 1890s, the representatives of farm states banded together with silver-mining interests in an effort to legislate silver purchases, which they were prepared to advocate even if initiating such purchases forced them to abandon the gold standard.

It was conceivable that Roosevelt would bow to these pressures. Anticipating this eventuality, investors withdrew money from the banks in order to convert it into gold and foreign exchange.[60] The new president did not take long to validate their expectations. Upon assuming office in March, he was met with bank runs in virtually every state and declared a bank holiday. In the third week of April he followed up by suspending gold convertibility. The dollar fell by more than 10 percent over the remainder of the month. Following a period of stability that coincided with discussion of a possible currency stabilization agreement at the London Economic Conference, the administration pushed the dollar down by purchasing gold at progressively higher prices set each morning by Roosevelt and a coterie of advisers breakfasting in the president's bedroom on eggs and coffee.[61] By January 1934, when the dollar was finally stabilized, the price of gold had risen from $20.67 to $35 an ounce.

America's departure from the gold standard encouraged other countries to follow. It led to the formation of a "little dollar bloc," which consisted of the United States, the Philippines, Cuba, and much of Central America, with Canada and Argentina following at a distance. The impact on the remaining gold-standard countries was predictable. Their depressions deepened, heightening pressure for the adoption of reflationary policies. Their payments positions weakened, threatening the maintenance of gold convertibility unless policies of austerity were reinforced. One by one the members of the gold bloc were forced to suspend convertibility: Czechoslovakia in

[60] For details, see Kennedy 1973 and Wigmore 1989. In Chapter 4 we will see that there are parallels with the market's reaction to the election of John F. Kennedy in 1960.

[61] Neither Roosevelt nor his advisers had a coherent vision of international economic policy. Fred Block (1977, p. 26) calls them "notoriously inept" in their grasp of economics. FDR's views were heavily influenced by the ideas of two Cornell University agricultural economists, George Warren and Frank Pearson. Warren and Pearson had uncovered a correlation between the prices of agricultural commodities (which they took as a proxy for the health of the economy) and the price of gold. To encourage the recovery of agricultural prices they urged Roosevelt to raise the dollar price of gold, indirectly bringing about the devaluation of the dollar. See Warren and Pearson 1935.

1934, Belgium in 1935, and France, the Netherlands, and Switzerland in 1936. The return to floating was complete.

Managed Floating

Exchange rates, though floating again, often varied by less than they had in the first half of the 1920s (see *managed floating* in the Glossary). Exchange Equalization Accounts intervened in the markets, leaning against the wind in order to prevent currencies from moving sharply. Monetary and fiscal policies were less erratic than they had been in high-inflation countries in the 1920s. For some exchange rates, notably the French franc–British pound rate shown in Figure 3.4, month-to-month real rate movements resembled those of the immediately preceding gold-standard years more than those of the first half of the 1920s. The volatility of most other exchange rates was greater, resembling that of the early 1920s.[62]

Having severed the link with the gold standard, governments and central banks had greater freedom to pursue independent economic policies. Britain could attach priority to stimulating recovery; the Bank of England was free to reduce Bank rate as long as it was prepared to allow sterling to decline against gold-backed currencies. Cutting the discount rate helped to reduce market interest rates, both nominal and real, which ignited a recovery led by interest-rate-sensitive sectors such as residential construction.[63] In an effort to reconcile interest-rate cuts with orderly currency markets, the Bank of England and the British Exchange Equalisation Account (which opened in July 1932) intervened to ensure that sterling declined in an orderly fashion.[64]

An internationally coordinated program of macroeconomic reflation would have been better still: had all countries agreed to reduce interest rates and expand their money supplies, they could have stimulated their economies

---

[62] One cannot reject the hypothesis that the variance of the franc-sterling rate was no different in the third period depicted in the diagram (September 1931–August 1936) than in the second (January 1927–August 1931). Differences in the behavior of the other three exchange rates shown in Figures 3.5–3.7 are more evident, but it is also true for the krona-sterling rate that one cannot reject the null of equal variances.

[63] Matte Viren (1994) shows that *central bank discount rates* had a powerful effect on real and nominal rates, which clearly dominated the effects of other macroeconomic determinants of interest rates.

[64] The Exchange Equalisation Account was initially authorized to issue £150 million in Treasury bills, which it used to acquire gold. Subsequently, it used those reserves to intervene in the foreign-exchange market to damp what it regarded as excessive fluctuations in the exchange rate. For details, see Howson 1980.

more effectively and done so without destabilizing their exchange rates. When the United States expanded, as it did in 1932, the dollar weakened, but had France expanded at the same time, the dollar would have strengthened. The gold standard and reflation could have been reconciled with each other. But internationally coordinated reflationary initiatives did not prove possible to arrange. The United States, France, and Britain were unable to agree on concerted action. In particular, their efforts to do so at the 1933 London Economic Conference came to naught. The French, preoccupied by the inflation of the 1920s, rejected monetary reflation as a source of speculative excesses and economic instability—as part of the problem rather than part of the solution. The British refused to tie their policies to those of a foreign partner of whose intentions they were unsure. The United States refused to wait.

Hence, the reflationary measures that were undertaken in the 1930s were initiated unilaterally. Inevitably they involved currency depreciation. Depreciation enhanced the competitiveness of goods produced at home, switching demand toward them and stimulating net exports. The improvement in the initiating country's competitiveness was, of course, a deterioration in the competitiveness of its trading partners. This led commentators to refer disparagingly to currency depreciation as *beggar-thy-neighbor devaluation*. But the fact that these depreciations were self-serving should not be allowed to obscure their effectiveness. The timing of depreciation goes a long way toward explaining the timing of recovery. The early devaluation of the British pound helps to explain the fact that Britain's recovery commenced in 1931. U.S. recovery coincided with the dollar's devaluation in 1933. France's late recovery was clearly linked to its unwillingness to devalue until 1936. The mechanism connecting devaluation and recovery was straightforward. Countries that allowed their currencies to depreciate expanded their money supplies. Depreciation removed the imperative of cutting government spending and raising taxes in order to defend the exchange rate. It removed the restraints that prevented countries from stabilizing their banking systems.[65]

Thus, currency depreciation in the 1930s was part of the solution to the Depression, not part of the problem. Its effects would have operated more powerfully if the decision to abandon the gold standard had occasioned the adoption of more expansionary policies. Had central banks initiated aggressive programs of expansionary open-market operations, the problem of inadequate aggregate demand would have been erased more quickly. The growth

[65] Evidence documenting these linkages is reported by Eichengreen and Sachs 1985. Campa 1990 and Eichengreen 1988 show that the same relationships hold in Latin America and Australasia.

in the demand for money that accompanied recovery could have been met out of an expansion of domestic credit rather than requiring additional imports of gold and capital from abroad. This would have diminished the gold losses suffered by countries that clung to the gold standard, attenuating the beggar-thy-neighbor effects of currency depreciation.

But because fears of inflation were rife, even in the slump, expansionary initiatives were tentative. Countries depreciating their currencies and shifting demand toward the products of domestic industry satisfied their growing demands for money and credit by strengthening their balances of payments and importing capital and reserves from abroad. Their reserve gains were reserve losses for countries still on gold. But the problem was not that devaluation took place; it was that the practice was not more widespread and that it did not prompt the adoption of even more expansionary policies. Abandoning the gold standard allowed countries to regain their policy independence. And by devoting some of that independence to policies of leaning against the wind in currency markets, they were able to do so without allowing the foreign exchanges to descend into chaos.

Why, if this managed float combined a modicum of exchange rate stability with policy autonomy, did it not provide a model for the international monetary system after World War II? To a large extent, postwar observers viewed the managed float of the 1930s through spectacles colored by the less satisfactory free float of the 1920s. Past experience continued to shape—some would say distort—contemporary perceptions of the international monetary regime. A further objection was that managed floating led to protectionism. Depreciation by the United Kingdom and the United States led France and Belgium to raise their tariffs and tighten import quotas in the effort to defend their overvalued currencies. It was not merely short-term exchange rate volatility as a source of uncertainty that policymakers opposed but also the predictable medium-term exchange rate swings that fueled protectionist pressures.[66]

In 1936, when the final round of devaluations loomed, France, the United States, and the United Kingdom negotiated the Tripartite Agreement. France promised to limit the franc's depreciation in return for the United States and Britain's promising to refrain from meeting one depreciation with another. The agreement committed the signatories to remove import quotas and to work for the reconstruction of the multilateral trading system. Even though

---

[66] Chapter 5 develops a similar argument in the context of European monetary unification and the European Union's Single Market Program. There I suggest that exchange rate swings could subvert efforts to construct a truly integrated market, as they undermined international trade in the 1930s.

trade conflict was not directly responsible for the war clouds darkening European skies, exchange rate fluctuations that created commercial conflicts were not helpful for cultivating cooperation among the countries that shared an interest in containing Germany's expansionist ambitions. When, during and after World War II, the United States led efforts to reconstruct the international monetary system, it sought arrangements that provided exchange rate stability specifically to support the establishment of a durable trading system.

CONCLUSIONS

The development of the international monetary system between the wars can be understood in terms of three interrelated political and economic changes. The first one was growing tension between competing economic policy objectives. Currency stability and gold convertibility were the unquestioned priorities of central banks and treasuries up to the outbreak of World War I. In the 1920s and 1930s things were different. A range of domestic economic objectives that might be attained through the active use of monetary policy acquired a priority they had not possessed in the nineteenth century. The trade-off between internal and external objectives began to bind. The single-minded pursuit of exchange rate stability that characterized central bank policy before the war became a thing of the past.

A second, related, change was the increasingly Janus-faced nature of international capital flows. Capital flows were part of the glue that bound national economies together. They financed the trade and foreign investment through which those economies were linked. When monetary policies enjoyed credibility, those capital flows relieved the pressure on central banks to defend temporarily weak exchange rates. But the new priority attached to internal objectives meant that credibility was not to be taken for granted. In the new circumstances of the interwar period, international capital movements could aggravate rather than relieve the pressure on central banks.

The third development that distinguished the prewar and interwar periods was the changing center of gravity of the international system; its weight shifted away from the United Kingdom and toward the United States. Before World War I, the international monetary system had fit the international trading system like a hand in a glove. Britain had been the principal source of both financial and physical capital for the overseas regions of recent settlement; it had provided the principal market for the primary commodity exports that generated the foreign exchange needed to service the borrowers' external debts. Between the wars, the United States overtook Britain as the leading player in the commercial and the financial domains. But America's foreign financial and commercial relations did not yet fit together in a way that produced a harmoniously working international system.

Hence, when postwar planners again contemplated the reconstruction of the international system, they sought a framework capable of accommodating these changed conditions. The solution to their problem was not straightforward.

The Bretton Woods System

To suppose that there exists some smoothly functioning automatic
mechanism of adjustment which preserves equilibrium if we only
trust to methods of laissez-faire is a doctrinaire delusion which
disregards the lessons of historical experience without having
behind it the support of sound theory.

(John Maynard Keynes)

Even today, more than three decades after its demise, the Bretton Woods international monetary system remains an enigma. For some, Bretton Woods was a critical component of the postwar golden age of growth. It delivered a degree of exchange rate stability that was admirable when compared with the volatility of the preceding and subsequent periods. It dispatched payments problems, permitting the unprecedented expansion of international trade and investment that fueled the postwar boom.

Other perspectives on Bretton Woods are less rosy. Ease of adjustment, it is argued, was a consequence rather than a cause of buoyant growth. And the notion that Bretton Woods reconciled exchange rate stability with open markets was largely an illusion. Governments restricted international capital movements throughout the Bretton Woods years. Foreign investment occurred despite, not because of, the implications of Brettton Woods for international capital mobility.

The Bretton Woods System departed from the gold-exchange standard in three fundamental ways. Pegged exchange rates became adjustable, subject to specific conditions (namely, the existence of what was known as "fundamental disequilibrium"). Controls were permitted to limit international capital flows. And a new institution, the International Monetary Fund, was created to monitor national economic policies and extend balance-of-payments financing to countries at risk. These innovations addressed the major worries that policymakers inherited from the 1920s and 1930s. The adjustable peg was an instrument for eliminating balance-of-payments deficits—an alternative to the deflationary increases in central bank discount rates that had proved so painful between the wars. Controls were designed to avert the threat posed by volatile capital flows of the sort that were disruptive in both interwar decades. And the IMF, armed with financial resources, powers of surveillance, and a *scarce-currency-clause*, could sanction governments responsible for policies that destabilized the international system and compensate countries that were adversely affected.

In principle, these three elements of the Bretton Woods System complemented one another. Pegged but adjustable exchange rates were feasible only because capital controls insulated countries seeking to protect their currencies from destabilizing capital flows and provided the breathing space needed to organize orderly adjustments. IMF resources provided an extra line of defense for countries attempting to maintain pegged exchange rates in the face of market pressures. And the Fund's surveillance discouraged the kind of changes in parities and controls that might have led to abuses of the system.

Unfortunately, the three elements of this triad did not function entirely harmoniously in practice. The adjustable peg proved to be an oxymoron: parity changes, especially by the industrial countries at the center of the system, were extraordinarily rare. IMF surveillance turned out to have blunt teeth. The Fund's resources were quickly dwarfed by the postwar payments problem, and the scarce-currency clause that was supposed to sanction countries whose policies threatened the stability of the system was never invoked.

Capital controls were the one element that functioned more or less as planned. Observers today, their impressions colored by the highly articulated financial markets of the late-twentieth century, are skeptical of the enforceability of such measures. But circumstances were different in the quarter-century after World War II. This was a period when governments intervened extensively in their economies and financial systems. Interest rates were capped. The assets in which banks could invest were restricted. Governments regulated financial markets to channel credit toward strategic sectors. The need to obtain import licenses complicated efforts to channel capital transactions through the current account. Controls held back the flood because they were not just one rock in a swiftly flowing stream. They were part of the series of levees and locks with which the raging rapids were tamed.

The efficacy of controls should not be exaggerated. They were more effective in the 1940s and 1950s than subsequently. As the white-water analogy suggests, the relaxation of domestic regulations and current-account restrictions weakened their operation. With the return to current-account convertibility in 1959, it became easier to over- and under-invoice imports and exports and otherwise channel capital transactions through the current account. But those who would minimize the effectiveness of capital controls in the Bretton Woods years overlook the fact that governments were continually testing their limits. The needs of postwar reconstruction were immense. Reducing unemployment and stimulating growth implied running the economy under high pressure of demand. Governments pushed to the limit the implications for the balance of payments, straining controls to the breaking point.

Indeed, in the 1950s, before the Bretton Woods System came into full operation, countries experiencing persistent balance-of-payments deficits and reserve losses tightened not just capital controls but also exchange restrictions and licensing requirements for importers, or at least slowed the rate at which they were relaxed, in order to strengthen the trade balance. Such restrictions on current-account transactions would not have been effective without the simultaneous maintenance of capital controls.

The retention of controls was essential because of the absence of a conventional adjustment mechanism. The commitment to full employment and growth that was integral to the postwar social compact inhibited the use of expenditure-reducing policies. The deflationary central bank policies that had redressed payments deficits under the gold standard were no longer acceptable politically. The International Monetary Fund lacked the power to influence national policies and the resources to finance the payments imbalances that resulted. Allowing countries to change their exchange rates only in the event of a fundamental disequilibrium prevented them from using *expenditure-switching policies* to anticipate problems. The exchange rate could be changed only in a climate of crisis; therefore in order to avoid provoking crisis conditions, the authorities could not even contemplate the possibility. As William Scammell put it, "By attempting a compromise between the gold standard and fixed rates on the one hand and flexible rates on the other the Bretton Woods planners arrived at a condition which . . . [was] not a true adjustment system at all."[1]

Exchange controls substituted for the missing adjustment mechanism, bottling up the demand for imports when the external constraint began to bind. But starting in 1959, with the restoration of current-account convertibility, this instrument was no longer available.[2] Controls remained on transactions on *capital account*, but their use did not ensure adjustment; it only delayed the day of reckoning. In the absence of an adjustment mechanism, the col-

[1] Scammell 1975, pp. 81–82.

[2] Some countries did maintain modest controls: the United Kingdom, for example, lifted exchange controls for nonresidents, as required by Article VIII of the IMF Articles of Agreement, but retained some controls on international financial transactions by residents. In any case, the scope for utilizing such restrictions for balance-of-payments purposes was greatly reduced.

lapse of the Bretton Woods international monetary system became inevitable. The marvel is that it survived for so long.

WARTIME PLANNING AND ITS CONSEQUENCES

Planning for the postwar international monetary order had been under way since 1940 in the United Kingdom and 1941 in the United States.[3] Under the terms of the Atlantic Charter of August 1941 and the Mutual Aid Agreement of February 1942, the British pledged to restore sterling's convertibility on current account and accepted the principle of nondiscrimination in trade in return for U.S. promises to extend financial assistance on favorable terms and to respect the priority the British attached to full employment. Attempting to reconcile these objectives were John Maynard Keynes, by now the grand old man of economics and unpaid adviser to the chancellor of the Exchequer, and Harry Dexter White, a brash and truculent former academic and U.S. Treasury economist.[4] Their rival plans passed through a series of drafts. The final versions, published in 1943, provided the basis for the "Joint Statement" of British and American experts and the Articles of Agreement of the International Monetary Fund.

The Keynes and White Plans differed in the obligations they imposed on creditor countries and the exchange rate flexibility and capital mobility they permitted. The Keynes Plan would have allowed countries to change their exchange rates and apply exchange and trade restrictions as required to reconcile full employment with payments balance. The White Plan, in contrast, foresaw a world free of controls and of pegged currencies superintended by an international institution with veto power over parity changes. To prevent deflationary policies abroad from forcing countries to import unemployment, Keynes's Clearing Union provided for extensive balance-of-payments financing (subject to increasingly strict conditionality and penalty interest rates) and significant exchange rate flexibility. If the United States ran persistent payments surpluses, as it had in the 1930s, it would be obliged to finance the total drawing rights of other countries, which came to $23 billion in Keynes's scheme.

---

[3] The failure of the Genoa Conference, which was convened three years after the conclusion of World War I, and the unsatisfactory operation of the international monetary system in the 1920s reminded the American and British governments not to neglect planning. The best review of wartime negotiations remains Gardner 1969.

[4] This is the Harry D. White whose research on the French balance of payments in the nineteenth century figures in Chapter 2.

Predictably, the Americans opposed Keynes's Clearing Union for "involving unlimited liability for potential creditors."[5] The Congress, American negotiators insisted, would not sign a blank check. The White Plan therefore limited total drawing rights to a much more modest $5 billion and the U.S. obligation to $2 billion.

The Joint Statement and the Articles of Agreement were a compromise, one that reflected the asymmetric bargaining power of the British and Americans. Quotas were $8.8 billion, closer to the White Plan's $5 billion than the Keynes Plan's $26 billion.[6] The maximum U.S. obligation was $2.75 billion, far closer to White's $2 billion than to Keynes's $23 billion.[7]

The less generous the financing, the greater the need for exchange rate flexibility. And so U.S. proposals for fixed rates went by the board. The compromise between U.S. insistence that exchange rates be pegged and British insistence that they be adjustable was, predictably, the "adjustable peg." Article XX of the agreement required countries to declare par values for their currencies in terms of gold or a currency convertible into gold (which in practice meant the dollar) and to hold their exchange rates within 1 percent of those levels. Par values could be changed to correct a "fundamental disequilibrium" by 10 percent following consultations with the Fund but without its prior approval, by larger margins with the approval of three-quarters of Fund voting power. The meaning of the critical phrase "fundamental disequilibrium" was left undefined. Or, as Raymond Mikesell put it, it was never defined in fewer than ten pages.[8]

In addition, the Articles of Agreement permitted the maintenance of con-

[5] See Harrod 1952, p. 3. There is an analogy with the situation in Europe in the 1970s. In 1978, when the creation of the European Monetary System was under discussion, the German Bundesbank was similarly reluctant to agree to a system that obligated it to unlimited support for weak-currency countries. See Chapter 5.

[6] This $26 billion figure is the sum of the $3 billion of drawing rights to which the United States would have been entitled under the Keynes Plan and the above-mentioned $23 billion of other countries.

[7] Quotas were, however, subject to quinquennial review under the provisions of the Articles of Agreement (Article III, Section 2) and could be increased with the approval of countries that possessed 80 percent of total voting power. White insisted to Keynes (in a letter dated July 24, 1943) that it would be impossible to marshal support for more than $2–3 billion from an isolationist Congress. See Keynes 1980, p. 336. Even that amount was not certain to receive congressional ratification. The timing of the Bretton Woods Conference was determined by the desire to finalize the Articles of the Agreement before the November 1944 congressional elections, in which isolationist Republicans were expected to make major gains. The venue, the Mount Washington Hotel in Bretton Woods, New Hampshire, was chosen in part to win over that state's incumbent Republican senator, Charles Tobey.

[8] See Mikesell 1994.

trols on international capital movements. This was contrary to White's early vision of a world free of controls on both trade and financial flows. In the same way that their insistence on limiting the volume of finance forced the Americans to accede to British demands for exchange rate flexibility, it forced them to accept the maintenance of capital controls.

Finally, the British secured a scarce-currency clause authorizing controls on imports from countries that ran persistent payments surpluses and whose currencies became scarce within the Fund. This would occur if, for example, the United States' cumulative surpluses reached $2 billion and its contribution to Fund resources were fully utilized to finance the dollar deficits of other countries. In addition, the British secured American agreement to a limited period in which controls on current transactions could be maintained. Under Article XIV, the IMF would report on countries' controls after three years, and after five it would begin advising members on policies to facilitate their removal, the implicit threat being that countries making insufficient progress could be asked to leave the Fund.

In retrospect, the belief that this system could work was extraordinarily naive. The modest quotas and drawing rights of the Articles of Agreement were dwarfed by the dollar shortage that emerged before the IMF opened for business in 1947. Postwar Europe had immense unsatisfied demands for foodstuffs, capital goods, and other merchandise produced in the United States and only limited capacity to produce goods for export; its consolidated trade deficit with the rest of the world rose to $5.8 billion in 1946 and $7.5 billion in 1947. In recognition of this fact, between 1948 and 1951, a period that overlapped with the IMF's first four years of operation, the United States extended some $13 billion in intergovernmental aid to finance Europe's deficits (under the provisions of the Marshall Plan). This was more than four times the drawing rights established on Europe's behalf and more than six times the maximum U.S. obligation under the Articles of Agreement. Yet despite support far surpassing that envisaged in the Articles of Agreement, the initial system of par values proved unworkable. In September 1949 European currencies were devalued by an average of 30 percent. And still import controls proved impossible to remove.

How could American planners have so underestimated the severity of the problem? Certainly, there was inadequate appreciation in the United States of the damage suffered by the European and Japanese economies and of the costs of reconstruction.[9] This bias was reinforced by the faith of American

[9] Europeans closer to the problem appreciated the magnitude of their prospective payments difficulties. The IMF, for its part, made note in its first two reports of the need for adjustment of rates.

planners in the power of international trade to heal all wounds. Cordell Hull, FDR's long-time secretary of state, had made the restoration of an open multilateral trading system an American priority. Extensive trading links, in his view, would heighten the interdependence of the French and German economies, suppress political and diplomatic conflicts, and prevent the two countries from again going to war. Trade would fuel recovery and provide Europe with the hard-currency earnings needed to import raw materials and capital goods. Once an open, multilateral trading system was restored, Europe could export its way out of the dollar shortage and out of its problems of postwar reconstruction, allowing the system of convertible currencies to be maintained.

The administration's free-trade orientation was supported by American industry, which saw export markets as vital to postwar prosperity and Britain's system of *imperial preference* as hindering its market access. War industry had boomed in the U.S. South and along the Pacific Coast; the growth there of aircraft and munitions manufacturers brought additional states into the free-trade camp.[10] There was more enthusiasm in the Congress for the trade-promoting thrust of the Bretton Woods Agreement than for its abstruse monetary provisions; without the emphasis placed on the former in the Articles of Agreement, it is unlikely that the Congress would have agreed to ratification.

Thus, the restoration of open, multilateral trade was to be the tonic that would invigorate the Bretton Woods System. The entire agreement was oriented toward this goal. As one author put it, "[To] provisions for the re-establishment of multilateral trade the Americans attached great importance, believing such re-establishment to be the main *raison d'etre* of the [International Monetary] Fund, equal in importance to its stabilization functions."[11] The Americans' insistence on a system of pegged exchange rates to be changed by substantial amounts only with IMF approval was intended to avoid the kind of international monetary turmoil that would hinder the reconstruction of trade. Along with negotiating the IMF Articles of Agreement, the delegates at Bretton Woods adopted a series of recommendations, including one to create a sister organization to be in charge of drawing down tariffs in the same way that the IMF was to oversee the removal of monetary impediments to trade. Article VIII prohibited countries from restricting payments on current account without Fund approval. Currencies were to be

---

[10] Frieden 1988 emphasizes that disruptions to the European economy that enhanced the export competitiveness of U.S. manufacturers also worked to shift them into the free-trade camp.

[11] Scammell 1975, p. 115.

convertible at official rates, and no member was to adopt discriminatory currency arrangements. Article XIV instructed countries to substantially remove monetary restrictions on trade within five years of the date the Fund commenced operations.

We will never know whether the rapid dismantling of controls on current-account transactions would have boosted European exports sufficiently to eliminate the dollar shortage. For instead of removing them, Western European countries maintained, and in some cases added to, their wartime restrictions. In Eastern Europe exchange controls were used to close loopholes that would have undermined state trading. Latin American countries used multiple exchange rates to promote import-substituting industrialization. While some countries made slow progress in removing monetary impediments to trade, others were forced to backtrack. Overall there was movement in a liberalizing direction, but the five-year transitional period stretched out to more than twice that length.

There are several explanations for this failure to liberalize at the anticipated pace. Sustaining a more liberal trading system would have required European countries to boost their exports, which in turn would have entailed a substantial depreciation of exchange rates to render their goods more competitive internationally. Governments resisted trade liberalization on the grounds that it would have worsened the terms of trade and lowered living standards. Import restrictions acted like tariffs; they turned the terms of trade in Europe's favor at the expense of the United States. A substantial worsening of the terms of trade and decline in living standards threatened to provoke labor unrest and disrupt the recovery process.[12] The IMF was aware that the par values submitted in 1945–46 implied that currencies would be overvalued if import restrictions were removed. While wartime inflation had proceeded much faster in Europe than in the United States, about half the exchange rates were as high against the U.S. dollar as they had been in 1939.[13] Rather than objecting, the Fund acceded to European claims that high exchange rates were necessary for domestic political reasons.[14]

Trade restrictions might be dismantled without creating unsustainable

---

[12] I pursue this line of thought in my 1993 book. Sometimes the argument is phrased differently: namely, that the substantial devaluations that would have been required by the removal of controls would not have worked because higher import prices would have provoked wage inflation (see Scammell 1975, p. 142 and passim). But the point is the same—that workers would not have acquiesced to the substantial reductions in living standards implied by a real depreciation.

[13] This was argued at the time; see, for example, Metzler 1947.

[14] It did, however, press for devaluation in 1948–49.

deficits or requiring substantial currency depreciation if government spending were cut and demand were reduced. If postwar governments had not attached priority to sustaining investment, the external constraint would not have bound so tightly.[15] Once again, domestic politics were the impediment to action. Where the Americans saw trade as the engine of growth, Europeans believed that investment was key. And curtailing investment, besides slowing recovery and growth, would be seen by European labor as reneging on the commitment to full employment.

Above all, efforts to liberalize trade were stymied by a coordination problem—by the need for European countries to act simultaneously. Countries could import more only if they exported more, but this was possible only if other countries also liberalized. The International Trade Organization (ITO) had been designed to cut this Gordian knot by coordinating the simultaneous reduction of tariffs and quotas. Hence, the failure of the United States to ratify the Havana Charter (the agreement to bring the ITO into being, finalized by the fifty-six countries participating in the United Nations Conference on Trade and Employment held in the Cuban capital) was a devastating blow. The agreement was squeezed between protectionists who opposed its liberal thrust and perfectionists who criticized the myriad exceptions from open trade extended to countries seeking to establish full employment, accelerate their economic development, or stabilize the prices of commodity exports.[16] Caught in the cross fire, the Truman administration declined to resubmit the charter to Congress in 1950.[17]

The General Agreement on Tariffs and Trade (GATT), thrust into the breach, made limited progress in its early years.[18] The first GATT round, in Geneva in 1947, led the United States to cut its tariffs by a third, but the other twenty-two contracting parties made minimal concessions. The second round at Annecy in 1949 involved no additional concessions by the twenty-three founding members. The third round (at Torquay in 1950–51) was a failure, the contracting parties agreeing on only 144 of the 400 items they had hoped to negotiate. The GATT's ambiguous status limited the scope for coordination with the IMF, complicating efforts to trade tariff concessions for the elimination of exchange controls. The IMF, for its part, did not see its place as arranging reciprocal concessions.

[15] This is the conclusion of Milward 1984.

[16] The definitive autopsy of the Havana Charter is Diebold 1952.

[17] In a sense, the ITO charter was also a casualty of the cold war. Once conflict with the Soviets broke out, the Marshall Plan (whose second appropriation bill was under congressional consideration) and NATO took precedence.

[18] For details, see Irwin 1995.

Thus, the kind of network externalities referred to in the preface to this book and emphasized in Chapter 2's analysis of the classical gold standard blocked a rapid transition to current-account convertibility. As long as other countries retained inconvertible currencies, it made sense for each individual country to do so, even though all countries would have been better off had they shifted to convertibility simultaneously. The framers of the Bretton Woods Agreement had sought to break this logjam by specifying a schedule for the restoration of convertibility and by creating an institution, the IMF, to oversee the process. In the event, the measures they provided were inadequate.

Eventually, the industrial countries created the European Payments Union to coordinate the removal of current-account restrictions. In the meantime they suffered through a series of upheavals, notably Britain's 1947 convertibility crisis and the 1949 devaluations.

THE STERLING CRISIS AND THE REALIGNMENT OF EUROPEAN CURRENCIES

The inability of one country to restore convertibility without the cooperation of others was illustrated by Britain's attempt to do so in 1947. Inflation had not proceeded as rapidly in Britain as on the European continent, and it was not clear that sterling was overvalued on purchasing-power-parity grounds.[19] Nor was war-related destruction of infrastructure and industrial capacity as extensive as in many European countries. But as long as other European countries maintained high tariffs and quantitative restrictions, the scope for expanding exports was limited. The country found itself unable to penetrate other European markets sufficiently to generate the export revenues needed to support a convertible currency.[20]

Britain's attempt to restore convertibility was further complicated by its delicate financial condition. The country had emerged from World War II with a monetary overhang (the money supply having tripled between 1938 and 1947 but nominal GNP having only doubled, reflecting the use of price controls to bottle up inflation). Private and official holdings of gold and dollars had fallen by 50 percent. Foreign assets had been requisitioned, and controls on foreign investment had prevented British residents from replac-

---

[19] Again, this was Metzler's conclusion (1947).

[20] The United Kingdom's response was to cultivate closer trade relations with its Commonwealth and Empire (as described in Schenk 1994). This did not bridge the dollar gap, however.

ing them. Between 1939 and 1945 the Commonwealth and Empire had accumulated sterling balances in return for supplying foodstuffs and raw materials to the British war machine. At the war's end, overseas sterling balances exceeded £3.5 billion, or one-third of the United Kingdom's GNP. U.K. gold and foreign-exchange reserves were barely half a billion pounds.

If the holders of overseas sterling attempted to rebalance their portfolios or to purchase goods in the dollar area, a fire sale of sterling-denominated assets would have followed. Shunning radical alternatives, such as the forced conversion of sterling balances into nonnegotiable claims, the British government sought to limit dollar convertibility to currently earned sterling, blocking existing balances through a series of bilateral agreements. But it was hard to know precisely how much sterling was newly earned, and incentives to evade the restrictions were strong.

Under the circumstances, the decision to restore convertibility in 1947 was the height of recklessness. It was an American decision, not a British one. In 1946 the United States extended Britain a $3.75 billion loan on the condition that the latter agree to restore current-account convertibility within a year of the loan's approval.[21] A prostrate United Kingdom had no choice. Convertibility was restored on July 15, 1947, nearly five years ahead of the deadline of the Bretton Woods Agreement.[22] Except for some previously accumulated balances, sterling became convertible into dollars and other currencies at the official parity of $4.03.

The six weeks of convertibility were a disaster. Reserve losses were massive. The government, seeing its reserves approaching exhaustion, suspended convertibility on August 20 with American consent. A loan that had been designed to last through the end of the decade was exhausted in a matter of weeks.

American insistence on the early resumption of convertibility was motivated by Washington's anxiety over imperial preference. Convertibility was the obvious way of guaranteeing American exporters a level playing field. In addition, American policymakers viewed Britain's restoration of convertibility as an important step toward the creation of an open, multilateral trad-

---

[21] An additional $540 million covered Lend-Lease goods already in the pipeline.

[22] Actually, convertibility was phased in. Toward the beginning of the year, the British authorities supplemented their bilateral clearing agreements with other countries with a system of transferable accounts. Residents of participating countries were authorized to transfer sterling among themselves, as well as to Britain, for use in current transactions. In February, transfers to residents of the dollar area were added. In return, participating countries had to agree to accept sterling from other participants without limit and to continue to restrict capital transfers. See Mikesell 1954.

ing system. Sterling was the most important reserve and vehicle currency after the dollar. Other countries were more likely to restore convertibility if their sterling balances were convertible and served as international reserves. But, as they had when specifying the modest quotas and drawing rights of the Articles of Agreement, American officials underestimated the difficulty of the task.

The 1947 sterling crisis lifted the scales from their eyes. No longer would the United States be so insistent about the early restoration of convertibility; thereafter it acquiesced to European policies stretching out the transition. Acknowledging the severity of Europe's problem, the United States acceded to modest discrimination against American exports. And it followed up with the Marshall Plan. Aid had been under discussion in Washington, D.C., before Britain's abortive restoration of convertibility, and General George Marshall's Harvard speech announcing the plan preceded Britain's July 15 deadline by more than a month. But Marshall aid had not been approved by Congress: the sterling crisis, by highlighting the weakened condition of the European economies, undermined the arguments of its opponents.

Significant quantities of Marshall aid were finally transferred in the second half of 1948. Until then, Britain's position remained tenuous. And problems were by no means limited to the British Isles. France, Italy, and Germany, in each of which the political situation remained unsettled, suffered capital flight. France ran persistent dollar deficits, depleting its reserves and forcing devaluation of the franc from 119 to the dollar to 214 at the beginning of 1948. While trade with most European countries took place at this rate, proceeds of exports to the dollar area could be sold half at the official rate and half at the rate quoted in parallel markets. Given that the free rate was more than 300 francs, the effective exchange rate for transactions with the United States was 264 francs. Making the dollar more expensive was designed to encourage exports to the United States and discourage imports in order to replenish France's dollar reserves. But the policy created inefficiencies and disadvantaged other countries; it provided an incentive to shunt British exports to the United States through third countries, for example. These were precisely the kind of discriminatory multiple exchange rates frowned on by the framers of the Bretton Woods Agreement. Over the objections of the French executive director, who denied that the Articles of Agreement provided a legal basis for the action, the IMF declared France ineligible to use its resources. The French government, in humiliation, was forced to devalue again and unify the rate at 264.

Eventually, Marshall aid lightened the burden under which the recipients labored. The United States instructed European governments to propose a scheme for dividing the aid among themselves; they did so on the basis of consensus forecasts of their dollar deficits. The $13 billion provided by the United States over the next four years would suffice, it was hoped, to finance the dollar deficits that would be incurred as the recipients completed their reconstruction and made final preparations for convertibility.[23]

Hopes that trade with the dollar area would quickly return to balance were dashed by the 1948–49 recession in the United States. The recession depressed U.S. demands for European goods, causing the dollar gap to widen. While the recession was temporary, its impact on European reserves was not. What the United States gave with one hand, it took away with the other.

The recession provided the immediate impetus for the 1949 devaluations. However attractive the terms-of-trade gains associated with overvalued currencies and import controls, there were limits to their feasibility. World War II had altered equilibrium exchange rates, as World War I had before it.[24] This became evident when American imports from the sterling area fell by 50 percent between the first and third quarters of 1949. The sterling area, which produced the raw materials that constituted the bulk of U.S. imports, and not the United Kingdom itself, felt the brunt of the deterioration. But residents of other sterling area countries sought to maintain the customary level of imports from the dollar area by converting their sterling balances into dollars. Controls restricted but did not eliminate their ability to do so. As its reserves dwindled, Britain further tightened its controls and got other Commonwealth countries to do likewise. Still the drain of gold and dollars continued. Between July and mid-September, it exceeded $300 million. Devaluation followed on September 18.

This episode laid to rest the belief that the devaluation of a major currency could be acted on as if it were an item on a committee agenda. Article IV entitled the Fund to seventy-two hours' notice of a parity change. Although foreign governments and the IMF were informed that devaluation was coming, the Fund was notified of its magnitude only twenty-four hours in advance to minimize the danger that the information would leak to the markets. Although there was time to make preparations, it was not possible to engage in the kind of international deliberations envisaged in the Articles of Agreement.[25]

---

[23] To prevent the recipients from "double dipping" and loosening Washington's financial control, the United States made the extension of Marshall aid contingent on IMF agreement not to extend credit to the recipient governments.

[24] As Triffin (1964) put it, recourse to controls only "slowed down, or postponed, the exchange-rate readjustments which had characterized the 1920s, and bunched up many of them in September 1949" (p. 23).

[25] See Horsefield 1969, Vol. 1, pp. 238–39.

Twenty-three additional countries devalued within a week of Britain, seven subsequently. Most had already come under balance-of-payments pressure, and sterling's devaluation implied that their problem was likely to worsen. The only currencies that were not devalued were the U.S. dollar, the Swiss franc, the Japanese yen, and those of some Latin American and Eastern European countries.

The devaluations had the desired effects. That this was disputed at the time and is questioned today testifies to the distrust of exchange rate changes inherited from the 1930s. British reserve losses halted immediately, and the country's reserves tripled within two years. Other countries also improved their positions. The French were able to relax their exchange restrictions, liberalizing the right of travelers to take bank notes out of the country and of others to transact on the forward market. The U.S. current-account surplus dropped by more than half between the first half of 1949 and the first half of 1950. Devaluation was not the only contributing factor; the American recession ended in late 1949, and the Korean War broke out in 1950.[26] But the improvement of trade balances was greatest in countries that devalued by the largest amounts, suggesting that the 1949 realignment had separate, economically significant effects.

The dollar shortage, while moderated, was not eliminated. In the first half of 1950, the U.S. current-account surplus was still running at an annual rate of $3 billion. It was by no means clear that other countries, their reserves limited and their deficits substantial, could complete the transition to convertibility in two years. Intra-European trade was still smothered by a suffocating blanket of restrictions on current-account transactions. By 1950 the countries involved concluded that solving this problem required extraordinary international monetary measures.

THE EUROPEAN PAYMENTS UNION

Those extraordinary steps involved supplementing the IMF with a regional entity, the European Payments Union, or EPU, to deal with Europe's trade and payments problems. The EPU came into operation in 1950, initially for two years, although it was wound down only at the end of 1958. At one

---

[26] The war had different effects on different economies: the sterling area, which was a net exporter of raw materials, benefited from the rise in the relative price of commodities it caused, while Germany, as a net importer of raw materials, suffered a deterioration in its terms of trade. This last point is emphasized by Temin 1995. It is contrary to much of the German literature, in which it is suggested that Germany benefited from the Korea boom.

level it was a straightforward elaboration of the Bretton Woods model. Its members, essentially the countries of Western Europe and their overseas dependencies, reaffirmed their intention of moving simultaneously toward the restoration of current-account convertibility. They adopted a Code of Liberalization, which mandated the removal of restrictions on currency conversion for purposes of current-account transactions. In February 1951, less than a year after the EPU came into existence, all existing restrictions were to be applied equally to all participating countries, and members were to reduce their barriers by one-half from initial levels and then by 60 and 75 percent. This, then, was a more detailed if geographically limited version of the commitment of the Bretton Woods Agreement to remove all restrictions on current-account transactions.

Countries running deficits against the EPU would have access to credits, although they would have to settle with their partners in gold and dollars once their quotas were exhausted. Here too inspiration derived from the Articles of Agreement: the credits to which participating countries were entitled resembled the quotas and drawing rights of the Bretton Woods Agreement. Like IMF quotas, their availability could be subject to conditions. Nearly $3 billion in credits were outstanding when the EPU was terminated in 1958; this was equivalent to an increase in the quotas provided for by the Articles of Agreement of nearly 50 percent.

At another level, the EPU departed from the Bretton Woods model and challenged the institutions established there. By acceding to the Code of Liberalization, the United States acknowledged the unrealism of the Bretton Woods schedule for restoring current-account convertibility. By helping to provide additional balance-of-payments credits, it acknowledged the inadequacy of the quotas provided by the Articles of Agreement. By allowing EPU countries to reduce barriers to trade among themselves more quickly than they abolished restrictions on imports from America, it acceded to discrimination in trade. It acknowledged that the dollar shortage was the central monetary problem of the postwar period, notwithstanding Marshall aid.[27] European countries, by designing an institution for the pursuit of discriminatory policies, admitted what had gone unsaid at Bretton Woods: that the postwar international monetary regime was an asymmetric system in which the United States and the dollar played exceptional roles.

That the EPU was a departure from Bretton Woods was acknowledged in

[27] Thus, the Second Annual Report of the OEEC acknowledged that Europe's dollar deficits would not be reduced to the point where monetary restrictions could be eliminated on a non-discriminatory basis by the end of the Marshall Plan. Organisation for European Economic Cooperation 1950, pp. 247–51.

several ways. Responsibility for clearing payments was vested with the Bank for International Settlements, a holdover from the 1930s, not the IMF. The managing board, which oversaw the EPU's operation, was housed in Basel, not Washington, D.C. The Code of Liberalization, rather than being appended to the Articles of Agreement, was a construct of the Organisation for European Economic Cooperation, or OEEC, which had been created to facilitate the division of Marshall aid. In effect, oversight of the restoration of convertibility and the rehabilitation of trade was withdrawn from the Bretton Woods institutions, whose authority was diminished as a result.

If one factor can explain these departures from the path cleared at Bretton Woods, it was the crises of 1947 and 1949. These episodes made it impossible for the United States to deny the severity of postwar adjustment problems. The advent of the cold war cemented its change of heart. The USSR had been present at Bretton Woods, even if its delegates were active mainly in after-hours drinking sessions. It had not yet established Eastern Europe as its sphere of influence or emerged as a threat to the political stability of the West. But by 1950 the cold war was under way and the Soviet Union had refused to assume the obligations of an IMF member. This left the United States more willing to countenance discrimination in trade if doing so facilitated recovery and economic growth in Western Europe.

The authority of the Bretton Woods institutions was weakened not just by the stillbirth of the ITO but by the decision of the IMF and World Bank to distance themselves from postwar payments problems. Although the Bank extended more credit to Europe than to any other continent in its first seven years, its total European commitments between May of 1947, when its first loan was made, and the end of 1953, a period that bracketed the Marshall Plan, amounted to only $753 million, or little more than 5 percent of Marshall aid.[28] Drawings on the IMF between 1947 and 1951, at $812 million, were scarcely larger. The Fund had been created to oversee the operation of convertible currencies and to finance temporary payments imbalances; it was slow to adapt to a world of inconvertibility and persistent payments problems. It acceded to U.S. demands that it withhold finance from countries receiving Marshall aid, to prevent governments from undermining U.S. efforts to control their financial affairs. Even after Britain's 1947 experiment had demonstrated the need for extensive support, it did not enlarge the resources available to countries that restored convertibility. *Stand-by arrange-*

[28] The World Bank made loans to Denmark, France, Luxembourg, and the Netherlands to finance imports of raw materials and capital goods from the dollar area. But with few funds of its own (the United States being the only country to pay in capital), the World Bank depended for liquidity on its ability to float loans on the U.S. capital market.

ments, inaugurated in 1952, simplified access to Fund resources but did not augment them. For all these reasons, the Fund proved incapable of offering assistance on the scale required to deal with postwar dislocations.

PAYMENTS PROBLEMS AND SELECTIVE CONTROLS

Britain, France, and Germany had long been at the center of European monetary affairs. Never was this truer than in the 1950s, although the three countries and their currencies had fallen into the shadow of the United States and the mighty dollar.

In all three countries, the second world war, like the first, strengthened the position of labor, rendering labor-based parties of the Left a force to be reckoned with. As they had after World War I, labor's spokesmen pressed for higher wages, higher taxes on wealth, and expanded social programs. To this list were now added demands to control interest rates, capital flows, prices, and rents and to expand the range of government activities. An accommodation with labor was vital if Europe was to avoid political and workplace disruptions to its recovery and growth.

The process by which this settlement was reached was complex. In France and Italy, for example, the United States provided encouragement by making Marshall aid conditional on the exclusion of Communist parties from government. But the critical steps were taken by the Europeans themselves.[29] Socialist parties moderated their demands in order to broaden their electoral base. Workers accepted the maintenance of private property in return for an expanded welfare state. They agreed to moderate their wage demands in return for a government commitment to full employment and growth.

From the perspective of balance-of-payments adjustment, the commitment to growth and full employment was key. The instrument used to eliminate external deficits under the gold standard had been increased interest rates.[30] A higher central bank discount rate placed upward pressure on the entire range of interest rates, depressing inventory investment and capital formation. A declining level of activity reduced the demand for imports at the

---

[29] Probably the best introduction to the relevant literature is Maier 1987. Esposito 1994 is expressly concerned with the relative importance of U.S. policy and indigenous factors in Europe's postwar political settlement.

[30] Again, this statement applies to countries whose central banks could influence domestic rates. Small open economies whose domestic-currency-denominated assets were perfect substitutes for foreign assets had no control of their interest rates and hence could make little use of the instrument. Canada is an example (see Dick and Floyd 1992).

109

expense of growth and employment at home. Any government's vigorous use of this instrument would have been regarded as an act of bad faith. Sacrificing growth and employment by raising interest rates in order to restore external balance would have jeopardized the accommodation between capital and labor.[31]

Hence, European countries, when experiencing balance-of-payments problems, could not adjust by raising interest rates. Their only recourse was to implement exchange controls. The fact that these restrictions were imposed in concert with the EPU rendered the policy acceptable to their trading partners. That controls were exceptions to an ongoing liberalization process and that their imposition was subject to EPU approval lent credibility to declarations that they were temporary.[32] It meant that controls were applied simultaneously to imports from all EPU countries, minimizing distortions.

Germany suffered a balance-of-payments crisis in the second half of 1950, the Korean War having worsened its terms of trade by raising the relative prices of imported raw materials. In the first five months of the EPU's operation (July–November 1950), the country exhausted its quota.[33] The German government then negotiated a special arrangement with the EPU. It reimposed exchange controls and received a special $120 million credit. In return, the government affirmed its commitment to the prevailing exchange rate and agreed to increase turnover taxes and reform personal and corporate income taxes in order to restrict consumption. Although import restrictions were not the only device used to eliminate external deficits, they were an important part of the package. Through their application, the crisis was surmounted. Germany's position strengthened sufficiently for it to repay the special EPU credit by the middle of 1951. Growth continued unabated, and Germany shifted to permanent surplus within the EPU.

---

[31] This description of the postwar settlement is stylized. It neglects variations across countries in the terms and effectiveness of the postwar social pact. While priority was attached to growth and full employment in Britain and France, the fragmentation of labor relations in both countries limited the effectiveness of labor-management collaboration. In Germany, labor's bargaining power was diminished by the presence of American troops and the influx of workers from the East. But even though Germany did not reach full employment until the end of the 1950s, the low living standards and levels of industrial production of the immediate postwar years still made the commitment to growth a priority.

[32] Credibility was further buttressed by the fact that the United States, though not a participant in the EPU, was a member of its managing board, having contributed $350 million in working capital to finance its operation. Hence, countries that failed to adhere to their bargain with the managing board risked jeopardizing their access to U.S. aid.

[33] That quota had been calibrated on the basis of 1949 exports and imports, which were dwarfed by the much higher level of trade that followed once the full effects of the 1948 monetary reform were felt.

The EPU managing board made the $120 million credit conditional on German reaffirmation that the exchange controls were temporary. The government had been tempted to reverse its trade liberalization measures unilaterally; Per Jacobsson, a special adviser to the EPU, convinced officials to mark time until import curbs could be reimposed in concert with the EPU. Moreover, the receipt of EPU credits allowed Germany's economics minister, Ludwig Erhard, to force through tax and interest-rate increases over the objections of the chancellor, Konrad Adenauer, who feared that these would damage the prospects for growth and social peace.[34]

Britain's crises and efforts to cope can be described in similar terms. Once the commodity boom caused by the Korean War tapered off and the revenues of the sterling area declined, a payments problem emerged.[35] In late 1951 Commonwealth finance ministers agreed to tighten controls on imports from the dollar area and to deviate from the liberalization schedule laid down by the OEEC code. Sterling recovered and it soon became possible to relax the controls.

As British economic growth gained vigor, the authorities reluctantly resorted to Bank rate to regulate the balance of payments. Although the annual average unemployment rate declined to 1.8 percent in 1953 and did not surpass that level until 1958, allowing the authorities to alter interest rates without exposing themselves to the accusation that they were causing unemployment, they remained reluctant to utilize the instrument. The result was the British policy of "Stop-Go," which involved cutting rates, inflating consumer demand, and allowing incomes to rise, especially with the approach of elections, followed by a rise in rates to restrict demand, generally too late to avert a crisis.

French experience in the 1950s also illustrates the importance of the trade-restriction instrument for balance-of-payments adjustment. Where Germany experienced a single payments crisis at the beginning of the decade, France endured a series of crises. The common factor in these episodes was deficit spending. Military expenditures in Indochina and elsewhere were superimposed on an ambitious program of public investment and on generous entitlement programs and housing subsidies. As in the 1920s, the country lacked a political consensus on how to pay for these programs. A third of the electorate voted for a Communist Party that favored increased taxes on the wealthy and resisted spending cuts. The remaining parties of the Fourth Republic formed a series of short-lived governments, none of which proved

[34] See Kaplan and Schleiminger 1989, pp. 102–4.

[35] That the government lost the October 1951 election, Iran nationalized British oil holdings, and repayment of the American and Canadian loans came due all served to exacerbate the problem.

capable of solving the fiscal problem. As a result, the financial consequences of the government's ambitious modernization program spilled over into balance-of-payments deficits.

The consequences became apparent in 1951. Expenditure on the war in Indochina was rising. Payments deficits depleted the reserves of France's stabilization fund and forced heavy utilization of its EPU quotas. In response, the government tightened import restrictions and extended tax rebates to exporters. It suspended the measures mandated by the OEEC Liberalization Code. The tighter import regime, together with financial assistance from the United States, allowed the crisis to be surmounted.

The removal of current-account restrictions under the OEEC code resumed in 1954, but military expenditures rose again in 1955–56 in response to unrest in Algeria and the Suez crisis. The Socialist government that took office in 1956 introduced an old-age pension scheme and increased other expenditures. France lost half its reserves between the beginning of 1956 and the first quarter of 1957. Again, import restrictions were tightened. Importers were required to deposit 25 percent of the value of their licensed imports in advance. In June 1957 the import deposit requirement was raised to 50 percent, and France's adherence to the OEEC code was suspended once more. The government obtained an IMF credit and utilized its position with the EPU.

While these measures provided breathing space, they did not eliminate the underlying imbalance. In August, in a step tantamount to devaluation (but one that did not require consultation with the IMF), a 20 percent premium was added to purchases and sales of foreign exchange, with the exception of those associated with imports and exports of certain primary commodities. Two months later, the measure was generalized to all merchandise. In return for liberalizing import controls, the government obtained $655 million in credits from the EPU, the IMF, and the United States.

But until the budgetary problem was addressed, the respite was only temporary. By the summer of 1957, this reality could no longer be denied. As it had during the "the battle of the franc" in 1924, public frustration with perpetual crisis eventually broke down resistance to compromise. A new Cabinet was formed with the economically conservative Felix Gaillard as finance minister. Gaillard then became prime minister and submitted to the Chamber of Deputies a budget that promised to significantly reduce the deficit. But, again as in 1924, the political will to sustain budget balance was in doubt. The situation in Algeria continued to deteriorate, and strikes broke out in the spring of 1958.[36] The crisis receded only when the war hero

---

[36] Workers complained that they were being forced to bear the costs of the nation's overseas commitments. See Kaplan and Schleiminger 1989, p. 281.

Charles de Gaulle formed a government and returned the financially ortho-dox Antoine Pinay to the Finance Ministry.[37] This made clear that the auster-ity measures would not be reversed. A committee of experts then recom-mended further increases in taxes and reductions of government subsidies. Although de Gaulle was unwilling to accept all the expenditure cuts it pro-posed, he agreed to raise taxes and limit the budget deficit. The committee of experts, along with the United States and France's EPU partners, de-manded that the country also restore its commitment to the OEEC code. To make this possible, the franc was devalued again, this time by 17 percent.

Together, devaluation and fiscal retrenchment had the desired effect. France's external accounts swung from deficit to surplus, and in 1959 the country added significantly to its foreign reserves. This permitted it to liber-alize 90 percent of its intra-European trade and 88 percent of its dollar trade.[38]

The importance of coordinating devaluation and fiscal correction, thereby addressing the sources of both internal and external imbalance, was a key lesson of the French experience. Import controls by themselves could not guarantee the restoration of equilibrium. As in Germany, they had to be accompanied by monetary and fiscal action. And retrenchment had to be cemented by political consolidation, as had also been the case in the 1920s. Until then, changes in the stringency of import restrictions were the princi-pal instrument through which the exchange rate was defended.

CONVERTIBILITY: PROBLEMS AND PROGRESS

These periodic crises should not be allowed to obscure the progress made toward the restoration of equilibrium. Yet many otherwise perceptive ob-servers continued to see the dollar gap as a permanent feature of the postwar world. Their perceptions colored by Europe's devastation and America's industrial might, they believed that U.S. productivity growth would continue to outstrip that of other countries. The United States would remain in peren-nial surplus, consigning its trading partners to perpetual crisis.[39]

No sooner were their studies warning of this dire scenario published than the dollar gap disappeared. As growth resumed in Europe and Japan, their respective trade balances strengthened. Europe became an attractive destina-

---

[37] Readers will recognize the parallels with the 1926 Poincaré stabilization, down to the extended fiscal deadlock, the formation of a new government by a charismatic leader, and the appointment of a committee of experts.

[38] See Kaplan and Schleiminger 1989, p. 284.

[39] For a sampling of pessimistic appraisals of Europe's postwar prospects, see Balogh 1946, 1949, Williams 1952, and MacDougall 1957.

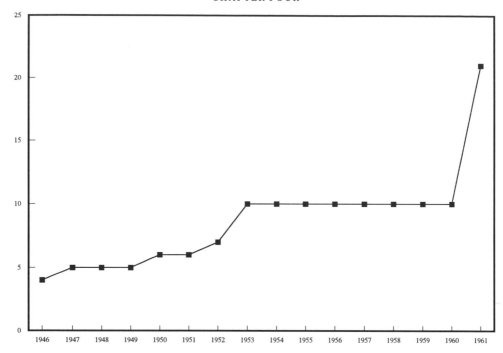

Figure 4.1. Number of IMF Members That Had Accepted Article VIII, 1946–61. *Source*: International Monetary Fund, *Annual Report on Exchange and Trade Restrictions*, various years.

tion for investment by American firms. U.S. military expenditures abroad and bilateral foreign aid, coming on the heels of the Marshall Plan, contributed an additional $2 billion a year to the flow. It was the United States, and not the other industrial countries, that lapsed into persistent deficit.

The redistribution of reserves from America to the rest of the world laid the basis for current-account convertibility. In 1948 the United States had held more than two-thirds of global monetary reserves; within a decade its share had fallen to one-half. On December 31, 1958, the countries of Europe restored convertibility on current account.[40] The IMF acknowledged the new state of affairs in 1961 by declaring countries in compliance with Article VIII of the Articles of Agreement (see Figure 4.1).

Operating a system of pegged exchange rates between convertible curren-

[40] The terms of intra-EPU settlements had already been hardened starting in 1954, making the currencies of member countries effectively convertible for transactions within Europe. Monetary restrictions on trade had been loosened under the provisions of the OEEC code. But it was only when the foreign-exchange markets opened for business in January 1959, with the major currencies fully convertible for current-account transactions, that the Bretton Woods System can be said to have come into full operation.

cies required credit to finance imbalances, as the framers of the Bretton Woods Agreement had recognized. The greater the reluctance to adjust the peg and to raise interest rates and taxes, the larger the requisite credits. And the more rapid the relaxation of capital controls, the greater the financing needed to offset speculative outflows. This was the context for the debates over *international liquidity* that dominated the 1960s. Weak-currency countries lobbied for more generous IMF quotas and increases in international reserves. Strong-currency countries objected that additional credits encouraged deficit countries to live beyond their means.

The situation was complicated by the fact that the Bretton Woods System, like the gold standard before it, generated its own liquidity. As they had under the gold standard, governments and central banks supplemented their gold reserves with foreign exchange. Given the dominant position of the United States in international trade and finance and America's ample gold hoard, they did so mainly by accumulating dollars. The United States could run payments deficits in the amount of foreign governments' and central banks' desired acquisition of dollars. The United States might limit this amount by raising interest rates, making it costly for foreign central banks to acquire dollars. Or by exercising inadequate restraint, it might flood the international system with liquidity. Either way, the system remained dependent on dollars for its incremental liquidity needs.

This dependence undermined the symmetry of the international monetary system. The Bretton Woods Agreement may have directed the United States to declare a par value against gold while permitting other countries to declare par values against the dollar, but there was a presumption that the system would grow more symmetric with time. The scarce-currency clause was supposed to ensure adjustment by surplus as well as deficit countries. And once Europe completed its recovery, IMF quotas were supposed to satisfy the world's demand for liquidity. Instead, the system grew less symmetric as the dollar solidified its status as the leading reserve currency. We might call this the de Gaulle problem, since the French president was its most prominent critic.

The historical consistency of the French position was striking.[41] Since the Genoa Conference in 1922, France had opposed any scheme conferring special status on a particular currency. That Paris was never a financial center comparable to London or New York limited the liquidity of franc-denominated assets and hence their attractiveness as international reserves; if there was to be a reserve currency, it was unlikely to be the franc, in other words.

---

[41] This is documented by Bordo, Simard, and White 1994.

In the 1920s and 1930s, as we saw in Chapter 3, France's efforts to liquidate its foreign balances in order to enhance the purity of the pure gold standard had contributed to the liquidity squeeze that aggravated the Great Depression. De Gaulle's criticism of America's "exorbitant privilege" and his threat to liquidate the French government's dollar balances worked in the same direction.[42]

A further problem was the Triffin dilemma. Robert Triffin, Belgian monetary economist, Yale professor, and architect of the EPU, had observed as early as 1947 that the tendency for the Bretton Woods System to meet excess demands for reserves through the growth of foreign dollar balances made it dynamically unstable.[43] Accumulating dollar reserves was attractive only as long as there was no question about their convertibility into gold. But once foreign dollar balances loomed large relative to U.S. gold reserves, the credibility of this commitment might be cast into doubt. U.S. foreign monetary liabilities first exceeded U.S. gold reserves in 1960, U.S. liabilities to foreign monetary authorities in 1963. If some foreign holders sought to convert their reserves, their actions might have the same effect as a queue of depositors forming outside a bank. Others would join for fear of being denied access. Countries would rush to cash in their dollars before the United States was forced to devalue.[44]

[42] Jacques Rueff, who had been financial attaché in the French embassy in London between 1930 and 1934 and a steadfast opponent of the gold-exchange standard, was head of the commission of experts that helped to frame de Gaulle's fiscal and monetary reform package in 1958. In both the 1930s and the 1960s, Rueff and his followers in the French government argued that the gold-exchange standard permitted reserve-currency countries to live beyond their means. This produced periods of boom and bust when the reserve-currency countries first became overextended and then were forced to retrench. (This interpretation of interwar events is discussed in Chapter 3. The solution was to restore a pure gold standard that promised to impose continuous discipline. Rueff published a series of articles, most notably in June 1961, that pointed to parallels between international monetary developments in 1926–29 and 1958–61, two instances when European countries accumulated the currencies of the "Anglo-Saxon countries" and inflation had accelerated in the United Kingdom and the United States. He called for the liquidation of the foreign-exchange component of the Bretton Woods System and a return to a more gold-standard-like system. See Rueff 1972.

[43] See Triffin 1947. Triffin repeated his warning at the beginning of Bretton Woods convertibility (Triffin 1960), and it was echoed by other observers (Kenen 1960).

[44] Triffin's fear was that the United States, to fend off the collapse of the dollar's $35 gold parity, would revert to deflationary policies, starving the world of liquidity. To defend their currencies, other countries would be forced to respond in kind, setting off a deflationary spiral like that of the 1930s. In fact, the Johnson and Nixon administrations continued to allow the supply of dollars and the rate of U.S. inflation to be governed by domestic considerations, rendering an excessive supply of dollars and inflation, not deflation, the actual problems. The

It is apparent that the de Gaulle and Triffin problems were related. De Gaulle was a large creditor of the U.S. Treasury threatening to liquidate his balance. This was precisely the kind of development that threatened to destabilize the dollar, as Triffin had warned.[45]

Special Drawing Rights

The logical response was to substitute other forms of international liquidity. The problem to which this was a solution was not a global liquidity shortage but the need to substitute a new reserve asset for the dollar in order to prevent the process described by Triffin from destabilizing the Bretton Woods System.[46] As mentioned above, this was favored by weak-currency countries and opposed by their strong-currency counterparts. Discussions were complicated by the fact that the dollar was both weak and strong. It was strong in that it remained the principal reserve currency and that the creation of alternative forms of liquidity threatened to diminish its role. It was weak in that the growth of foreign dollar balances sowed doubts about its convertibility; the development of alternative liquidity sources promised to slow the growth of U.S. external monetary liabilities and therefore to contain the pressures undermining the currency's stability. Given these conflicting considerations, it is no surprise that the United States was less than consistent in its approach to the problem.

Negotiations over the creation of additional reserves were initiated by the *Group of Ten (G-10)*, the club of industrial countries that viewed itself as the successor to the U.S. and British delegations that had dominated the Bretton

---

United States attempted to bottle up the consequences by establishing the Gold Pool with its European allies and encouraging the latter to refrain from converting dollars into gold. Eventually, however, conversions of dollars into gold by the private markets undermined the currency's position. See Williamson 1977 and De Grauwe 1989.

[45] Although the United States had foreign assets as well as foreign liabilities, the maturity imbalance between the assets and liabilities exposed it to the danger of the international equivalent of a bank run. Neglect of the bank-run problem was the flaw of the view of Emile Deprés and Charles Kindleberger that U.S. payments deficits were benign because the country was simply acting as banker to the world, borrowing short and lending long.

[46] One can imagine that markets could have solved this problem on their own by elevating other countries to reserve-currency status. But the prevalence of controls and the narrowness of markets prevented currencies like the deutsche mark, franc, and yen from acquiring a significantly expanded reserve role. The only currency with a sufficiently wide market, sterling, became progressively less attractive as a form of reserves for reasons explained elsewhere in this chapter.

Woods negotiations. In 1963 it formed the Group of Deputies, a committee of high officials, which recommended increasing IMF quotas. It proposed allocating reserves to a small number of industrial economies and making the latter responsible for extending conditional credit to other countries.

While this approach seemed logical enough to officials of the industrial countries, they had not reckoned with the emergence of the Third World.[47] Developing countries participated fully in the Bretton Woods System: many of them maintained pegged exchange rates for long periods behind the shelter of trade restrictions and capital controls. Not unlike experience under the gold standard, they were subject to exceptionally severe balance-of-payments shocks, which they met by devaluing more frequently than was the practice in the industrial world.[48] Having gained in numbers and formed organizations of their own, Third-World leaders countered that their balance-of-payments financing needs were at least as great as those of the industrial countries. They argued that the additional resources should be allocated directly to the countries in the greatest need (namely, themselves). They viewed the G-10 as an inappropriate forum for resolving the issue. Efforts to increase the level of reserves thus became bound up with the issue of their distribution.

IMF quotas amounted to $9.2 billion at the end of 1958, up slightly from the original $8.8 billion as a result of the admission to the Fund of countries that had not been represented at Bretton Woods (as well as the nonparticipation of the Soviet Union and the withdrawal of Poland). In acknowledgment of the expansion of the world economy since 1944, a 50 percent increase in quotas was agreed to in 1959.[49] But since the dollar value of world trade had more than doubled since 1944, this did not restore Fund resources to even the modest levels, in relation to international transactions, of the White Plan. In 1961 the ten industrial countries that would subsequently form the G-10 agreed to lend up to $6 billion of their currencies to the Fund through the *General Arrangements to Borrow*. But this was not an increase in Fund quotas; it merely augmented supplies of particular currencies that the Fund could make available, and access to these funds was conditioned on terms satisfactory to the G-10 finance ministers.[50] Fund quotas were raised in

[47] This is a theme of the introduction to Gardner 1969 and of Eichengreen and Kenen 1994.

[48] Edwards (1993, p. 411) identifies sixty-nine substantial devaluations between 1954 and 1971 in some fifty developing countries.

[49] The United States, then the strong-currency country, had opposed increased quotas in the first two quinquennial reviews.

[50] See Horsefield 1969, Vol. 1, pp. 510–12.

1966, but by only 25 percent, because Belgium, France, Italy, and the Netherlands objected to larger increases.[51]

Ultimately, a solution was found in the form of the First Amendment to the Articles of Agreement, which created *special drawing rights* (SDRs). The conflict between industrial and developing countries, both of which insisted that they be allocated a disproportionate share of the additional resources, found a straightforward solution in the decision to increase all quotas by a uniform percentage. But the conflict between weak- and strong-currency countries within the industrial world proved more difficult to resolve. The weak-currency countries desired additional credits for balance-of-payments settlement purposes, while the strong-currency countries feared the inflationary consequences of additional credits. The United States initially opposed the creation of an SDR-like instrument for fear of diminishing the dollar's key-currency role. At the IMF annual meetings in 1964, the French, for whom the dollar's asymmetric position was a particular bone of contention, proposed creating such an instrument, but the idea was torpedoed by the United States. De Gaulle, never one to shy away from provocation, then proposed returning to the gold standard as the only remaining way of restoring symmetry to the international system, and the Bank of France accelerated its conversion of dollars into gold.

These veiled threats hastened the transformation of official opinion in the United States. It was five years since U.S. external dollar liabilities had first exceeded the country's gold reserves and since the price of gold in London had risen significantly above the level at which the U.S. Treasury pegged it in New York, signaling that traders attached a nonnegligible probability to dollar devaluation. The realization having dawned that the country's international monetary position was no longer impregnable, the United States reversed itself in 1965, siding with the proponents of an SDR allocation. The details were finally agreed upon at the Fund's Rio de Janeiro meeting in 1967. France's pound of flesh was a proviso that the scheme could be activated only when there existed a "better working" of the adjustment process—when the United States eliminated its balance-of-payments deficit, in other words.

By the time the United States had demonstrated the requisite payments surplus in 1969, permitting the first SDR allocation to be disbursed in 1970, the problem was no longer one of inadequate liquidity. The U.S. payments deficits of the 1960s had inflated the volume of international reserves, and

---

[51] They were raised a third time in 1970 by about 30 percent.

there was good reason to think that the restrictive monetary policy of 1969 was only temporary. Liquidity was augmented further by the increasingly expansionary monetary policies of the other industrial countries. Still more liquidity, in the form of an SDR allocation, was not what was needed in this inflationary environment. The inevitable delays built into negotiations meant that policymakers were solving yesterday's problems with counterproductive implications for today's.

Would these instabilities have been averted by a more generous SDR allocation at an earlier date? To be sure, had liquidity needs been met from such sources, there would have been no need to augment the stock of official dollar balances. The United States, to defend the dollar, would have been forced to rein in its deficits, solving both the Triffin and de Gaulle problems. The question is whether the country possessed instruments for doing so. Given U.S. military commitments and the pressure to increase spending on social programs, expenditure-reducing policies were not available. External imbalances could be addressed only by adjusting the supposedly adjustable peg, something that neither the United States nor other countries were yet willing to contemplate.

DECLINING CONTROLS AND RISING RIGIDITY

Meanwhile, the limitations of the Bretton Woods adjustment mechanism were underscored by the removal of trade restrictions. With the restoration of current-account convertibility, it was no longer possible to tighten import licensing requirements.[52] One's trading partners might still be induced to reduce their tariffs, a strategy the United States followed by proposing a new round of GATT negotiations when its trade balance deteriorated in 1958. But as indicated by the delay of four years until the conclusion of the Dillon Round in 1962, this mechanism hardly operated with the speed needed to cope with speculative pressures.

Governments could still attempt to correct an imbalance by manipulating the capital account. Controls on capital movements could be tightened. Measures such as the U.S. *Interest Equalization Tax*, which discouraged residents from investing in foreign bonds, might be deployed. But attempts to discourage capital outflows bought only time. They did not remove the underlying problem that had prompted the tendency for capital to flow out in

[52] However, there were echoes of the 1950s strategy in the 10 percent surcharge on customs and excise duties imposed by Britain in 1961, its 15 percent surcharge in 1964, and President Nixon's ten per cent import surcharge in 1971.

the first place. In other words, they provided some temporary autonomy for domestic policy but did not provide an effective adjustment mechanism.

One measure of the effectiveness of capital controls is the size of covered interest differentials (interest-rate differentials adjusted for the forward discount on foreign exchange). Maurice Obstfeld computed these for the 1960s, finding that they were as large as two percentage points for the United Kingdom and larger than one percentage point for Germany.[53] Differentials of this magnitude, which cannot be attributed to expected exchange rate changes, confirm that capital controls mattered. Richard Marston compared covered interest differentials between Eurosterling (offshore) rates and British (onshore) rates. (The advantage of this comparison is that it eliminates country risk—the danger that one country is more likely to default on its interest-bearing obligations.) Between April 1961, when Eurosterling interest rates were first reported by the Bank of England, and April 1971, the beginning of the end for the Bretton Woods System, the differential averaged 0.78 percent. Marston concludes that controls "clearly . . . had a very substantial effect on interest differentials."[54]

The implications for the balance of payments were explored in a 1974 study by Pentti Kouri and Michael Porter.[55] Kouri and Porter found that roughly half of a change in domestic credit was neutralized by international capital flows in the cases of Australia, Italy, and the Netherlands, and on the order of two-thirds to three-quarters in the case of Germany. Their results suggested that although international capital flows responded to changes in credit conditions, there was still some scope for autonomous monetary policy. Central banks could still alter monetary conditions without seeing domestic credit leak abroad dollar for dollar. Given the reluctance of governments to change the exchange rate or compress domestic demand, the use of controls to influence capital flows was the only mechanism left to reconcile internal and external balance in the short run.

To be sure, with the restoration of current-account convertibility, capital controls became more difficult to enforce. It was easier to over- and underinvoice trade and to spirit funds abroad. The growth of multinational corporations created yet another conduit for capital-account transactions, as did the development of the Euro-currency markets. Once controls on banking transactions in Europe were relaxed, London-based banks began to accept dollar deposits, bidding away funds from American banks whose deposit

---

[53] See Obstfeld 1993b. Aliber 1978 and Dooley and Isard 1980 undertake similar analyses and reach similar conclusions.

[54] Marston 1993, p. 523.

[55] Kouri and Porter 1974.

rates were capped by Regulation Q. Euro-dollar depositors, when they began to fear for the stability of the dollar, could exchange their balances for Euro–deutsche marks. Although the volume of Euro-currency transactions was limited, controls on capital movements enforced by the U.S. government at the border were less effective to the extent that a pool of dollars already existed offshore.

Why countries were so reluctant to devalue in response to external imbalances is perhaps the most contentious question in the literature on Bretton Woods. In fact, the architects of the system, worried about the disruptions to trade that might be caused by frequent parity adjustments, had sought to limit them. Requiring countries to obtain Fund approval before changing their parities discouraged the practice because of the danger that their intentions might be leaked to the market. Frequent small devaluations and revaluations, which could be taken without consulting with the Fund, might only be destabilizing; they would be viewed as too small to remove the underlying disequilbrium but as proof that the authorities were prepared to contemplate further exchange rate changes, on both grounds exciting capital flows. This was the lesson drawn from the German and Dutch revaluations in 1961. And permitting a country to devalue by a significant amount only if there were evidence of a fundamental disequilibrium precluded devaluation in advance of serious problems. The possibility that mounting pressures might not ultimately constitute a fundamental disequilibrium forced governments to reiterate their commitment to the prevailing exchange rate in order to avoid provoking capital outflows and exacerbating existing difficulties. To reverse course would be a source of serious embarrassment.[56]

The inflexibility of exchange rates under this system of "managed flexibility" followed from these perverse incentives. The problem intensified with the growth of capital mobility and increasing porousness of capital controls. External weakness could unleash a torrent of capital outflows. A government had to make even stronger statements and commit to even more

---

[56] As Akiyoshi Horiuchi (1993, p. 102) writes of Japan, which suffered balance-of-payments problems until the mid-1960s, the government "refused to try to restore the exernal balance of payments by devaluing the yen for fear that devaluation might be regarded as a public admission of some fatal errors in its economic policies." As John Williamson (1977, p. 6) put it, "exchange rate changes were relegated to the status of confessions that the adjustment process had failed." Richard Cooper's (1971) evidence that currency devaluation in developing countries often was followed by the dismissal of the finance minister illustrates that this embarrassment could have significant costs. Revaluation was less embarrassing for the strong-currency countries, of course. But it penalized producers of traded goods, a concentrated interest group, and therefore had political costs. It could not be resorted to with a freedom that would have resolved the dilemmas of Bretton Woods.

draconian steps to defend its currency. To devalue was to admit to an all-too-visible failure.[57]

There was also not much scope for increasing interest rates and applying restrictive fiscal measures to rein in payments deficits. The postwar social contract, in which workers moderated their wage demands as long as capitalists invested their profits, remained attractive only as long as the bargain delivered high growth. Thus, John F. Kennedy ran for president in 1960 on a promise of 5 percent growth. In the 1962 British general election, both parties promised 4 percent growth.[58] Commitments such as these left little room for expenditure-reducing policies.

All this makes the survival of the Bretton Woods System until 1971 something of a surprise. A large part of the explanation is international cooperation among governments and central banks.[59] Much as regime-preserving cooperation supported the gold standard in times of crisis, international support for its key currencies allowed Bretton Woods to stagger on. Central bank governors and officials gathered monthly at the BIS in Basel. Working Party 3 of the OECD's Economic Policy Committee provided a forum for the exchange of information and advice.[60] In 1961, responding to pressure on sterling associated with Germany's March 4 revaluation of the deutsche mark, the leading central banks agreed to *swap arrangements*, whereby they would temporarily retain their balances of weak currencies rather than demanding their conversion into gold. In 1961 Britain received nearly $1 billion in support under the provisions of these arrangements. In 1964, when sterling again came under attack, the Federal Reserve Bank of New York offered Britain a special $3 billion line of credit. In effect, the kind of central bank cooperation that had been characteristic of the 1920s was revived after a hiatus of more than thirty years.

Other examples of cooperation include the General Arrangements to Borrow and German and Swiss bans on interest on foreign deposits.[61] The *Gold Pool* established in November 1961 by Britain, Switzerland, and the members of the *European Economic Community* (EEC) can also be understood in this light. By 1961 the ratio of dollars to gold outside the United States had

[57] Leland Yeager, writing in 1968, emphasized governments' reluctance to adjust exchange rates "for fear of undermining confidence and aggravating the problem of speculation." See Yeager 1968, p. 140.

[58] For more discussion of this point, see James 1995.

[59] While this is a theme that runs through the present book, its particular relevance for the Bretton Woods period is emphasized by Fred Block (1977).

[60] On these initiatives, see Roosa 1965 and Schoorl 1995.

[61] Germany banned interest only on new foreign deposits, while the Swiss actually imposed a 1 percent tax on foreign deposits.

risen above levels that would be willingly held at \$35 per ounce of gold. The relative price of the dollar began to fall (in other words, the market price of gold began to rise above \$35). The incentive for central banks to demand gold for dollars from the U.S. Treasury mounted accordingly. The industrial countries therefore created the Gold Pool, an arrangement under which they pledged to refrain from converting their dollar exchange and sold gold out of their reserves in an effort to relieve the pressure on the United States.[62]

Foreign support was not costless for the governments and central banks extending it, for they had no assurance of prompt repayment of their short-term credits.[63] They were reluctant to offer support unless the countries receiving it committed to adjust, assuring them that support would be limited in magnitude and that it would produce the desired results. When the United States declined to subordinate other economic and political objectives to defending the dollar price of gold, its partners grew less enthusiastic about supporting the greenback. Britain, Switzerland, and the members of the European Economic Community had contributed fully 40 percent of the gold sold on the London market; as America's reluctance to adjust became apparent, they concluded that they would be forced to provide an ever-growing fraction of the total. France, skeptical as always of such arrangements, withdrew from the Gold Pool in June 1967, forcing the United States to increase its contribution. When sterling's devaluation undermined confidence in the dollar, forcing the members of the pool to sell \$800 million of gold in a month, the writing was on the wall. The arrangement was terminated the following spring. To prevent the Fed from being drained of gold, its price in private transactions was allowed to rise, although the price at which it was traded in official transactions was kept unchanged. When the price on private markets shot up to more than \$40, there was a considerable incentive for other central banks to obtain gold from the Fed for \$35 an ounce. The cost of supporting the dollar became clear for other central banks to see. The collapse of the Bretton Woods international monetary system followed as a matter of logic.

That collapse was several years in coming because the United States tight-

[62] In practice, the arrangement operated through foreign central banks and the BIS providing loans of foreign currencies and dollars. The Fed typically borrowed to purchase dollars held abroad instead of selling gold.

[63] When the short-term credits obtained through the operation of the Gold Pool began to mature, the U.S. Treasury attempted to place Roosa bonds (U.S. government bonds that carried a guarantee against capital loss due to dollar devaluation) with foreign central banks, increasing the maturity of the borrowings. This is an example, then, of a situation in which short-term borrowings were not quickly repaid. See Meltzer 1991.

ened capital controls. The Interest Equalization Tax of September 1964 had been followed by restraints on banking and corporate transfers of funds abroad, as described above. These were tightened in 1965, coincident with the escalation of U.S. involvement in Vietnam, and again in 1966 and 1968.

THE BATTLE FOR STERLING

Two manifestations of these pressures were the battles for the British pound and the U.S. dollar. As we saw above, the struggle to make and keep sterling convertible for current-account transactions dated to 1947. The United States saw sterling as the dollar's first line of defense. The pound remained the second-most-important reserve currency; for members of the British Commonwealth it was the principal form of international reserves. For sterling to be devalued would shake confidence in the entire reserve currency system. Few observers had forgotten 1931, when Britain's abandonment of the gold standard had ignited a flow of funds out of the dollar and forced the Fed to ratchet up interest rates.

British governments, seeking to defend the exchange rate of $2.80, operated under significant handicaps. Output grew slowly by the standards of Western Europe and the United States.[64] The fragmented structure of the British union movement made it difficult to coordinate bargaining, restrain wages, and encourage investment in the manner of the more corporatist European states. External liabilities were extensive, and efforts to preserve sterling's reserve-currency status heightened the country's financial vulnerability. If any country had an argument for floating its currency, it was Britain. The possibility of making sterling convertible and floating it was canvassed in 1952 (as the so-called ROBOT Plan named after its originators *Ro*wan, *Bol*ton, and *Ot*to Clarke) but rejected for fear that a floating pound would be unstable and that sudden depreciation would provoke inflation and labor unrest.[65] Instead, Britain trod the long and rocky road that led to the resumption of convertibility at a fixed rate at the end of 1958.

---

[64] It grew by 2.7 percent per year in the 1950s, compared to 3.2 percent in the United States, and 4.4 percent in Western Europe as a whole. The comparable figures for the 1960s were 2.8 percent for the United Kingdom, 4.3 percent for the United States, and 4.8 percent for Western Europe. Calculated from van der Wee 1986.

[65] Sterling would have been allowed to fluctuate within a wide band, from $2.40 to $3.20. A floating rate would have violated the Articles of Agreement, however, and precluded access to Fund resources. Admittedly, a couple of countries, most notably Canada, did float their exchange rates in the 1950s, but Canada enjoyed capital inflows throughout the period and never had occasion to contemplate IMF drawings.

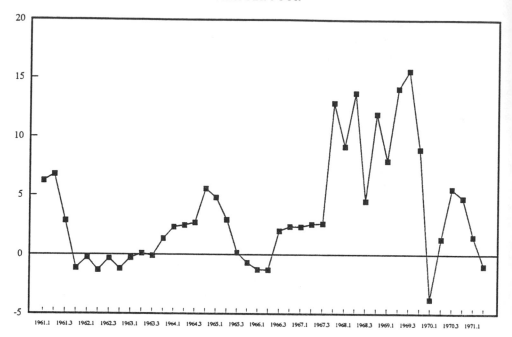

Figure 4.2. Expected Rate of Sterling Devaluation against the Deutsche Mark, 1961–71 (percent per year). *Sources*: Calculations by author. Sterling interest rates from Bank of England, *Quarterly Bulletin*, various issues. Other data from International Monetary Fund, *International Financial Statistics*, various years.

Figure 4.2 shows an estimate of expected devaluation rates (the implicit probability of devaluation times the expected magnitude of the devaluation in the event that it occurred).[66] The upward march of devaluation expectations in 1961 is striking. Growth had accelerated in 1959–60, sucking in imports and transforming a modest current-account surplus into a substantial deficit. Problems of price competitiveness prevented exports from respond-

[66] This is estimated by the trend-adjustment method—that is, by subtracting the expected rate of depreciation of the exchange rate within the band (calculated by regressing the actual change in the exchange rate on a constant term and the rate's position in the band) from the percentage forward discount. The figures plotted in Figure 4.2 are derived using a regression, which adds a dummy variable for the period before the third quarter of 1967 as an additional independent variable (although its coefficient turns out to be small and statistically insignificant). Capital controls create complications for this approach, since differences in the domestic-currency-denominated rate of return on sterling and dollars will incorporate not only expected exchange changes but also the costs of evading controls. While using Euro-currency differentials avoids this problem, it introduces another, since for the early part of this period the Euro-markets were relatively thin. Reassuringly, estimates using Euro-market interest differentials in place of the forward discount deliver very similar results.

ing. Invisible earnings were stagnant, in a disturbing echo of 1931. The gap was bridged by short-term capital inflows attracted by higher interest rates. Bank rate was raised by a point to 5 percent in January 1961 and by a further two percentage points in June. After being cut back to 5½ and then 5 percent in October and December, it was ratcheted back up to 7 percent the following July. Interest-rate increases were accompanied by fiscal retrenchment. The government's April 1961 budget projected a reduction in the overall deficit. In July the chancellor of the Exchequer announced a 10 percent surcharge on imports, excise duties, and a variety of spending cuts. As Figure 4.2 shows, these measures succeeded in calming the markets.

These were the kind of expenditure-reducing policies that countries typically resisted under Bretton Woods. Britain was no exception; retrenchment in 1961 was not particularly great. In any case, the fiscal measures were described as temporary. Unemployment was only allowed to rise from 1.6 percent in 1961 to 2.1 percent in 1962. Policy was adjusted by just enough to assure the international community of the government's resolve. In March of 1961, European central banks intervened heavily on behalf of sterling. Britain drew $1.5 billion from the IMF, which made an additional $500 million available under a standby arrangement. One can argue that it was the foreign support as much as the domestic measures that reassured the markets.

1962 was uneventful, but 1963 was marked by the harshest winter in more than a century (which raised unemployment), de Gaulle's veto of Britain's membership in the European Economic Community, and pre-election uncertainty. January 1964 saw a record deficit in merchandise trade, with the economy again expanding rapidly, and a Conservative government reluctant to take deflationary action just before an election. October saw the election of the first Labour government in thirteen years.

Harold Wilson's newly formed Cabinet rejected devaluation. It feared the inflationary consequences in an economy already approaching full employment and worried that Labour would come to be seen as the party that habitually devalued.[67] The government's only remaining alternative was to impose deflationary fiscal measures, which it hesitated to do. When this reluctance was confirmed in the chancellor's budget speech in November, the crisis escalated. It was surmounted only when the government tightened capital controls and arranged a $1 billion standby credit with the IMF and an additional $3 billion line of credit with eleven foreign countries. The United States urged the British to resist devaluation, fearing that speculative pres-

---

[67] See Cairncross and Eichengreen 1983, p. 164. This motive for resisting devaluation on the part of left-wing governments is a commonplace. See, for comparison, Chapter 5 on France's Socialist government in 1981.

sures would spill over to the dollar, and took the lead in organizing foreign support.

But in the absence of more fundamental adjustments, foreign support could only delay the inevitable. Figure 4.2 indicates renewed bearishness in 1966 but also that the deterioration in expectations was halted in the first half of 1967 by fiscal retrenchment and an additional $1.3 billion in foreign credits. The closing of the Suez Canal during the Six-Day War in 1967, by auguring a further disruption to trade, did not help, but Wilson hoped that he could ride it out, anticipating that the American economy was soon to boom, 1968 being an election year. However, when Maurice Couve de Murville, the French foreign minister, disappointed by the British government's failure to adopt adequate adjustment measures, voiced doubts about sterling's stability, raising the question of whether further foreign support could be expected, conditions deteriorated markedly.[68]

Against this background, capital took flight. The IMF made the extension of credits conditional on strict deflationary measures, which the British government was reluctant to accept. This left no alternative to devaluation. Sterling's external value was reduced by 17 percent on November 18, 1967. Reflecting the liberalization of capital markets and the speed with which events unfolded, the IMF received only an hour's notice (having received twenty-four hours' notice in 1949).

The Crisis of the Dollar

In October 1960, the price of gold in private markets shot up to $40 an ounce. John F. Kennedy's victory in the presidential election the following month led to capital outflows and further increases in the dollar price of gold. It was as if the markets, echoing their reaction to FDR's election in 1932, were worried that the new president, who pledged to "get America moving again," might find it necessary to devalue.[69]

That the markets reacted this way is indicative of how far things had come

[68] Readers familiar with recent financial history will recognize a parallel with the comments made by Bundesbank president Helmut Schlesinger in 1992. The absence of crisis conditions until the final weeks before devaluation resembled both 1931 and 1992 (as we shall see in the next chapter). Prime Minister Wilson's memoirs confirm the impression conveyed by our estimates of devaluation expectations: that the markets did not attach a significant probability to devaluation until immediately before the crisis. Wilson 1971, p. 460.

[69] In fact, Kennedy was entirely unwilling to do so, regarding the stability of the dollar as a matter of prestige. See Sorensen 1965, pp. 405–10.

since the 1940s, when the $35 gold price seemed etched in stone.[70] The dynamics of the Bretton Woods System, which generated reserves by pyramiding more U.S. official foreign liabilities on the country's dwindling gold, placed the currency in a position that increasingly resembled that of the pound sterling in the wake of World War II. The consequences were manageable only if the United States strengthened its current account; as they had in the United Kingdom in the 1940s, observers speculated that a devaluation might be required. The American government, like the British government before it, sought to contain the pressure by placing controls on capital movements and then, as the end drew near, tacking a surcharge on imports.

Before leaving office in January 1961, President Dwight D. Eisenhower issued an executive order prohibiting Americans from holding gold abroad. Kennedy then prohibited U.S. citizens from collecting gold coins. He increased commercial staffs in U.S. embassies in an effort to boost exports. Visa requirements were simplified in an effort to boost tourist receipts, and the export credit insurance facilities of the *Export-Import Bank* were expanded. The Treasury experimented with denominating bonds in foreign currency, and the Federal Reserve, as its agent, intervened on the forward market.[71] In 1962, in order to encourage the maintenance of official foreign dollar balances, Congress suspended the ceilings that had been placed on time deposits held by foreign monetary authorities. The Interest Equalization Tax on American purchases of securities originating in other industrial countries, proposed in July 1963 and implemented in September 1964, reduced the after-tax yield of long-term foreign securities by approximately one percentage point. Voluntary restraints on lending abroad by U.S. commercial banks were introduced in 1965 and extended to insurance companies and pension funds. In January 1968 some of these restrictions on financial intermediaries were made mandatory.

The array of devices to which the Kennedy and Johnson administrations resorted became positively embarrassing. They acknowledged the severity of the dollar problem while displaying a willingness to address only the symptoms, not the causes. Dealing with the causes required reforming the international system in a way that diminished the dollar's reserve-currency role, something the United States was still unwilling to contemplate.

---

[70] The message was reinforced when the Germans and Dutch revalued by 5 percent on March 5, 1961, again suggesting that there might be more attractive currencies in which to invest than the dollar.

[71] In 1962 the Federal Reserve resumed foreign-exchange-market intervention on its own account for the first time since World War II.

Bolstering this otherwise untenable situation was international cooperation. We have considered one example, the London Gold Pool. In addition, in 1962–63 the Federal Reserve negotiated a series of swap arrangements under which foreign central banks loaned it currencies. The Fed intervened on spot and forward markets to support the dollar, and the German Bundesbank and other European central banks engaged in coordinated intervention on its behalf. Foreign central banks purchased Roosa bonds (U.S. government bonds that carried a guarantee against capital loss due to dollar devaluation, named after Undersecretary of the Treasury Robert Roosa) despite their limited negotiability.

America's ultimate threat was to play bull in the china shop: to disrupt the trade and monetary systems if foreign central banks failed to support the dollar and foreign governments failed to stimulate merchandise imports from the United States. Foreign governments supported the dollar because it was the linchpin of the Bretton Woods System and because there was no consensus on how that system might be reformed or replaced.

But there were limits to how far foreign governments and central banks would go. No one, in the prevailing climate of uncertainty about reform, welcomed the breakdown of Bretton Woods, but there might come a time where the steps required to support it were unacceptable. The idea that the Bundesbank might engage in large-scale purchases of dollars, for example, fed German fears of inflation. For Germany to support the dollar through foreign-exchange intervention would require German and American prices to rise in tandem over the medium term. Even though U.S. inflation was not yet excessive from the German viewpoint, there was the danger that it might become so, especially if the escalation of the Vietnam War caused the United States to subordinate the pursuit of price and exchange rate stability to other goals. And the more extensive the foreign support, the stronger the temptation for the United States to disregard the consequences of its policies for inflation and the balance of payments, and the less acceptable the consequences for Germany, which was fearful of inflation, and France, which recalled the refusal of other countries to help finance its own military ventures. That cooperation was arranged on an ad hoc basis rather than through the IMF made effective conditionality that much more difficult to arrange. This left foreign governments less confident that they could expect adjustments in U.S. policy.

In fact, the evidence of excessive inflation, money growth, and budget deficits in the United States is far from overwhelming.[72] Between 1959 and

---

[72] This fact is emphasized by Cooper 1993.

1970, the period of Bretton Woods convertibility, U S. inflation, at 2.6 percent, was lower than that in any of the other G-7 countries. The rate of money growth, as measured by M1, was slower in the United States than in the rest of the G-7 in every year between 1959 and 1971.[73] And despite widespread complaints about the laxity of American fiscal policy, U.S. budget deficits were not exceptionally large.[74]

How then could inadequate monetary and fiscal discipline in the United States have caused a run on the dollar? The answer is that it did not suffice for the United States simply to match the inflation rates of other countries. Once postwar reconstruction was sorted out, the poorer economies of Europe and Japan could grow faster than the United States simply by virtue of having started out behind the technological leader. And fast-growing countries starting off from low levels of income could afford to run relatively rapid rates of inflation (as captured by economywide measures such as the GNP deflator). As incomes rose, so did the relative price of services, the output of the sector in which the scope for productivity growth is least (a phenomenon known as the *Balassa-Samuelson effect*). Since few products of the service sector are traded internationally, the relatively rapid rise in sectoral prices showed up in the GNP deflator but did not damage competitiveness. Hence, Europe and Japan, which were growing faster than the United States, could run higher inflation rates.[75] Japan, for example, ran inflation rates that were high by international standards throughout the Bretton Woods period (see Figure 4.3).

By absorbing dollars rather than forcing the United States to devalue, foreign central banks allowed their inflation rates to rise still further.[76] But there were limits on the process: Germany, for example, was unwilling to

[73] Adjusting for the faster rate of growth of output (and money demand) outside the United States modifies the picture only slightly; 1961 was the last year in which the money growth rate minus the output growth rate in the rest of the G-7 fell below that of the United States, and then only marginally. And the behavior of these variables did not augur an acceleration of inflation in the future. The excess of money growth rates in the rest of the G-7 relative to those of the United States rose in the final years of Bretton Woods.

[74] On monetary policy, inflation, and budget deficits, see Darby, Gandolfi, Lothian, Schwartz, and Stockman 1983 and Bordo 1993.

[75] This same point arises in our discussion of the causes of the crisis in the European Monetary System in 1992. One popular explanation for that crisis focuses on inflation in countries such as Spain and Portugal. But because these were two of the relatively low-income countries of the European Community experiencing the fastest growth, the inflation differential may again overstate the loss of competitiveness due to the Balassa-Samuelson effect.

[76] This is one way to understand how U.S. inflation could be lower than foreign inflation but that the United States could still be the engine of the process.

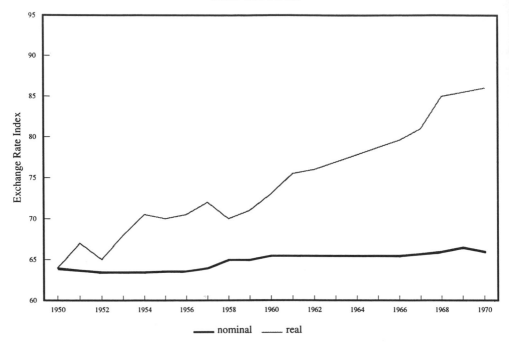

Figure 4.3. Real and Nominal Japanese Yen Exchange Rate, 1950–70. *Source*: Penn World Table (Mark V), described in Summers and Heston 1991. *Note*: Real exchange rate index is Japan's price level divided by geometric average of dollar price level of eleven OECD countries.

countenance inflation rates much in excess of 3 percent.[77] In the absence of changes in the exchange rate of the dollar, U.S. inflation therefore had to be kept significantly below that level. While Germany revalued modestly in 1961 and 1969, there was a hesitancy, for the reasons detailed above, to alter exchange rates. Adjustment could occur only by depressing the rate of U.S. inflation below that of the rest of the G-7.[78] And in a world of liquid

[77] The average rate of increase of Germany's GDP deflator was 3.2 percent over the period of Bretton Woods convertibility. The mean for the G-7 countries was 3.9 percent. Again, see Bordo 1993.

[78] The parallels with the 1992 EMS crisis are striking. In 1992 it was again necessary for other countries' price levels to rise less quickly than Germany's, in that instance because of the shift in demand toward the products of German industry associated with German unification. Because the Bundesbank refused to countenance a significant acceleration of inflation and was unwilling to alter intra-EC exchange rates, adjustment could occur only through deflation abroad, which Germany's EMS partners found difficult to effect (as the United States did in the 1960s). In 1991–92, inflation rates in other EMS countries, such as France, actually fell below Germany's, but not by the margin required for balance-of-payments and exchange rate stability. In all these respects, then, the predicament of these countries was similar to that of the United States in the 1960s.

markets, even a small divergence from sustainable policies could provoke a crisis.[79]

The spring of 1971 saw massive flows from the dollar to the deutsche mark. Germany, fearing inflation, halted intervention and allowed the mark to float upward. The Netherlands joined it. Other European currencies were revalued. But flight from the dollar, once started, was not easily contained. In the second week of August, the press reported that France and Britain planned to convert dollars into gold. Over the weekend of August 13, the Nixon administration closed the gold window, suspending the commitment to provide gold to official foreign holders of dollars at $35 an ounce or any other price. It imposed a 10 percent surcharge on merchandise imports to pressure other countries into revaluing, thereby saving it the embarrassment of having to devalue. Rather than consulting with the IMF, it communicated its program to the managing director of the Fund as a fait accompli.

Over the following four months the industrial countries engaged in extended negotiations over reform of the international monetary system, culminating in an agreement at the Smithsonian Conference in Washington. At European insistence, the devaluation of the dollar was limited to a modest 8 percent. The rest of the change in relative prices was effected by revaluing the yen, the Swiss franc, the deutsche mark, and the Benelux currencies. Fluctuation bands were widened from 1 to 2¼ percent. The U.S. import surcharge was abolished. But the United States was not compelled to reopen the gold window; if exchange rate pegs were maintained, this would now occur purely through intervention on the part of the relevant governments and central banks. Adjustment would depend on the effects of the revaluations of European currencies that had occurred in the summer of 1971.

Clearly, nothing fundamental had changed, notwithstanding Nixon's statement, in retrospect tinged with irony, that the Smithsonian Agreement was "the most significant monetary agreement in the history of the world." The Triffin dilemma had not been removed; the dollar value of global gold reserves had been raised only marginally. The revaluation of European currencies improved the competitiveness of U.S. exports, but, absent adjustments in other policies, the effect was only temporary. U.S. policy remained too expansionary to be compatible with pegging the dollar to foreign currencies; the monetary aggregates grew at more than 6 percent per year as the 1972 U.S. elections loomed. The dollar having been devalued once, there was no reason to doubt that it could happen again.

Another attack on sterling, prompted by the inflationary policies of British

[79] Peter Garber (1993) shows how the cumulation of small policy divergences culminated in a speculative attack on the dollar in 1971.

prime minister Edward Heath, forced Britain to float the currency out of its Smithsonian band in 1972. This set the stage for the final act. Flight from the dollar in early 1973 led Switzerland and others to float their currencies. A second devaluation of the dollar, by 10 percent against the major European currencies and a larger amount against the yen, was negotiated, but without assuring the markets that the underlying imbalance had been removed. Flight from the dollar resumed, and this time Germany and its partners in the EEC jointly floated their currencies upward. The Bretton Woods international monetary system was no more.

THE LESSONS OF BRETTON WOODS

In 1941 John Maynard Keynes, in the statement reproduced at the head of this chapter, dismissed the notion that there existed an automatic balance-of-payments adjustment mechanism as a "doctrinaire delusion." Not for the first time was he looking forward with remarkable prescience. There is little question that such a mechanism had once existed. When a country experienced an external deficit under the prewar gold standard, the price-specie flow mechanism—that deficits reduced stocks of money and credit, depressing the demand for imports and restoring balance to the external accounts—automatically came into play. The decline in the demand for imports was produced not by large-scale gold outflows, of course, but by higher discount rates and other restrictive policy measures. Keynes was right that this was hardly laissez faire; the mechanism depended on central bank management and rested on political conditions.

By the time current-account convertibility was restored at the end of 1958, the notion that such a mechanism still existed was a delusion indeed. Changed political circumstances made it difficult for central banks and governments to eliminate payments deficits by tightening financial conditions. The substitute developed in the 1950s, adjustments in the speed with which controls were relaxed, had always been regarded as temporary. It was vitiated by the restoration of current-account convertibility and by the development of the Euro-markets and other financial innovations that made capital controls increasingly difficult to enforce.

This left only parity adjustments for eliminating a disequilibrium. And these the Bretton Woods Agreement had sought to deter. Its articles discouraged anticipatory adjustments. They forced governments to deny that parity changes were contemplated and to suffer embarrassment if forced to devalue. As international capital mobility rose over the 1960s, the conflict sharpened. Governments thought to be contemplating devaluation exposed their currencies to attack by speculators. A willingness to devalue once gave rise to expectations that the authorities might devalue again, given their manifest reluctance to pursue deflationary policies. This produced a refusal to devalue at all. The inadequacy of the available adjustment mechanisms and the very great difficulty of operating a system of pegged exchange rates in the presence of highly mobile capital is a first lesson of Bretton Woods.

That this system functioned at all is testimony to the international cooperation that operated in its support. This is a second lesson of Bretton Woods. Unlike the late-nineteenth century, when foreign assistance was limited to instances when the stability of the system was threatened, cooperation among governments and central banks was continuous. It took place in the context of an alliance in which the United States, Western Europe, and Japan were partners in the cold war. Other countries supported the dollar and hence the Bretton Woods System in return for the United States bearing a disproportionate share of the defense burden. A third lesson of Bretton Woods is therefore that cooperation in support of a system of pegged currencies will be most extensive when it is part of an interlocking web of political and economic bargains.

But there were limits to how far Europe and Japan would go. U.S. military expenditures in Southeast Asia were less to their liking than NATO commitments. As supporting the dollar came to jeopardize price stability and other economic objectives at home, Germany and other industrial countries evinced growing reservations. In the nineteenth century, international cooperation was viable—and the need for it was limited—because there was no reason to question governments' overriding commitment to defending their gold parities. Ultimately, governments and central banks were certain to take the measures required for adjustment, which limited the need for foreign support. Under Bretton Woods, in contrast, there were reasons to doubt that adjustment would take place. Cooperation, while extensive, ran up against binding limits. The inevitability of such limits in a politicized environment is a fourth lesson of Bretton Woods.

From Floating to Monetary Unification

It's our currency but it's your problem.
(U.S. Treasury Secretary John Connally)

T HE DEMISE of the Bretton Woods international monetary system in 1973 was a watershed. Even more than the reconstruction of the gold standard in 1925 or the restoration of convertibility in 1958, it transformed international monetary affairs. Ever since central banks and governments had been aware of the existence of the instrument that came to be known as monetary policy, the stability of the exchange rate had been the paramount goal to which it was directed. Monetary policy was used to peg the exchange rate except during exceptional and limited periods of war, reconstruction, and depression. In 1973 policy was cut loose from these moorings, and exchange rates were allowed to float.

This transition was a consequence of the rise of international capital mobility. Throughout the Bretton Woods years, capital controls had provided some insulation from balance-of-payments pressures for governments that felt a need to direct monetary policy toward other targets. Controls offered the breathing space to organize orderly adjustments of the adjustable peg. Policymakers could contemplate changing the peg without provoking a destabilizing tidal wave of international capital flows. But the effectiveness of controls had been eroded over the preceding decades. The recovery of international financial markets and transactions from the disruptions of depression and war had been delayed, but by the 1960s it was well under way. With the reestablishment of current-account convertibility, it became difficult to distinguish and segregate purchases and sales of foreign currency related to transactions on current and capital accounts. Market participants found new and clever ways of circumventing barriers to international capital flows.

Stripped of this insulation, governments and central banks found the operation of pegged but adjustable exchange rates increasingly problematic. The merest hint that a country was considering a parity change could subject it to massive capital outflows, discouraging officials from even contemplating such a change. Defending the parity did not prevent balance-of-payments pressures on pegged rates from continuing to mount, of course, or the markets from challenging pegs they suspected were unsustainable. In a world of high capital mobility, defending a parity required unprecedented levels of foreign-exchange-market intervention and international support. Support of this magnitude was something countries hesitated to extend when they doubted the willingness and ability of a government to eliminate the source of the payments imbalance.

The alternatives to pegged but adjustable rates were polar extremes: floating and attempting to peg once and for all. Large countries like the United States and Japan, for whom the importance of international transactions was still limited, opted to float. For them, the uncertainties of a fluctuating exchange rate, while not pleasant, were tolerable. For smaller, more open economies, especially developing countries with thin financial markets, floating exchange rates were even more volatile and disruptive. They opted for the other alternative: attempting to establish a fixed currency peg. Developing countries maintained tight capital controls in an effort to support currency pegs against major trading partners.[1] The countries of Western Europe, for whom intra-European trade was exceptionally important and whose *Common Agricultural Policy* (CAP) could be seriously disrupted by exchange rate swings, sought to peg their currencies to one another, there too behind the shelter of controls. They created new institutions to structure the international cooperation needed to support a collective currency peg.

But there was no turning back the clock. The ongoing development of financial markets, powered by advances in telecommunications and information processing technologies, hampered efforts to contain international financial flows. Doing so was not only difficult but also increasingly costly: with the development of competing financial centers, countries imposing onerous controls risked losing their financial business to offshore markets. Developing countries that failed to liberalize risked being passed over by foreign investors. Liberalization, though inevitable, exacerbated the difficulty of pegging the exchange rate, leading a growing number of developing countries to float (see Figure 5.1).

The same trend was evident in Europe, although there the transformation took a different form. The interdependent economies of Western Europe had repeatedly sought to operate collective currency pegs. In the 1970s they had attempted to maintain the 2¼ percent fluctuation bands of the Smithsonian Agreement in an arrangement known as the *European Snake*. In the 1980s

---

[1] Many of these countries tightened controls in the 1970s and 1980s in response to the rise of capital mobility. Edwards and Losada 1994 document that this was the case in a number of Central American countries, for example, which had long pegged their exchange rates to the dollar.

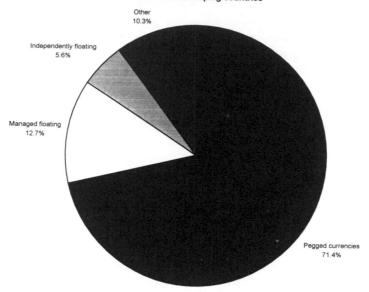

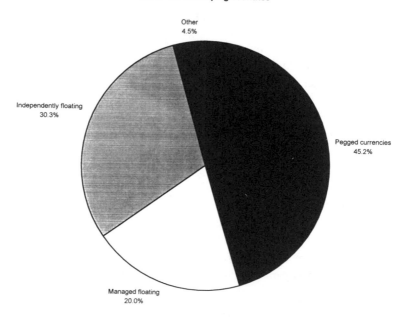

Figure 5.1. Exchange Rate Arrangements in Developing Countries, 1984 and 1994 (percent of total). *Source*: International Monetary Fund, *International Financial Statistics*, February 1985 and May 1995.

they sought to limit exchange rate fluctuations by creating the *European Monetary System* (EMS). But with the removal of capital controls at the end of the 1980s, the EMS became increasingly difficult to operate. Orderly changes in parities became all but impossible. Strong-currency countries grew reluctant to support their weak-currency partners, given that effective support would have to be virtually unlimited in a world of liquid markets and high capital mobility. The limits to international cooperation in a Europe of sovereign monetary authorities became clear to see. A series of crises then forced the members of the EC to widen the fluctuation bands of the EMS from 2¼ to 15 percent in 1993.

The other option was to move further in the direction of hardening the exchange rate peg. A few countries—Hong Kong, Bermuda, the Cayman Islands, and more recently, Argentina and Estonia—did so by establishing *currency boards*. They adopted parliamentary statutes or constitutional amendments requiring the government or central bank to peg the currency to that of a trading partner. A monetary authority constitutionally required to peg the exchange rate was insulated from political pressure to do otherwise and enjoyed the confidence of the markets. The problem with currency boards was that monetary authorities were constrained even more tightly than under the nineteenth-century gold standard from engaging in lender-of-last-resort intervention. Currency boards were attractive only for countries in special circumstances: typically they were very small, their banks were closely tied to institutions overseas and hence could expect foreign support, they possessed exceptionally underdeveloped financial markets, or they had particularly lurid histories of inflation.

The other way of hardening the peg was to move toward monetary union. Notwithstanding detours, this was the avenue pursued by the members of the European Community. In 1991 they adopted a plan to establish a *European Central Bank* (ECB) to assume control of their monetary policies, irrevocably peg their exchange rates, and replace their national monies with a single European currency. Whether they will succeed remains to be seen. What is clear is that informally pegged or pegged-but-adjustable exchange rates are no longer a feasible option. In most cases, the only alternative to monetary union has become more freely floating rates.

FLOATING EXCHANGE RATES IN THE 1970s

The transition to floating following the breakdown of Bretton Woods was a leap in the dark. Officials—especially those of organizations like the IMF that were heavily committed to the old system—did not jump willingly; they had to be pushed. In July of 1972 the governors of the International Monetary Fund set up the Committee of Twenty (C-20), composed of representatives of each of the twenty country groups represented by an IMF executive director, to prepare proposals for reforming the par value system.[2] Their "grand design" assumed, at odds with reality, the maintenance of adjustable pegs and concentrated on the provision of international reserves and on measures to encourage adjustment. Work on this proposal continued even after currencies were floated out of their Smithsonian bands in 1973 and the adjustable peg had expired.

While the Europeans and Japanese hoped for the restoration of par values, the United States, having endured repeated attacks on the dollar, was inclined to continue floating (especially once George Shultz replaced John Connally as secretary of the Treasury). The Americans saw the problem as one of European countries intent on running surpluses and the solution— shades of the Keynes Plan—as a set of "reserve indicators" that would compel their governments to take corrective action. The governments of the surplus countries—particularly Germany—hesitated to submit to sanctions that could compel them to inflate. They opposed the use of IMF resources to buy up the overhang of dollars. Failure to surmount these obstacles forced the C-20 to abandon work on its grand design in 1974.

The members of the IMF then groped toward the Second Amendment to the Articles of Agreement, which legalized floating. At Bretton Woods thirty years earlier, a small group of countries had held the fate of the monetary system in its hands. And the same was again true: after the collapse of the C-20 process, the G-10, which had been responsible for the ill-fated Smithsonian negotiations, resumed its deliberations. The IMF established the ironically named Interim Committee (ironic because it still exists today). The most important forum was the G-5, composed of finance ministers from the United States, Japan, France, Germany, and the United Kingdom, plus invited guests.

The French advocated pegged rates and a system that would prevent reserve currency countries from living beyond their means. They sought to limit America's exorbitant privilege of financing its external liabilities with dollars. U.S. Treasury secretary Shultz and his undersecretary, Paul Volcker, were prepared to contemplate stabilizing the dollar only if bands were sufficiently wide that U.S. policy would not be significantly constrained and if the par-

---

[2] The United States had come to feel isolated from the rest of the G-10 and realized that an amendment to the IMF Articles of Agreement regularizing a new system would require the assent of countries not represented there. It consequently backed the idea of negotiations with representatives of a larger group of countries within the framework of the IMF.

ticipating countries agreed on indicators whose violation would compel surplus countries to revalue or otherwise share the adjustment burden. This inversion of the positions held by the United States and the Europeans at Bretton Woods, which mirrored the changing balance-of-payments positions of their respective economies, did not go unremarked upon.

The French, forced to acknowledge the depth of American resistance, agreed at the Rambouillet summit in 1975 to the face-saving formula of a "stable system" of exchange rates rather than a "system of stable rates." This concession opened the door to the Second Amendment to the Articles of Agreement, which came into effect in 1978. The Second Amendment legalized floating and eliminated the special role of gold. It obligated countries to promote stable exchange rates by fostering orderly economic conditions and authorizing the Fund to oversee the policies of its members.

Forecasts of the operation of the new system ran the gamut. Jacques Rueff, the French critic of Bretton Woods, predicted that the collapse of par values would provoke the liquidation of foreign exchange reserves and a deflationary scramble for gold like that which had aggravated the Great Depression.[3] This view neglected the learning that had occurred in the interim. From the experience of the 1930s, governments and central banks had learned that when the exchange rate constraint was relaxed, policymakers and not markets could control the money supply. Indeed, they had learned this lesson too well; they started up the monetary printing presses to finance budget deficits and oil-import bills. The problem of the 1970s became inflation, not the deflation Rueff had feared.

And there was no consensus forecast of the behavior of floating rates. Some believed that the demise of par values removed the problem of one-way bets and persistent misalignments. Floating rates would settle down to equilibrium levels from which they would have little tendency to diverge. The contrary view was that the world was about to enter a dangerous era of financial turmoil and instability.

Today we know that both positions were oversold. Nominal and real exchange rates proved to be more volatile than when currencies were pegged and than predicted by academic proponents of floating. Nominal rates frequently moved by 2 or 3 percent a month; their variability greatly exceeded that of relative money supplies and other economic fundamentals.[4] Real rates were nearly as volatile (see Figures 5.2 and 5.3). Still, there was not the financial chaos the opponents of floating had anticipated.

At first, it seemed that the pessimists would be proven correct. The dollar depreciated by 30 percent against the deutsche mark in the first six months

[3] See Rueff 1972, chap. 5 and passim.
[4] This regularity, now well known, is perhaps best documented by Rose 1994.

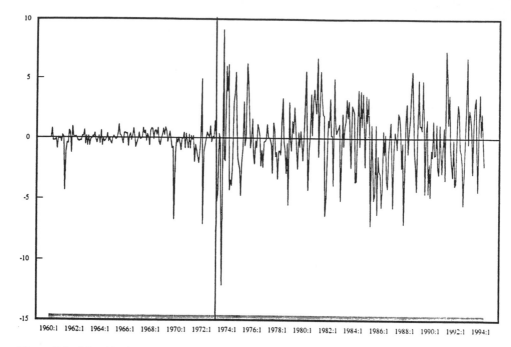

Figure 5.2. Monthly Change in the Deutsche Mark–U.S. Dollar Real Exchange Rate, February 1960–March 1994 (monthly percentage change in relative wholesale prices). *Source*: International Monetary Fund, *International Financial Statistics*, various years.

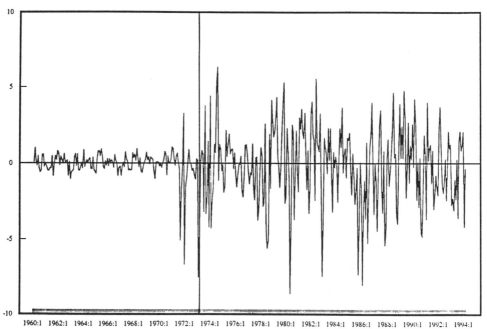

Figure 5.3. Monthly Change in the Japanese Yen–U.S. Dollar Real Exchange Rate, February 1960–March 1994 (monthly percentage change in relative wholesale prices). *Source*: International Monetary Fund, *International Financial Statistics*, various years.

of floating. After that, however, it settled down. Much of the dollar's de-cline had been needed to eliminate its earlier overvaluation. Misalignments, though a subject of complaint, were not as severe as feared by the critics of floating (see *misaligned currency* in the Glossary). Sterling may have been undervalued in 1976, the dollar overvalued in 1978. The undervalued yen may have appreciated excessively in 1977–79. But none of these currencies was as seriously misaligned as the dollar would become in the mid-1980s. This was an achievement, given that economies were buffeted in the 1970s by two oil shocks and other commodity-price disturbances.

The absence of 1980s-style misalignments in the second half of the 1970s reflected two factors: that governments intervened in the currency markets, and that there was some willingness—in contrast to U.S. policy in the first half of the 1980s—to adjust monetary and fiscal policies with the exchange rate in mind. The Canadian dollar, French franc, Swiss franc, lira, yen, and pound sterling were actively managed. Intervention was on both sides of the market: it was used to support weak currencies and to limit the appreciation of strong ones. The Bank of Japan intervened both to support the yen in 1973–74 and then to stem its appreciation in 1975–77, for example.

The dollar/deutsche mark rate was only lightly managed; through 1977 intervention was modest. For the first two years of floating, the Federal Reserve confined itself to smoothing day-to-day fluctuations without at-tempting to influence the trend. But when the dollar fell by more than 11 percent against the deutsche mark in the six months ending in March 1975, the Federal Reserve, with the reluctant support of the German Bundesbank and the Swiss National Bank, undertook concerted intervention. For a time, their operations halted the currency's fall. But in 1977, responding to expec-tations of accelerating U.S. inflation provoked by the Carter administration's policies of demand stimulus, the dollar's depreciation resumed.

This time the Bundesbank agreed to make available a special credit to the U.S. Treasury's Exchange Stabilization Fund. Swap lines between the Bun-desbank and the Fed were doubled. Intervention rose from DM 2 billion in the first three quarters of 1977 to more than DM 17 billion in the two quar-ters that followed.[5] The dollar recovered for a time. When it weakened again in the second half of 1978, the two central banks undertook another DM 17 billion of intervention.[6]

Critical to the success, however limited, of these operations were domes-tic policy adjustments. To be sure, policies were not continuously directed

[5] *Reports* of the Deutsche Bundesbank for 1977, 1978, and 1979, cited in Tew 1988, p. 220.

[6] There was also U.S. and foreign intervention in the markets for the Swiss franc and Japa-nese yen.

toward exchange rate targets. The macroeconomic stimulus applied by the administration of President Jimmy Carter when it assumed office at the beginning of 1977 was adopted with full knowledge that its inflationary effects would weaken the dollar. The administration's hope was that other countries would also adopt more expansionary policies, limiting currency instability. Fearing inflation, the Japanese and Europeans refused to do so despite their awareness that the currency problem would be compounded.

But when currency fluctuations threatened to get out of hand, compromise ensued. The details were hammered out at the Bonn summit meeting in July 1978. The Carter administration announced an anti-inflation package to restrain wages and public spending. It agreed to raise domestic oil prices to world levels, eliminating a discrepancy that in the European and Japanese view aggravated the external deficits responsible for the dollar's decline. In return, the Europeans and Japanese agreed to expand. Japanese prime minister Takeo Fukuda submitted a supplementary budget that increased government spending by 1.5 percent of GNP in 1978. The Japanese authorities reduced the discount rate to an unprecedented 3.5 percent in March 1978. Bonn agreed to increase federal government expenditures and cut taxes by amounts sufficient to augment German domestic demand by approximately 1 percent in 1979. The French government made a similar commitment. "Remarkably, virtually all the crucial pledges of the Bonn summit were redeemed," in the words of Putnam and Henning.[7] These cooperative adjustments in policy may have been too modest to stabilize exchange rates, but they prevented the major currencies from diverging further.[8]

How did governments reconcile domestic policy objectives with the imperatives of exchange rate stabilization? In fact, the two did not always conflict. In all the countries that participated in the Bonn summit, there was a powerful faction that favored on domestic grounds the policy changes needed to stabilize exchange rates. And where conflicts occurred, governments resorted to capital controls to mitigate the trade-off between domestic policy autonomy and currency stability. In 1977–78, as an alternative to more inflationary policies, the German authorities revoked the authorization for nonresidents to purchase certain classes of German bonds and raised reserve ratios on nonresident deposits with German banks in order to limit capital inflows into Germany and prevent further appreciation of the mark. The Japanese government supported the yen in 1973–74 by revising capital

[7] See Putnam and Henning 1989, p. 97. Implementation of the U.S. promise to decontrol oil prices was delayed, however, until after the 1978 election, to the irritation of the Europeans.

[8] See Henning 1994, p. 129; Gros and Thygesen 1991, p. 37; and Sachs and Wyplosz 1986, p. 270.

controls to favor capital inflows and discourage outflows.[9] In 1977 it imposed 50 percent reserve requirements on most non-resident deposits, in 1978 raising these to 100 percent and prohibiting purchases by foreigners of most domestic securities on the over-the-counter market.

Readers should not come away with the idea that the 1970s were copacetic. With the transition to floating, real as well as nominal exchange rates became more volatile than before. The contrast is evident in the behavior of both the yen/dollar and deutsche mark/dollar rates (again, see Figures 5.2 and 5.3). Not only were month-to-month changes in real rates larger than before, but movements in one direction could persist. But these problems, however serious, were not as severe as those that arose with the dollar's dramatic misalignment in the 1980s. The difference in the 1970s was more concerted intervention, more extensive use of capital controls, and greater willingness to adapt policies to the imperatives of the foreign-exchange markets.

FLOATING EXCHANGE RATES IN THE 1980s

Three events transformed the international monetary environment at the end of the 1970s. One, the advent of the European Monetary System, I discuss later. The others were shifts in the stance of U.S. and Japanese policies.

Few nations had been more committed than Japan to exchange market intervention. Like Germany, Japan experienced a period of rapid inflation after World War II and valued its nominal anchor. In an economy heavily dependent on exports, powerful interests resisted revaluation. Symptomatic was the Bank of Japan's effort to continue pegging the yen to the dollar at the level of 360 established in April 1949 even after Nixon closed the gold window in August 1971.[10] After two weeks, however, the Bank of Japan was forced to allow the currency to float up to 308 to the dollar, where it was repegged following the Smithsonian negotiation. When the Smithsonian Agreement collapsed in February 1973, the yen was again allowed to float. At first, intervention was used to hold the currency within a narrow trading range. Starting with the first oil shock, however, the exchange rate was permitted to fluctuate more widely (see Figure 5.4).

This transition to a more flexible policy had important implications for the international monetary system. By the 1970s, with the considerable growth of the Japanese economy, the level of the yen had become an issue of con-

[9] See Horiuchi 1993, pp. 110–13.
[10] See Volcker and Gyohten 1992, pp. 93–94.

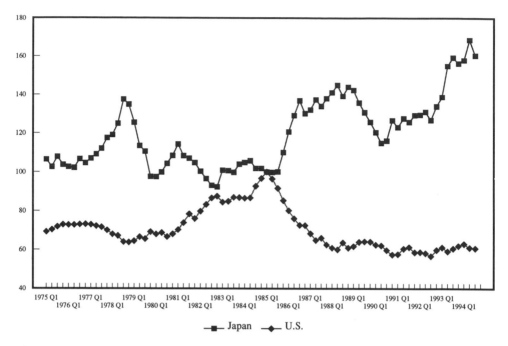

Figure 5.4. U.S. and Japanese Real Exchange Rates, 1975–94 (1985 = 100). *Source*: International Monetary Fund, *International Financial Statistics*, various years.

cern to other countries. While the Japanese government continued to intervene selectively in the foreign-exchange market, the behavior of the dollar/yen rate came to resemble that of the dollar/deutsche mark rate: increasingly it was left to be determined by market forces and allowed to fluctuate over a considerable range.

The United States also gravitated toward greater exchange rate flexibility. If there had been any doubt about American priorities, it was removed by the appointment of Paul Volcker as chairman of the Federal Reserve Board in 1979 and Ronald Reagan's election as president in 1980. Volcker was prepared to let interest rates rise and the growth of the money supply fall to whatever levels were required to bring inflation down from double digits. The well-known Dornbusch model of exchange rate determination, which had gained wide currency in the 1970s, suggested that the exchange rate would overshoot its long-run equilibrium level in response to a change in rates of inflation and money growth.[11] This is what happened: Germany and Japan having abandoned policies of exchange rate targeting, the dollar ap-

[11] See Dornbusch 1976. While the Dornbusch model suggested that the appreciation of the dollar should have occurred all at once, at the moment when the change in U.S. monetary policy took place, the currency actually strengthened gradually over the 1980–82 period. Mi-

146

preciated by 29 percent in nominal terms and 28 percent in real terms between 1980 and 1982.

The Reagan administration followed with cuts in personal income taxes. It indexed tax brackets for inflation and increased military spending. As the budget deficit widened, U.S. interest rates rose: the differential in relation to foreign rates was a full point larger in 1983–84 than it had been in 1981–82. "The textbooks [did not] have much trouble explaining the source of this increase in U.S. interest rates," as Jeffrey Frankel put it.[12] The same can be said of the increase in the foreign-exchange value of the dollar. Foreign capital was attracted to the United States by high interest rates, pushing up the currency still further.

Initially this dramatic appreciation elicited little in the way of a policy response. There was scant willingness on the part of the United States to contemplate tax increases, cuts in government spending, or changes in Federal Reserve policy to bring U.S. interest rates down and render the dollar less attractive to foreign investors. Volcker's Fed still attached priority to the reduction of inflation; Treasury Secretary Donald Regan believed in entrusting the exchange rate to the market.

The dollar's appreciation in 1983–85 highlighted the need for cooperative adjustments of macroeconomic policies to counter misalignments. But in the 1980s, as on prior occasions, intellectual disputes precluded cooperation. U.S. policymakers such as Treasury Undersecretary Beryl Sprinkel were committed to the monetarist proposition that a stable rate of monetary growth would produce stable inflation and a stable exchange rate.[13] They denied that the dollar's strength reflected the crowding-out effects of deficit spending and high interest rates, ascribing it instead to the administration's success in containing inflation.[14] Not only was foreign exchange intervention inappropriate, in this view, but it was unnecessary since, by assumption, exchange rates were driven by the market to efficiency-maximizing levels.

The Europeans and Japanese continued to attach more importance to exchange rate stability. For historical reasons they had more faith in intervention and cooperation, and they subscribed to a model of the economy in

---

chael Mussa (1994) suggests that this reflected a gradual realization on the part of the public that the change in policy that had taken place was credible and permanent.

[12] See Frankel 1994, p. 296.

[13] This was the view of exchange rate determination espoused by Milton Friedman in his influential 1953 article on floating rates. See Friedman 1953.

[14] Disinflation could indeed explain the real appreciation experienced by the United States in 1980–81 when U.S. monetary policy shifted in a more contractionary direction (this being the implication of the Dornbusch model), but it was more difficult to account for the further real appreciation of subsequent years. See discussion below.

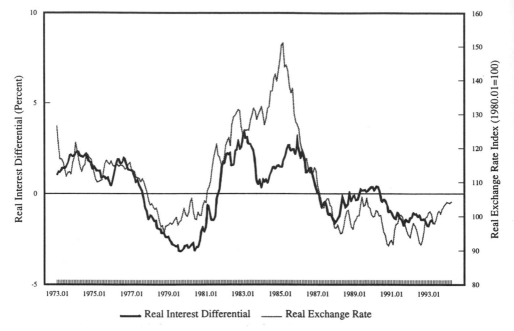

Figure 5.5. U.S. Dollar Real Exchange Rate and Long-Term Interest Differential, 1973–94.
Source: International Monetary Fund, *International Financial Statistics*, various years. *Note*:
Real exchange rate is U.S. consumer price index relative to trade-weighted average of consumer
prices of other G-7 countries. Real interest rates are long-term government bond yields minus
twenty-four-month moving average of inflation. Interest differential is real U.S. rate minus
weighted average of real interest rates of other G-7 countries.

which budget deficits and high interest rates were the source of misalignments. But however desirous they were of harmonizing policies, collaboration also required a course correction on the part of the United States.[15] Left
to their own devices, the Europeans withdrew into the EMS, while the Japanese made the most of their improved export competitiveness.

Figure 5.5 shows that the difference between U.S. interest rates and for-

[15] This was something which neither the Treasury nor the Fed was willing to contemplate. At
the G-7 summit in Williamsburg, Virginia, in 1983, the Europeans pushed for reductions in
U.S. deficits to stem the dollar's rise. The American response was that the strong dollar was not
the result of U.S. deficits and high interest rates. See Putnam and Bayne 1987, p. 179 and
passim. By the end of 1983 American producers of traded goods had begun to complain of the
injury they suffered as a result of the dollar's appreciation. Treasury Secretary Regan therefore
sought to pressure Japan to take steps to strengthen the yen. His initiative, which pressed the
Japanese to open their capital markets to international financial flows, ironically led to an
outflow of capital from Japan and a further weakening of the yen. The United States for its part
offered little in the way of policy adjustments. See Frankel 1994, pp. 299–300.

eign interest rates closely tracked the dollar's rise through the first half of 1984. After June, however, the dollar rose further to an extent that was not readily explained by interest rates and macroeconomic fundamentals. The currency continued to appreciate, by an additional 20 percent through February 1985, even though the U.S. interest rate premium began to fall.

This movement, widely interpreted as a speculative bubble, eroded the Reagan administration's resistance to foreign-exchange-market intervention.[16] At a secret meeting at New York City's Plaza Hotel in September 1985, G-5 finance ministers and central bank governors agreed to try to push the dollar down. They were united by their desire to head off protectionist legislation wending its way through the U.S. Congress as a result of the damage inflicted on domestic producers of traded goods. For the Reagan administration, congressional protectionism threatened its agenda of deregulation and economic liberalization; for the Japanese and Europeans it jeopardized their access to the American market. The five governments issued a joint statement of the desirability of an "orderly appreciation of the non-dollar currencies" (a typically prosaic way for politicians to refer to dollar depreciation) and of their readiness to cooperate in attaining it.

The dollar fell by 4 percent against the yen and the deutsche mark the day the Plaza communiqué was released, and it continued to decline thereafter. However, no change in monetary and fiscal policies had been discussed at the Plaza, much less undertaken. This, in conjunction with the fact that the dollar had already begun to decline six months earlier, led some to conclude that the negotiation was inconsequential—that the currency's fall was simply the unwinding of an unsustainable appreciation. The contrary view is that the Plaza Accord and *sterilized intervention* undertaken in its wake signaled an impending policy shift—a new willingness to adapt policy in the directions needed to stabilize the exchange rate.[17] That the dollar began to fall before the Plaza meeting can in fact be reconciled with this argument. Some months earlier (after the 1984 presidential election), the more pragmatic and interventionist James Baker and Richard Darman had replaced Donald Regan and Beryl Sprinkel at the Treasury, suggesting that new policies might be in the offing. Intervention had been agreed to at a G-5 meeting in January 1985, and the Bundesbank had intervened heavily (see Figure 5.6). All this suggests that intervention and cooperation in fact played a role in halting the dollar's rise.

Once it began falling, the dollar depreciated rapidly. The United States

---

[16] Paul Krugman (1985) and Stephen Marris (1985) provided analytical grounding for the bubble interpretation of the 1984–85 appreciation.

[17] See Feldstein 1986 and Frankel 1994 for the competing views.

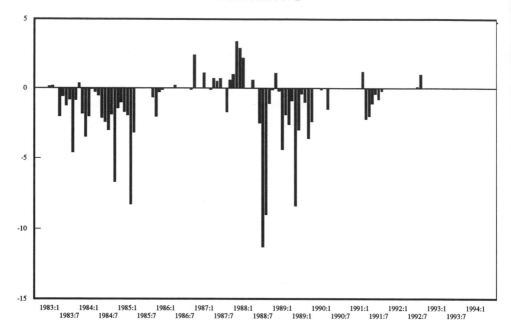

Figure 5.6. Bundesbank Operations in the Deutsche Mark–U.S. Dollar Market, 1983–94 (billions of D-marks). *Source*: Deutsche Bundesbank, *Annual Reports*, various years. *Note*: Positive entries denote Bundesbank intervention on behalf of the U.S. dollar.

had run down its net foreign assets as a result of the external deficits of the early 1980s; a lower exchange rate was needed to offset a weaker invisibles account.[18] Even so, by the second half of 1986 the Europeans and Japanese began to complain that the process had gone too far. The dollar had lost 40 percent of its value against the yen from the peak the year before, creating problems of cost competitiveness for Japanese producers. The Japanese government intervened extensively to support the dollar. In September a bilateral deal between the United States and Japan, trading Japanese fiscal expansion for U.S. abstention from talking the dollar down, sought to stabilize the exchange rate. But absent a willingness to adjust macroeconomic policies in the United States and Europe, the effects were limited.

This realization prompted the Louvre meeting of G-7 finance ministers in February 1987, where more fundamental policy adjustments were discussed. The ministers agreed to stabilize the dollar around current levels; some observers went so far as to suggest that the ministers established a "reference

[18] Some argued that in addition U.S. exporters had lost their foothold in international markets and that foreign producers had gained a permanent beachhead in American markets as a result of the early-1980s misalignment; a lower exchange rate was needed to offset this.

range" of 5 percent.[19] The central banks concerned undertook intervention. The Japanese agreed to further stimulus measures, the Germans to limited tax cuts, the United States to more nebulous adjustments in domestic policy. The Federal Reserve in fact allowed U.S. interest rates to rise (reversing the downward trend that had begun in 1984), although whether its decision was motivated by the decline of the dollar or by signs of impending inflation remains unclear.

The International Monetary Fund played a surprisingly small role in these developments. The Second Amendment to the Articles of Agreement, in suggesting that the IMF's role was to encourage policy coordination among its members, removed the Fund's responsibility for overseeing a system of par values but spoke of the need for "firm surveillance" of national policies. But the leading industrial countries showed little interest in a forum where scores of smaller nations might have some say in their decisions. As a result, governments relied less on changes in underlying monetary and fiscal policies and more on foreign-exchange-market intervention than the Fund may have wished. The IMF is portrayed in the academic literature as a mechanism for applying sanctions and rewards to encourage countries to follow up on cooperative agreements.[20] In practice, the fact that the Fund was an unattractive venue in which to conduct negotiations, and that none of the countries concerned drew on Fund resources to finance their foreign-exchange-market intervention, prevented it from effectively carrying out this role.

The U.S. currency rallied in mid-1988 and again in mid-1989. But as with the Plaza and the 1986 bilateral United States–Japan accord, there was little willingness on the part of the United States to follow through with changes in domestic (in particular, fiscal) policies. Sterilized intervention not backed by a commitment to adjust domestic policies had only transient effects.[21] And the United States, Germany, and Japan lacked the web of interlocking agreements needed to lock in policy adjustments.

[19] See Funabashi 1988, pp. 183–86. Karl Otto Pöhl, who was president of the Bundesbank, recalls some confusion among G-7 ministers over what they had agreed upon. Pöhl's understanding was that formal *target zones* had not been established but that a first step toward their implementation had been taken. But others, especially finance ministers of the smaller countries involved, may have interpreted discussions as implying a formal commitment. See Pöhl 1995, p. 79.

[20] In technical terms, the IMF is portrayed as a "commitment technology." See Dominguez 1993, pp. 371–72.

[21] This had been the finding of the Jurgensen Committee, an intergovernmental working group commissioned to study foreign-exchange intervention. See Working Group on Exchange Market Intervention 1983.

The dollar's decline resumed in the second half of 1989, and the United States settled into the policy of benign neglect of the exchange rate pioneered by the Carter administration. The administrations of Presidents George Bush and Bill Clinton displayed little readiness to adjust policies to stop the currency's fall. A typical Bush reaction to a question about the declining dollar was, "Once in a while, I think about those things, but not much."[22] With this response, Bush was only swimming with the political tide. An overvalued currency, like the dollar in the mid-1980s, imposes high costs on concentrated interests (producers of traded goods who find it difficult to compete internationally) who powerfully voice their objections. In contrast, an undervalued currency, like the dollar in the mid-1990s, imposes only modest costs on diffuse interests (consumers who experience higher inflation and import prices) who have little incentive to mobilize in opposition. Thus, there was little domestic opposition to the dollar's decline. Its depreciation was driven by domestic considerations, such as the Fed's decision to cut interest rates in 1991 in response to the U.S. recession, and a second set of cuts in 1994, again taken to counter signs of a weakening economy.

The situation was reversed in other countries, where an undervalued dollar meant an overvalued local currency. By 1992 the low level of the dollar had become a huge problem for Japan, where the profits of tradable goods producers were squeezed, and for Europe, the one place where it could be argued that there existed the interlocking web of commitments needed to support the maintenance of pegged rates.

THE SNAKE

The countries of Europe followed the other path, seeking to create an institutional framework within which they could stabilize their currencies against one another. That European countries were more open to trade than the United States heightened their sensitivity to exchange rate fluctuations.[23] Europe, not the United States or Japan, was where floating currencies had been associated with hyperinflation in the 1920s. Europe was where the devaluations of the 1930s had most corroded good economic relations.

Still, Europe's steadfast pursuit of pegged exchange rates in a period marked by the quadrupling of oil prices, the breakdown of Bretton Woods,

[22] Cited in Henning 1994, p. 290.
[23] This is argued by Giavazzi and Giovannini 1989.

and the most serious business-cycle fluctuation of the postwar era is one of the most striking features of the period. Its motivation must be understood in terms of the development of the European Economic Community. The EEC was seen by its European founders and their American allies as a mechanism for binding Germany and France together and, by heightening their economic interdependence, for discouraging them from going to war. It helped prevent these and other European countries from reneging on their commitment to cooperate in the economic domain. The EEC created an interlocking web of agreements and side-payments that would be jeopardized if a country followed noncooperative monetary policies. The success of the Community, which by the 1970s had gone a considerable distance toward liberalizing intra-European trade, increased the share of member countries' total trade that took place with one another. To the extent that exchange rate stability was desirable for encouraging the expansion of trade (a proposition for which the evidence provides limited support), focusing on the liberalization of trade within Europe made it possible to achieve that objective by stabilizing intra-European rates. European experience thus supports those who suggest that stable and extensive trade relations are a prerequisite for a smoothly functioning international monetary system.

The EEC completed its customs union ahead of schedule by the end of the 1960s. Monetary unification was the next logical step, especially for those who saw the EEC as a nascent political entity. In 1969 the *European Council* reaffirmed its intention of moving ahead to full economic and monetary union (EMU). It was motivated in part by the incipient instability of the dollar and by fears that a disorderly revaluation of European currencies would endanger the EEC.[24] This led in 1970 to the formation of a study group of high-level officials chaired by the prime minister of Luxembourg, Pierre Werner.[25]

The Werner Report described a process by which monetary union could be achieved by 1980. It recommended creating a central authority to guide and harmonize national economic policies, concentrating fiscal functions at the Community level, and accelerating the integration of factor and commodity markets. It did not recommend creating a single European currency or a

---

[24] This is the interpretation of Harry Johnson (1973).

[25] See Werner et al. 1970. The Werner Report was not the EEC's first discussion of monetary integration. The Treaty of Rome had already acknowledged that the exchange rates of member countries should be regarded as a matter of "common interest." The revaluation of the Dutch guilder and German mark in 1961 then prompted discussion of how the customs union could be extended to the monetary domain. By the mid-1960s this had led to the creation of the *Committee of Central Bank Governors*.

European Central Bank, however, instead assuming that responsibility for exchanging European currencies at par could be vested in a European "system of national central banks." The transition was to be accomplished by a progressive hardening of exchange rate commitments (narrowing of fluctuation bands) and closer harmonization of macroeconomic policies. The recommendations of Werner's group were endorsed by the politicians, who set out on the path it delineated.

In retrospect, it was naive to think that Europe would be ready for monetary union in 1980, much less that it could achieve that goal without building institutions to support the operation of such an arrangement. Admittedly, it had established a customs union and created the Common Agricultural Policy that was the European Community's most visible function. The desire to avoid jeopardizing the CAP, whose administration would be complicated by frequent and sizable exchange rate movements, was a source of support for the Werner Report. But few political functions had been transferred to the *European Parliament* or the *European Commission*. The web of interlocking agreements needed to bond national governments to monetary unification—to prevent them from reneging on a commitment to follow guidelines for macroeconomic policy set down by the Community—remained underdeveloped. And the enlargement of the Community to incorporate Denmark, Ireland, and the United Kingdom in 1973 introduced new diversity that further complicated integration efforts.

If nothing else, the discussions surrounding the Werner Report provided a basis for responding to the collapse of the Bretton Woods System. The Smithsonian Agreement of December 1971 tripled the width of fluctuation bands against the dollar, allowing intra-European exchange rates to vary by as much as 9 percent. For the members of the EEC, exchange rate variability of this magnitude was an alarming prospect. They therefore sought to limit the fluctuation of their bilateral rates to 4½ percent in an arrangement known as the Snake. They maintained that arrangement even after the Smithsonian "tunnel" collapsed in 1973.[26]

Denmark, Ireland, and the United Kingdom, which were not yet members of the EEC, agreed to participate in the Snake within a week of its founding. Norway linked up a month later. The members of the Snake established *Short-Term* and *Very-Short-Term Financing Facilities* to extend credits to weak-currency countries. The *European Monetary Cooperation Fund*, with a board made up of governors of national central banks, was established to

---

[26] Following the collapse of the Smithsonian arrangement, the floating Snake was referred to, not entirely seriously, as "the snake in the lake" to distinguish it from its predecessor, "the snake in the tunnel."

monitor European monetary policies, oversee the operation of credit facilities, and authorize realignments, mimicking the global role of the IMF. Countries were authorized to retain controls on capital movements within Europe, but current transactions were unrestricted as under the Articles of Agreement. The inspiration derived from the Bretton Woods System of pegged but adjustable rates was clear.

The Snake soon encountered difficulties (see Table 5.1). While all of Europe suffered a loss of competitiveness due to the dollar's post-1973 decline and the first OPEC (Organization of Petroleum Exporting Countries) oil-price shock, the weaker currencies were disproportionately affected.[27] Both foreign support and domestic policy adjustments remained limited, however, and could not contain exchange market pressures. In January 1974 France was forced to float; it rejoined the Snake in July 1975. The German Bundesbank then adopted a strategy of targeting monetary aggregates, which prevented it from accommodating the inflationary pressures caused by higher oil prices. The French government of Jacques Chirac, in contrast, adopted expansionary fiscal policies, forcing it to again leave the Snake in 1976.

All the while, Germany intervened in support of the currencies of its small northern European neighbors. But officials of both the Bundesbank and the Free Democratic Party on which the governing coalition relied grew increasingly concerned about the inflationary consequences. Purchases of foreign currencies for deutsche marks, if they remained unsterilized, threatened to bring German inflation rates up to those prevailing in the countries to which the Bundesbank lent support.[28] This tension was resolved by the Frankfurt realignment of October 1976 in which the currencies of the Benelux and Scandinavian countries were devalued against the deutsche mark, inaugurating a period of more frequent parity changes. While the complete story of the Frankfurt realignment is yet to be told, German officials appear to have demanded greater exchange rate flexibility as the price for continued cooperation. Any notion that monetary union could be achieved by pegging exchange rates within unchanging bands was thereby dealt a blow.

In the end, the Snake failed to provide exchange rate stability at the regional level. Intra-European rates were stabilized for limited periods, but efforts to hold them within narrow bands were frustrated. Not only did coun-

---

[27] The Bundesbank was forced to intervene on their behalf. This was the first instance of what became a familiar pattern, in which a weak dollar was associated with a strong deutsche mark within Europe. The same problem afflicted the European Monetary System in 1992, as we shall see below.

[28] Alternatively, if the Bundesbank's intervention were sterilized, there would be good reason to worry that its effects would be neutralized. See note 21 above.

TABLE 5.1
Chronological History of the Snake

1972	
April 24	Basel Agreement enters into force. Participants are Belgium, France, Germany, Italy, Luxembourg, and the Netherlands.
May 1	The United Kingdom and Denmark join.
May 23	Norway becomes associated.
June 23	The United Kingdom withdraws.
June 27	Denmark withdraws.
October 10	Denmark returns.
1973	
February 13	Italy withdraws.
March 19	Transition to the joint float: interventions to maintain fixed margins against the dollar ("tunnel") are discontinued.
March 19	Sweden becomes associated.
March 19	The deutsche mark is revalued by 3 percent.
April 3	Establishment of a European Monetary Cooperation Fund is approved.
June 29	The deutsche mark is revalued by 5.5 percent.
September 17	The Dutch guilder is revalued by 5 percent.
November 16	The Norwegian krone is revalued by 5 percent.
1974	
January 19	France withdraws.
1975	
July 10	France returns.
1976	
March 15	France withdraws again.
October 17	Agreement on exchange rate changes ("Frankfurt realignment"): The Danish krone is devalued by 6 percent, the Dutch guilder and Belgian franc by 2 percent, and the Norwegian and Swedish kroner by 3 percent.
1977	
April 1	The Swedish krona is devalued by 6 percent, and the Danish and Norwegian kroner are devalued by 3 percent.
August 28	Sweden withdraws; the Danish and Norwegian kroner are devalued by 5 percent.
1978	
February 13	The Norwegian krone is devalued by 8 percent.
October 17	The deutsche mark is revalued by 4 percent, the Dutch guilder and Belgian franc by 2 percent.
December 12	Norway announces decision to withdraw.

Source: Gros and Thygesen 1991, p. 17.

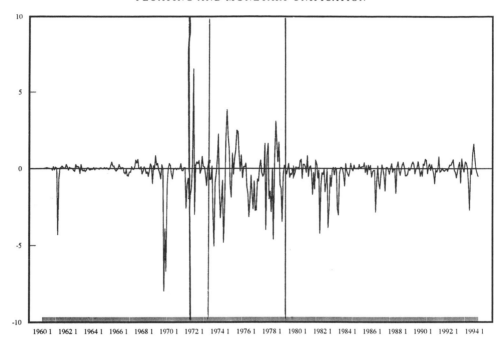

Figure 5.7. Monthly Change in the Deutsche Mark–French Franc Real Exchange Rate, February 1960–April 1994. *Source*: International Monetary Fund, *International Financial Statistics*, various years.

tries engage in serial realignments, but several were compelled to withdraw from the Snake entirely. Figures 5.7–5.9 distinguish four periods: a first before the closing of the gold window, a second through the collapse of the Smithsonian Agreement, a third corresponding to the European Snake, and a fourth denoting the European Monetary System. It is apparent that the critical French franc/deutsche mark exchange rate was less stable under the Snake than during Bretton Woods.[29]

Why was the Snake so troubled? For one thing, the economic environment, marked by oil shocks and commodity market disruptions, was unpropitious for efforts to peg exchange rates. The liberation of the Snake from the Smithsonian tunnel coincided with the first OPEC oil-price shock in 1973 and the 1974 commodity-price boom. Because different European countries relied to differing degrees on imported petroleum and raw materials, the impact was felt asymmetrically. Some countries experienced more

[29] Note the contrast with the deutsche mark/Belgian franc rate, which was relatively stable during the years of the Snake, reflecting Belgium's success in staying in the system.

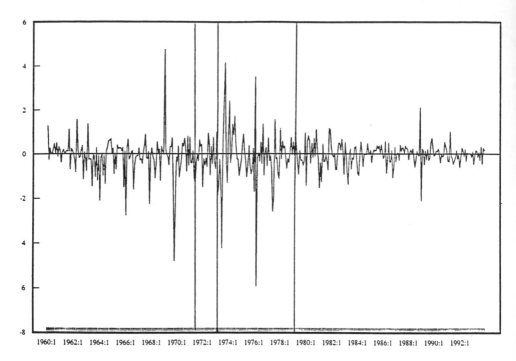

Figure 5.8. Monthly Change in the Deutsche Mark–Dutch Guilder Real Exchange Rate, February 1960–December 1992 (monthly percentage change in relative wholesale prices). *Source*: International Monetary Fund, *International Financial Statistics*, various years.

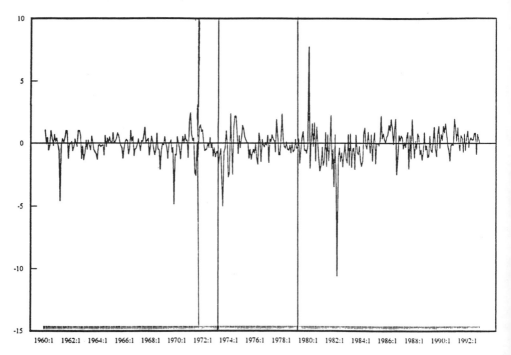

Figure 5.9. Monthly Change in the Deutsche Mark–Belgian Franc Real Exchange Rate, February 1960–December 1992. *Source*: International Monetary Fund, *International Financial Statistics*, various years.

unemployment than others. Some governments were exposed to more intense pressure to respond in expansionary ways. These dislocations interrupted the upward trend in France and Germany's intra-European trade, dimming enthusiasm in both countries for integration initiatives. In the same way that the goal of monetary union by the end of the century tied down intra-European exchange rates in the early 1990s—and questions about whether the *Maastricht Treaty on European Union* would be ratified undermined the stability of prevailing rates—the hope that the Snake might be a stepping stone to monetary union by 1980 encouraged the markets to support Europe's narrow bands only until the shocks of the 1970s made the Werner Report obsolete.[30]

Moreover, officials in different countries had different views of the appropriate response to disturbances. That monetary policy should be directed toward the maintenance of price stability was not yet an intellectual consensus. Some European policymakers, not having had the freedom to experiment with expansionary monetary initiatives under Bretton Woods, failed to appreciate how attempts to aggressively utilize monetary policy, especially in an environment of unbalanced budgets, could stimulate inflation rather than output and employment. Given Germany's aversion to inflation, the result was a lack of policy cohesion.[31]

Ultimately, the disturbances of the mid-1970s were so disruptive to the Snake because the political and institutional preconditions for the harmonization of monetary and fiscal policies remained underdeveloped. The fiscal federalism and centralization foreseen by the authors of the Werner Report, which might have helped weak-currency countries cling to the Snake, remained wholly unrealistic. There was no entity in Brussels accountable to fiscal constituencies at the national level; governments consequently resisted ceding fiscal responsibility to the Community. The adjustments in national fiscal policies needed to hold exchange rates within the Snake were not made.

Analogous problems afflicted monetary policy. The European Monetary Cooperation Fund possessed little authority, central bank governors being unprepared to delegate their prerogatives. Meeting separately as the Committee of Central Bank Governors, they were supposed to set guidelines for national monetary policies but did little more than coordinate foreign-ex-

[30] On the Maastricht Treaty and ratification difficulties in 1992, see discussion later in the text.

[31] Note the parallel with the failure to coordinate reflationary responses to the Depression of the 1930s, when incompatible conceptual frameworks in different countries stood in the way of international cooperation.

change-market intervention.[32] In the end, there existed no regional analogue to the International Monetary Fund to monitor policies and press for adjustments. The absence of such an institution meant that the strong-currency countries could not be assured that their weak-currency counterparts would undertake policy adjustments. Therefore the foreign support they were willing to provide was necessarily limited.

The Snake had been established as a symmetric system in reaction to French objections to the dollar's asymmetric role under Bretton Woods. But once the Snake was freed from the Smithsonian tunnel, the deutsche mark emerged as the Europe's reference currency and its anti-inflationary anchor. The Bundesbank set the tone for monetary policy continentwide. Yet there existed no mechanism through which other countries could influence the policies of the German central bank and no option other than exit through which they could control their own monetary destinies. This "accountability deficit" was the ultimate obstacle to the success of the Snake.

THE EUROPEAN MONETARY SYSTEM

The French sought to rectify these deficiencies by creating the European Monetary System in 1979. They sought to strengthen the oversight powers of the Monetary Committee of the European Community with the goal of creating an EC body to which national monetary policymakers could be held accountable. And they secured a provision in the EMS Act of Foundation authorizing governments to draw *unlimited* credits from the Very-Short-Term Financing Facility, seeming to oblige the strong-currency countries to extend unlimited support to their weak-currency partners. In practice, however, neither provision of the new system worked as intended by France and the small EC countries that depended on German policy.

The French had never wavered in their support for pegged rates; when the country was forced at Rambouillet to abandon the effort to establish such a system globally, President Valéry Giscard d'Estaing redirected his efforts to stabilizing the critical franc/deutsche mark rate. France's inability to stay in the Snake demonstrated that this was easier said than done. The experience inspired French officials to seek the construction of a sturdier structure within which intra-European exchange rates could be held. Critical to the success of their initiative was the cooperation of the German government. Giscard's German counterpart, Federal Chancellor Helmut Schmidt, saw the

---

[32] See Gros and Thygesen 1991, pp. 22–23.

creation of the EMS as a logical step toward a federal Europe—as a way of salvaging the vision of the Werner Report and of "bringing the French back in."[33] Linking the franc and other European currencies to the deutsche mark would also help to insulate the German economy from the effects of a depreciating dollar. In the same way that the dominance of the British and American delegations simplified the Bretton Woods negotiations, the fact that the EMS arose out of a meeting of the minds between the leaders of the two dominant EC member states finessed free-rider and coordination problems. Schmidt and Giscard's bilateral agreement received the endorsement of the European Council in July 1978, leading to the creation of the European Monetary System in 1979.[34]

Negotiating the EMS Act of Foundation still required reconciling French and German interpretations of the failure of the Snake. German officials argued that the Snake had operated satisfactorily for countries that subordinated other goals to the imperatives of price and currency stability. Their French counterparts complained that the Snake was a German-led system that accorded other countries inadequate input into policy. The Schmidt-Giscard initiative thus sought to create a new institution to reconcile France's desire for symmetry with Germany's insistence on discipline. The moribund European Monetary Cooperation Fund would be replaced by a European Monetary Fund (EMF) to manage the combined foreign-exchange-rate reserves of the participating countries, to intervene in currency markets, and to create *ecu* reserves to serve as European SDRs. The EMS would feature a "trigger mechanism," which would be set off when domestic policies jeopardized currency pegs. Violation of agreed-upon indicators would force strong-currency countries to expand and weak-currency countries to contract.

Thus, Keynes's preoccupation at Bretton Woods, that surplus countries be forced to revalue or expand so as not to saddle deficit countries with the entire burden of adjustment, again took center stage. But as at Bretton Woods and again in the early 1970s when the U.S. sought to salvage the system of pegged but adjustable rates by appending a set of "reserve indicators" to compel surplus countries to adjust, the strong-currency countries, whose support for any reform was indispensable, were reluctant to agree. The Bundesbank realized that if the trigger mechanism failed, requiring it to

---

[33] As Schmidt put it in his memoirs, "I had always regarded the EMS not only as a mere instrument to harmonize the economic policies of the EC member countries, but also as part of a broader strategy for political self-determination in Europe." Cited in Fratianni and von Hagen 1992, pp. 17–18.

[34] On the chronology of EMS negotiations, see Ludlow 1982.

purchase weak EMS currencies for marks, its mandate to pursue price stability could be compromised. If the EMF created unbacked ecu reserves to meet the financing needs of the deficit countries, the inflationary threat would be heightened.[35] The Bundesbank Council therefore objected to the agreement.[36]

Intense negotiations followed.[37] The French and German governments dropped their proposal for a trigger mechanism that might require changes in Bundesbank policy and for the transfer of national exchange reserves to a European Monetary Fund. Although the EMS Act of Foundation still spoke of foreign support "unlimited in amount," and although no restrictions were placed on drawings on the Very-Short-Term Financing Facility, an exchange of letters between the German finance minister and the president of the Bundesbank conceded the German central bank the right to opt out of its intervention obligation if the government were unable to secure an agreement with its European partners on the need to realign.[38] If it proved impossible to reestablish appropriate central rates, raising fears that its commitment to price stability would be threatened, the Bundesbank could discontinue its intervention.

Thus, not only was Germany's obligation to provide foreign support effectively circumscribed, but it was made contingent on the willingness of other countries to realign. Germany assumed the strong-currency-country role that had been occupied by the United States at Bretton Woods. It fol-

---

[35] It remained unclear to what extent the EMF would be empowered to create additional ecus. The Brussels Resolution of December 5, 1978 authorized only swaps of ecus for gold and dollar reserves, which did not imply net liquidity creation. However, an annex to the Bremen conclusion (reached at the Bremen meeting of the European Council in early 1978) had spoken cryptically of ecus created against subscriptions in national currencies "in comparable magnitude." See Polak 1980.

[36] There was resistance to the mandatory triggering of interventions and policy adjustments in other branches of the German government as well, and in Denmark and the Netherlands.

[37] Schmidt, by his own account, threatened to change the Bundesbank law, compromising the central bank's independence if it failed to go along. His account is as yet uncorroborated, and some authors doubt that he would have carried out the threat. See Kennedy 1991, p. 81.

[38] See Emminger 1986. Extracts from the correspondence appear in Eichengreen and Wyplosz 1993. This correspondence remained secret, and not until the 1992 EMS crisis was its import fully appreciated. This secrecy accounts for the appearance in the interim of passages like the following: "But the most important single feature of the EMS has not yet been mentioned. A self-fulfilling speculative crisis cannot take place unless the market can commit larger sums of money than governments can mobilize. The market must be able to swallow their reserves. That cannot happen in the EMS, where governments can mobilize infinite amounts by drawing on reciprocal credit facilities." Kenen 1988, p. 55. I suggest below that self-fulfilling attacks were in fact possible precisely because foreign support was not infinite.

lowed that the Bundesbank Council, like the U.S. delegation at Bretton Woods, sought to limit the surplus country's intervention obligations and the balance-of-payments financing that would be made available to weak-currency countries.

Unlike the United States in 1944, however, Germany had a third of a century of experience suggesting that deficit countries would hesitate to adjust; hence, it acknowledged the necessity of allowing the latter to devalue (in less embarrassing EMS-ese, to *realign*). Experience with the Snake had fallen into two periods: a first before the Frankfurt realignment when the system had been strained by the failure to realign; and a second of greater exchange rate flexibility that had been more satisfactory. Germany and its EMS partners drew the obvious conclusion.[39]

The parallels with Bretton Woods extended beyond the desire for managed flexibility. The currencies of countries agreeing to abide by the *Exchange Rate Mechanism* (ERM) were to be held within 2¼ percent bands, as they had been in the final years of the Bretton Woods System.[40] Capital controls were permitted as a way of preserving governments' limited policy autonomy and of giving them the breathing space to negotiate orderly realignments. Clearly, the postwar international monetary agreement cast a long shadow.

Eight of the nine EC countries participated in the ERM from the outset (the United Kingdom being the exception). Italy, saddled with stubborn inflation, was permitted to maintain a wide (6 percent) band for a transitional period.[41] None of the original participants in the ERM had to withdraw from the system over the course of the 1980s, in contrast to experience with the Snake, although France came close at the start of the decade.

Central rates were modified on average once every eight months in the first four years of the EMS (see Table 5.2). Over the next four years, through January 1987, the frequency of realignments declined to once every twelve months. The change reflected the gradual relaxation of capital controls, which made orderly realignments more difficult to carry out. In addition, it reflected changes in global economic conditions. The first four EMS years were punctuated by a recession that, like the post-1973 downturn that

---

[39] Moreover, in contrast to the early years of the Snake, when it was hoped that the stability of exchange rates could be tied down by the Werner Report commitment to complete the transition to monetary union by 1980, the EMS Act of Foundation entailed no such commitment, implying the need for greater exchange rate flexibility.

[40] Countries in weak financial positions were permitted to operate wider 6 percent bands for a transitional period after entry.

[41] That transitional period was extended to 1990.

TABLE 5.2

Revaluations of the Deutsche Mark against other EMS Currencies
(measured by bilateral central rates, in percent)

	Belgian/Luxembourgian franc	Danish krone	French franc	Dutch guilder	Irish pound	Italian lira	Total EMS[a]
Weight[b] (in %)	16.6	4.0	32.0	17.4	1.8	27.5	100
Realignment date with effect from:							
September 24, 1979	+2.0	+5.0	+2.0	+2.0	+2.0	+2.0	+2.1
November 30, 1979	—	—	—	—	—	—	+0.2
March 23, 1981	—	—	—	—	—	+6.4	+1.7
October 5, 1981	+5.5	+5.5	+8.8	—	+5.5	+8.8	+6.5
February 22, 1982	+9.3	+3.1	—	—	—	—	+1.6
June 14, 1982	+4.3	+4.3	+10.6	—	+4.3	+7.2	+6.3
March 21, 1983	+3.9	+2.9	+8.2	+1.9	+9.3	+8.2	+6.7
July 22, 1983	—	—	—	—	—	+8.5	+2.3
April 7, 1986	+2.0	+2.0	+6.2	—	+3.0	+3.0	+3.8
August 4, 1986	—	—	—	—	+8.7	—	+0.2
January 12, 1987	+1.0	+3.0	+3.0	—	+3.0	+3.0	+2.6
January 8, 1990	—	—	—	—	—	+3.7	+1.0
Cumulative since start of the EMS on March 13, 1979	+31.2	+35.2	+45.2	+4.0	+41.4	+63.5	+41.8

Source: Gros and Thygesen 1991, p. 68.

a. Average revaluation of the deutsche mark against the other EMS currencies (geometrically weighted); excluding Spain.

b. Weights of the EMS currencies derived from the foreign trade share between 1984 and 1986, after taking account of third-market effects, and expressed in terms of the weighted value of the deutsche mark.

— = not applicable.

had marked the birth of the Snake, magnified policy divergences in Europe. The pressure of unemployment in some EMS countries greatly aggravated the strains on the new system.

This became evident in 1981, when France's new Socialist government, led by Francois Mitterrand, initiated expansionary policies. The budget deficit was allowed to rise by more than 1 percent of GDP, and the annual M2 growth rate exceeded the government's 10 percent target. The franc weakened as soon as the markets began to anticipate that the electorate would install a government ready to hit the fiscal and monetary accelerator. Incoming officials, led by Minister of Economic Affairs Jacques Delors, recommended an immediate realignment as a way of starting the new government off with a clean slate. This was rejected on the grounds that it would stigmatize the Socialists as the party that always devalued.

In the new Mitterrand government's first four months in office, the French and German central banks were forced to intervene extensively in support of the franc. By September, devaluation could no longer be resisted. Face was saved by placing the change in the context of a general realignment of EMS currencies.[42]

But absent fiscal and monetary retrenchment, the French balance of payments was bound to weaken further. The market acted on the expectation, selling francs and forcing intervention that drained reserves from the Bank of France. Tightening capital controls put off the day of reckoning but could not do so indefinitely.[43] The franc was devalued against the deutsche mark again in June 1982 and a third time in March 1983.[44] The French government was driven to ponder withdrawing from the EMS and even from the EC.[45]

In the end, this option proved too radical, given France's investment in European integration. The day was carried by the moderate wing of the

[42] The parallel with the 1936 Tripartite Agreement extended beyond the attempt to salvage the Socialist government's reputation by placing the realignment in the context of a broader agreement. In 1936 the newly appointed government of Léon Blum had also initiated expansionary fiscal policies, reduced hours of work, and stimulated demand. It had considered but rejected the possibility of devaluing upon taking office. It was then forced to allow the franc to depreciate four months later.

[43] On changes in French capital controls, see Neme 1986.

[44] On both occasions the franc/deutsche mark adjustment was dressed up by also realigning other rates.

[45] That the French government considered this last option might seem incredible. But, as noted above, France's withdrawal from the EMS would have jeopardized the CAP, the EC's central program, which meant that withdrawing from the EMS could have seriously eroded European solidarity. See Sachs and Wyplosz 1986.

Mitterrand government, led by Delors and Treasury Director Michel Camdessus, and the government scaled back its policies of demand stimulus. It was not that expansionary fiscal and monetary policies were incapable of spurring the economy. To the contrary, they were quite effective: French GDP growth, unlike that of other countries, did not go negative even in the depths of the European recession. What French policymakers did not anticipate was how quickly the external constraint would bind.

The Socialists' policies of demand stimulus provoked such rapid reserve losses because of the lack of policy coordination between France and Germany. Just when the French embarked on their expansionary initiative, the Bundesbank took steps to suppress inflationary pressures. Any hope that the Bundesbank might be pressured into lowering interest rates was dashed in October 1982 when Germany's Socialist-Liberal coalition was replaced by the more conservative government of Helmut Kohl. Unlike the Schmidt government, Kohl and his colleagues had no desire to encourage the Bundesbank to reduce German interest rates.[46] It became clear that the European economy would not emerge from recession at the rate assumed in French forecasts. Lower levels of demand in Europe, in conjunction with a widening inflation differential between France and Germany, implied more serious losses of French competitiveness.[47] Fortunately for the EMS, the French Socialists ultimately bowed to these realities.

The second four years of the EMS were consequently less turbulent than the first. As the European economy began to recover, policies of austerity became more palatable. The threat to policy convergence receded. The dollar's appreciation in the first half of the 1980s made it easier for European governments to live with a strong exchange rate against the mark. The Mitterrand debacle had served as a caution, effectively reconciling Germany's most important EMS partner to policies of currency stability.

The dispersion of inflation rates across countries, as measured by their standard deviation, fell by half between 1979–83 and 1983–87. Although capital controls were partially relaxed, important restrictions remained, providing governments some time to negotiate realignments. None of the four realignments that took place in the 1983–87 period exceeded the cumulative inflation differential. None therefore provided devaluing governments an ad-

---

[46] See Henning 1994, pp. 194–95.

[47] In addition, supply-side rigidities afflicting the French economy meant that demand stimulus produced more inflation and less output than the government had hoped. Additional social security taxes, higher minimum wages, and reduced hours of work caused employers to hesitate before taking on workers. With the aggregate supply curve shifting in at the same time the aggregate demand curve shifted out, inflation rather than growth resulted.

ditional boost to their competitiveness that might permit them to continue running more inflationary policies than Germany without suffering alarming losses of competitiveness. Thus, policy signaled a hardening commitment of EMS countries to nominal convergence. Europe's "minilateral Bretton Woods" appeared to be gaining resilience.

Renewed Impetus for Integration

While the European Community seemed on the road to solving its exchange rate problem, other more fundamental difficulties remained. Unemployment was disturbingly high, often in the double digits, and policymakers felt hamstrung by their commitment to peg the exchange rate.[48] They worried about European producers' ability to compete with the United States and Japan. All this led them to contemplate a radical acceleration of the process of European integration as a way of injecting the chill winds of competition into the European economy and helping producers to better exploit economies of scale and scope. The initiative turned out to have profound and not wholly anticipated consequences for the evolution of the European Monetary System.

The dynamics that followed were complex. In their most schematic form, the interplay between monetary unification and the integration process unfolded as follows.

- The renewed commitment to pegging exchange rates on the part of the member states of the European Community and the emergence of Germany as the European Monetary System's low-inflation anchor limited the freedom of European countries to use independent macroeconomic policies in pursuit of national objectives.
- Governments therefore turned when pursuing distributional objectives and social goals to microeconomic policies of wage compression, enhanced job security, and increasingly generous unemployment and other social benefits. These reduced the flexibility and efficiency of the labor market, leading to high and rising unemployment.[49]

[48] I suggest below that the unemployment problem of the 1980s was in fact related to the advent of the EMS, but not for the reasons emphasized by policymakers at the time and echoed in most historical accounts.

[49] I am suggesting, in other words, that the two popular explanations for high unemployment in Europe—which emphasize, respectively, the commitment to a strong exchange rate and social policies that introduced microeconomic rigidities into the labor market—are not incom-

- This problem, "Eurosclerosis," lent additional impetus to the integration process. The Single Market Program, embodied in the *Single European Act* of 1986, sought to bring down unemployment and end the European slump by simplifying regulatory structures, intensifying competition among EC member states, and facilitating European producers' exploitation of economies of scale and scope.

- The attempt to create a single European market in merchandise and factors of production accelerated the momentum of monetary integration. Eliminating currency conversion costs was the only way of removing hidden barriers to internal economic flows—of forging a truly integrated market. Abolishing the opportunity for countries to manipulate their exchange rates was necessary to defuse protectionist opposition to the liberalization of trade. Both arguments pointed to the need for a single currency as a concomitant of the single market. This vision found expression in the *Delors Report* of 1989 and the Maastricht Treaty adopted by the European Council in December 1991.

- Integral to the creation of the single market was the removal of capital controls. But the elimination of controls rendered the periodic realignments that had vented pressures and restored balance to the European Monetary System more difficult to effect. After the beginning of 1987 there were no more realignments of ERM currencies. This came to be known, for obvious reasons, as the period of the "hard EMS."[50]

- Thus, the same dynamic that heightened the desire for currency stability removed the safety valve that had permitted the members of the ERM to operate a system of relatively stable exchange rates. No sooner did this occur than, starting in 1990, a series of shocks intervened. A global recession elevated unemployment rates in Europe; the dollar's decline further undermined European competitiveness; and German unification raised interest rates throughout the European Community.

- At this point, national political leaders began to question the Maastricht blueprint for monetary union. The markets, in turn, began to question the commitment of political leaders to the defense of their EMS pegs. Ultimately, the pressures that mounted within the EMS could not be contained, and the whole structure came tumbling down.

---

patible with or even entirely distinct from each other. The policies that led to wage compression and increased hiring and firing costs were themselves a response to limits on the autonomous use of macroeconomic policy imposed by the EMS.

[50] The adjustment of the lira's band in 1990, when Italy moved from 6 to 2¼ percent margins, did not involve a change in the lira's lower limit.

Two milestones along this route were the Delors Report in 1989 and the Maastricht Treaty in 1991. Since the days of the Snake, French governments had bridled at their lack of input into the Europe's common monetary policy. By the second half of the 1980s it had become clear that the EMS had not solved this problem. In a 1987 memo to the ECOFIN Council (a council of EC-member economics and finance ministers), French finance minister Edouard Balladur argued for a new system. "The discipline imposed by the exchange-rate mechanism," he wrote, "may, for its part, have good effects when it serves to put a constraint on economic and monetary policies which are insufficiently rigorous. [But] it produces an abnormal situation when its effect is to exempt any countries whose policies are too restrictive from the necessary adjustment."[51] A monetary union governed by a single central bank in whose policies all the member states had a say was one solution to this problem.

The presidency of the European Commission having been assumed by the former French economic affairs minister Jacques Delors, Balladur's appeal was received warmly in Brussels. More surprising was the German government's broadly sympathetic response. Revealingly, the critical reaction came not from the German Finance Ministry but from Foreign Minister Hans-Dietrich Genscher, who expressed a willingness to consider replacing the EMS with a monetary union in return for accelerating the process of European integration. Germany desired not just an integrated European market in which economies of scale and scope could be efficiently exploited, but also deeper political integration in the context of which the country might gain a foreign policy role. Monetary union was the quid pro quo.

The Delors Committee, consisting of the governors of the central banks of EC member states, a representative of the EC Commission, and three independent experts, met eight times in 1988 and 1989. Its report, like the Werner Report before it, supported the achievement of monetary union within a decade, although it did not set an explicit deadline for the conclusion of the process. Like its predecessor, the Delors Committee envisaged a gradual transition. But whereas the Werner Report had recommended removing capital controls at the end of the process, the Delors Report advocated removing them at the beginning, reflecting the linkage between monetary union and the single market. And the Delors Report, in a concession to political realities, did not propose ceding fiscal functions to the EC. Instead, it recommended rules imposing ceilings on budget deficits and excluding

[51] Cited in Gros and Thygesen 1991, p. 312.

governments' access to direct central bank credit and other forms of money financing.[52]

Most striking, the Delors Committee recommended the complete centralization of monetary authority. Whereas the Werner Report had described a system of national central banks joined together in a monetary federation, the Delors Report proposed the creation of a new entity, a European Central Bank (ECB), to execute the common monetary policy and to issue a single European currency. National central banks, like regional Reserve banks in the United States, would become the central bank's operating arms.

In June of 1989 the European Council accepted the Delors Report and agreed to convene an intergovernmental conference to negotiate the amendments to the Treaty of Rome required for its implementation. Again it is revealing that the intergovernmental conferences, which started in December 1990 and were completed at Maastricht one year later, took both EMU and political union as their charge.

Following the Delors Report, the Maastricht Treaty described a transition to be completed in stages. Stage I, which commenced in 1990, was to be marked by the removal of capital controls.[53] Member countries were to fortify the independence of their central banks and to otherwise bring their domestic laws into conformance with the treaty. Stage II, which began in 1994, was to be characterized by the further convergence of national policies and by the creation of a temporary entity, the *European Monetary Institute* (EMI), to encourage the coordination of macroeconomic policies and plan the transition to monetary union.[54] If the Council of Ministers decided during Stage II that a majority of countries met the preconditions, it could recommend the inauguration of Stage III, monetary union. But to prevent Stage II from continuing indefinitely, the treaty required the EU heads of state or government to meet no later than the end of 1996 to determine whether a majority of member states satisfied the conditions for monetary union and whether to specify a date for its commencement. If no date were set by the end

[52] Committee for the Study of Economic and Monetary Union 1989, p. 30.

[53] A few countries, Greece, Ireland, Portugal, and Spain among them, were permitted to retain their controls beyond this deadline. In addition, other countries were permitted during Stage I to reimpose controls for no more than six months in response to financial emergencies. As we shall see in the next section, these provisions were utilized in the 1992–93 EMS crisis.

[54] Creating a temporary entity, the European Monetary Institute, to carry out these functions in Stage II, the transitional phase, was a step back from the Delors Report, which had proposed establishing the European Central Bank at the start of Stage II and not merely at the start of Stage III, monetary union. This compromise was in deference to German opposition to any arrangement that entailed the delegation of significant national monetary autonomy before full monetary union was achieved.

of 1997, Stage III would commence on January 1, 1999, if even a minority of member states qualified. When Stage III began, the exchange rates of the participating countries would be irrevocably fixed. The EMI would be succeeded by the ECB, which would execute the common monetary policy.

Germany was reluctant to consent to these deadlines and did so only after obtaining safeguards to ensure that the monetary union would be limited to countries with a record of currency stability.[55] To that end, the treaty specified four "convergence criteria." These required a qualifying country to hold its currency within the normal ERM fluctuation bands without severe tensions for at least two years immediately preceding entry. They required it to run an inflation rate over the preceding twelve months that did not exceed the inflation rates of the three lowest-inflation member states by more than 1.5 percentage points. They required it to reduce its public debt and deficit toward reference values of 60 and 3 percent of GDP, respectively.[56] They required it to maintain for the preceding year a nominal long-term interest rate that did not exceed by more than two percentage points that of the three best-performing member states in terms of price stability.

In December 1991, when treaty negotiations were concluded, satisfying these conditions appeared to be within the reach of a majority of member states. Little did observers know how quickly the situation would change.

THE EMS CRISIS

The intergovernmental conference having been successfully concluded the previous December, the European Monetary System entered 1992 on a wave of optimism. It had been five years since the last realignment of ERM currencies. All the member states of the European Community but Greece and Portugal were participating, and Portugal was about to join.

The optimism with which the stewards of the European Monetary System were imbued had been fed by the system's success in surmounting a series of shocks. The collapse of the Soviet Union's trade dealt a blow to European economies (such as Finland) that depended on exports to the East. The end of the cold war called for an infusion of aid to the transforming economies

---

[55] This reluctance was characteristic of the Bundesbank in particular, which expressed strong opposition to any blueprint for the transition that entailed binding deadlines. See Bini-Smaghi, Padoa-Schioppa, and Papadia 1994, p. 14.

[56] These last conditions were weakened by a number of qualifications. For example, debts and deficits may exceed their reference values if they are judged to do so for reasons that are exceptional and temporary or if they are declining toward those values at an acceptable pace.

of Eastern Europe; this left fewer resources for the structural funds and the EC's other cohesion programs. German economic and monetary unification in 1990 spawned budget deficits, capital imports, and a surge of spending that placed upward pressure on interest rates continentwide. The dollar's decline against the deutsche mark and other ERM currencies further damaged Europe's international competitiveness. The continent then entered one of its deepest recessions in the postwar period. And with the conclusion of negotiations at Maastricht, the public debate over monetary union intensified. Yet despite these disturbances, the countries participating in the ERM were able to resist the pressure to alter their exchange rates. Countries outside the EC that shadowed the EMS—Austria, Norway, and Sweden—continued to do so successfully.[57]

Denmark's June 2 referendum on the Maastricht Treaty was the turning point. The Danish no raised questions about whether the Maastricht Treaty would come into effect. If the treaty were repudiated, the incentive for countries to hold their currencies within their ERM bands in order to qualify for monetary union would be weakened, and high-debt countries like Italy would have less reason to cut their deficits. The lira, which had been in the narrow band since 1990, plunged toward its lower limit. The three currencies of the wide band (sterling, the peseta, and the escudo) weakened.

Pressure mounted with the approach of France's September 20 referendum on the treaty. On August 26 the pound fell to its ERM floor. The lira fell through its floor two days later. Other ERM member countries were forced to intervene in support of their currencies. The Bundesbank intervened extensively on their behalf (see Figure 5.10).

On September 8, the Finnish markka's unilateral ecu peg was abandoned. Currency traders, some of whom were said to have been unable to distinguish Sweden from Finland, turned their attention to the krona; over the subsequent week the Riksbank was forced to raise its marginal lending rate to triple digits. All the while, the lira remained below its ERM floor. A crisis meeting on September 13 led to a 3.5 percent devaluation of the lira and 3.5 percent revaluation of other ERM currencies.

But what European monetary officials hoped would end the crisis only marked its start. The first discontinuous realignment in five years reminded

[57] The one exception was Finland, which suffered the collapse of its Soviet trade and a banking crisis. In November 1991 the Bank of Finland, which pegged the markka to the ecu but, not being a member of the EMS, did not enjoy the support provided ERM countries through the Very-Short-Term Financing Facility, devalued by 12 percent. Despite this, the British pound remained firmly within its fluctuation band. The Portuguese escudo joined the wide band in April. Divergences between ERM exchange rates actually moderated, with the French franc moving up from the bottom of its band and the deutsche mark, Belgian franc, and Dutch guilder moving down.

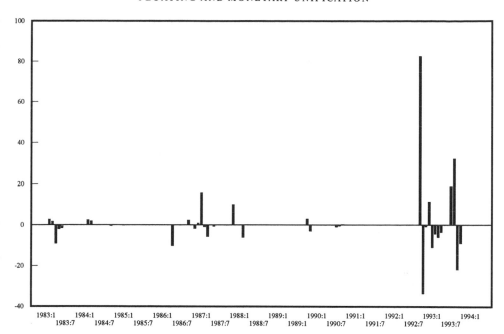

Figure 5.10. Bundesbank Operations in the European Monetary System, 1983–94 (billions of D-marks). *Source*: Deutsche Bundesbank, *Annual Reports*, various years. *Note*: Positive entries denote Bundesbank intervention on behalf of other EMS currencies.

observers that changes in EMS exchange rates were still possible. Pressure mounted on Britain, Spain, Portugal, and Italy (whose realignment, many observers believed, had been too small). Despite further interest-rate increases and intervention at the margins of the EMS bands, these countries suffered massive reserve losses. British ERM membership was suspended on September 16, and the two interest-rate increases taken earlier in the day were reversed. That evening Italy announced to the Monetary Committee that the inadequacy of its reserves in the face of speculative pressure forced it to float the lira.[58]

Following Italy and Britain's exit from the ERM, pressure was felt by the French franc, the Danish krone, and the Irish pound. The outcome of the French referendum, a narrow *oui*, failed to dispel it. The franc hovered just above the bottom of its band, requiring the Bank of France and the Bundesbank to undertake extensive interventions.[59] Pressure on Spain, Portugal, and Ireland led their governments to tighten capital controls.

[58] The committee also authorized a 5 percent devaluation of the peseta.

[59] One-hundred-sixty-billion French francs (about $32 billion) were reportedly spent on the currency's defense in the week ending September 23. Bank for International Settlements 1993, p. 188.

Six additional months of instability were inaugurated by Sweden's decision in November to abandon its unilateral ecu peg after the government failed to obtain all-party support for austerity measures. The Riksbank had suffered massive reserve losses in the course of defending the krona; in all, it spent a staggering $3,500 for each resident of Sweden![60] Spain was forced to devalue again, this time by 6 percent, as was its neighbor and trading partner, Portugal. Norway abandoned its ecu peg on December 10, and pressure spread to Ireland and France. While the franc was successfully defended, the punt was not. In the face of Ireland's removal of controls on January 1, 1993, increases in Irish market rates to triple-digit levels did not suffice.[61] The punt was devalued by 10 percent on January 30. In May, the uncertainty surrounding Spain's springtime elections forced yet another devaluation of the peseta and the escudo.

Once again there were reasons to hope that unsettled conditions had passed. In May the Danish electorate, perhaps chastened by the fallout from its earlier decision, endorsed the Maastricht Treaty in a second referendum. The Bundesbank lowered its discount and *Lombard rates*, moderating the pressure on its ERM partners. The French franc and other weak ERM currencies strengthened.

With French inflation running below that of Germany, French officials incautiously suggested that the franc had assumed the role of the anchor currency within the ERM. Oblivious to the fragility of the position, they encouraged the Bank of France to reduce interest rates in the hope of bringing down unemployment. The Bank of France lowered its discount rate, anticipating that the Bundesbank would follow. But when on July 1 the cut in German rates came, it was disappointingly small. The French economics minister then called for a Franco-German meeting to coordinate further interest-rate reductions, but the Germans canceled their plans to attend, leading the markets to infer that Germany lacked sympathy for France's potentially inflationary initiative. The franc quickly fell toward its ERM floor, requiring Bank of France and Bundesbank intervention. It was joined there by the Belgian franc and the Danish krone. A full-blown crisis was at hand.

The last weekend of July was the final chance to negotiate a concerted response. A range of alternatives is said to have been mooted, including devaluation of the franc (which France vetoed), a general realignment of ERM curren-

---

[60] Reserve losses incurred in the six days preceding the devaluation are reported to have amounted to $26 billion, or more than 10 percent of Sweden's GNP. Bank for International Settlements 1993, p. 188.

[61] Ireland's difficulties were aggravated by the descent of the pound sterling (fueled by further British interest-rate cuts). Between September 16 and the end of the calendar year, sterling declined by 13 percent against the deutsche mark.

cies (which other countries vetoed), floating the deutsche mark out of the ERM (which the Dutch vetoed), and imposing deposit requirements on banks' open positions in foreign currencies (suggested by Belgium but vetoed by the other countries). The diversity of these proposals indicated the lack of a common diagnosis of the problem. By Sunday evening the assembled ministers and central bankers were faced with the impending opening of financial markets in Tokyo. With no course on which they could agree, they opted to widen ERM bands from 2¼ percent to 15 percent. European currencies were set to float more freely than had ever been allowed in the age of par values, snakes, and central rates.

Understanding the Crisis

Three explanations for the crisis can be distinguished: inadequate harmonization of past policies, inadequate harmonization of future policies, and speculative pressures themselves.

According to the first explanation, some countries, most notably Italy, Spain, and the United Kingdom, had not yet brought their inflation rates down to those of their ERM partners. Excessive inflation cumulated into overvaluation, aggravating deficits on current account. These problems were exacerbated by the weakness of the dollar and the yen. Currency traders, for their part, understood that substantial current-account deficits could not be financed indefinitely. In this view, the move to the hard EMS in 1987 was premature; countries should have continued to adjust their central rates as needed to eliminate competitive imbalances.[62]

Yet the data do not support this interpretation unambiguously.[63] Table 5.3

---

[62] Two clear expositions of this view are Branson 1994 and von Hagen 1994. Understandably, it has found its way into official accounts. See Bank for International Settlements 1993, Commission of the European Communities 1993, and Committee of Governors of Central Banks of the Member States of the European Economic Community 1993a, b.

[63] One reason that these data speak less than clearly is that Europe experienced a massive asymmetric shock: German unification. The increase in consumption and investment associated with unification raised the demand for German goods. In the short run this pushed up German prices relative to those prevailing in other ERM countries. The implication is that inflation rates elsewhere in Europe not only had to stay as low as Germany's; they had to lag behind. Unfortunately, it is impossible to know by precisely how much inflation rates in countries other than Germany had to fall. One way of going about this is to look at the "competitiveness outputs" to which relative prices are an input. Eichengreen and Wyplosz 1993 considered the current account of the balance of payments and profitability in the manufacturing sector as two variables whose values would deteriorate in the event of inadequate adjustment to changing competitive

TABLE 5.3

Indicators of Cumulative Competitiveness Changes, 1987–August 1992

(in percent)

	Relative to Other EC Countries[a]		Relative to Industrial Countries	
Country	Producer Prices	Unit Labor Costs[b]	Producer Prices	Unit Labor Costs[b]
Belgium	4.0	5.6	1.3	2.7
Denmark	3.6	6.4	− 0.5	3.8
Germany (western)	1.7	0.5	− 3.8	− 5.5
Greece	n.a.	n.a.	− 10.2	− 15.6
France	7.9	13.3	3.3	7.2
Ireland	6.4	35.7	1.3	27.9
Italy	− 3.0	− 7.0	− 6.4	− 9.8
Netherlands	1.5	5.2	− 1.4	1.9
From ERM Entry[c]–August 1992				
Spain	− 2.1	− 7.5	− 8.1	− 13.8
Portugal	n.a.	− 4.6	n.a.	− 6.9
United Kingdom	− 1.7	− 0.4	− 4.0	8.3

Source: Committee of Governors of the Central Banks of the Member States of the European Economic Community 1993a.

a. Excluding Greece.

b. Manufacturing sector.

c. Spain: June 1989; Portugal: April 1992; United Kingdom: October 1990.

n.a. = not available.

shows the EC's Committee of Governors of Central Banks' own estimates of cumulative competitiveness changes on the eve of the 1992 crisis.[64] Of the countries that participated in the EMS from 1987, only Italy shows an obvious deterioration in competitiveness. Italian unit labor costs rose by 7 percent relative to other EC countries, by 10 percent relative to the industrial

conditions. Only for Italy do both measures deteriorate in the period leading up to the crisis. For Spain the current account deteriorates, but profitability does not; for the United Kingdom the opposite is true. Other countries whose currencies were attacked—Denmark, France, and Ireland, for example—experienced a significant deterioration in neither of these variables in the period preceding the crisis.

[64] It distinguishes two indicators, producer prices and unit labor costs, and two comparison groups, other EC countries and all industrial countries. The latter should pick up the effect of the depreciation of the dollar and the yen.

countries.[65] The only other country in this group whose labor costs rose at comparable rates is Germany, which did not suffer a speculative attack. In other words, there is nothing in Table 5.3 that obviously justifies the attacks on the French franc, Belgian franc, Danish krone, and Irish punt.[66]

It is also not clear from the unit labor cost and producer price data in Table 5.3 that sterling was overvalued. One might object that the problem lay in the period before the country entered the ERM in October 1990.[67] It is unclear that this was the markets' perception, however: sterling's one-year-ahead forward rate also remained within its ERM band until only weeks before the September crisis. Indeed, this is the fundamental flaw of explanations that attribute the crisis to excessive inflation and overvaluation: if the attacks were prompted by the cumulative effects of excessive inflation and current-account deficits, the markets' doubts should have found reflection in the behavior of forward exchange rates and interest differentials. Because inflation and deficits are slowly evolving variables, their effects should have been mirrored in the gradual movement of forward rates to the edges of the ERM bands and the gradual widening of interest differentials. Yet little movement in these variables was apparent until they suddenly jumped up on the eve of the crisis.[68] Until then, they continued to imply expected future exchange rates well within the prevailing ERM bands. None of these measures suggests that the markets attached a significant probability to devaluation until just before the fact.[69]

The obvious complement to this emphasis on past policy imbalances is future policy shifts. Countries that had been pursuing policies of austerity in

[65] While the second figure is higher for Greece, that country had not yet joined the ERM.

[66] The evidence for the three countries that entered the ERM between June 1989 and April 1992, Spain, Portugal, and the United Kingdom, is less clear-cut. Spain and Portugal experienced more inflation than their richer ERM partners, but this was to be expected of rapidly growing countries moving into the production of higher-value-added goods. See the discussion of the Balassa-Samuelson effect in the penultimate section of Chapter 4. Even though countries like Spain had more scope to run inflation than their more industrialized ERM partners, one can still argue that the Spanish government overdid it.

[67] See Williamson 1993.

[68] A careful study of the evidence is Rose and Svensson 1994.

[69] This skepticism should not be overstated. Even if the data fail to speak clearly, their muffled voices still suggest that ERM currencies were not attacked randomly. Italy is the one country for which the evidence of competitive imbalances is unambiguous, and the lira was the first ERM currency to be driven from the system. Some indicators do suggest problems in the United Kingdom, Spain, and Portugal; theirs were the next ERM currencies to be attacked and to be realigned or driven out of the system. Yet the fact that the evidence of competitive imbalances is far from overwhelming and that other currencies were attacked as well suggests that this is not the entire story.

TABLE 5.4
Unemployment Rates, 1987–92[a]

	Percentage of Civilian Labor Force			
Country	1987–89 Average	1990	1991	1992[b]
Belgium	10.0	7.6	7.5	8.2
Denmark	6.6	8.1	8.9	9.5
Germany (western)[c]	6.1	4.8	4.2	4.5
Greece	7.5	7.0	7.7	7.7
Spain	19.1	16.3	16.3	18.4
France	9.9	9.0	9.5	10.0
Ireland	17.0	14.5	16.2	17.8
Italy	10.9	10.0	10.0	10.1
Luxembourg	2.1	1.7	1.6	1.9
Netherlands	9.2	7.5	7.0	6.7
Portugal	5.9	4.6	4.1	4.8
United Kingdom	8.7	7.0	9.1	10.8
EEC				
Average	9.7	8.3	8.7	9.5
Dispersion[d]	2.7	2.6	3.3	3.7
ERM original narrow band				
Average	8.1	7.2	7.1	7.4
Dispersion[d]	2.2	2.2	2.8	2.9
United States[e]	5.7	5.5	6.7	7.3
Japan	2.5	2.1	2.1	2.2

Source: Eurostat.

a. Standardized definition.

b. Estimates.

c. For 1992, unemployment rates (national definition) are: 14.3 percent for eastern Germany and 7.7 percent for the whole of Germany.

d. Weighted standard deviation.

e. Percentage of total labor force.

order to maintain external balance experienced mounting unemployment. (Table 5.4 tabulates their unemployment rates in the years leading up to the crisis.) The German unification shock required a rise in German prices relative to those prevailing elsewhere in Europe. As long as exchange rates remained pegged, this change in relative prices could be accomplished only by faster inflation in Germany or slower inflation abroad. Predictably, the

Bundesbank preferred the second alternative. It raised interest rates to ensure that adjustment did not take place through German inflation. Hence, adjustment could occur only through disinflation abroad. With European labor markets slow to adjust, disinflation meant unemployment.

In turn, rising unemployment meant waning support for the policies of austerity needed to defend ERM pegs. There might come a time when a government dedicated to such policies would be thrown out of office by a disaffected electorate or when, in order to head off this possibility, the authorities would choose to abandon their policies of restraint. Anticipating this eventuality, the markets attacked the currencies of the countries with the highest unemployment rates and weakest governments.[70] As predicted, there is a correlation between the incidence of the crisis and the countries with the most serious unemployment problems.

This explanation also provides a link between market behavior and the controversy over the Maastricht Treaty. If the treaty were not going to be ratified (which seemed possible in the interval between the Danish and French referendums), it would not pay to endure unemployment as a way of demonstrating one's commitment to participate in the monetary union. It is no coincidence, then, that exchange rate tensions surfaced when the Danes rejected the treaty in June or that they peaked immediately before France's September 20 referendum.

Yet this explanation also sits uneasily with the observed behavior of forward exchange rates. If observers attached a significant probability to an expansionary policy shift, why then did the one-year-ahead forward rates of the ERM currencies that were attacked in the second week of September not move outside their ERM bands in July or August? Aside from the Italian lira, the only ERM currency whose forward rate fell out of its band before September was the Danish krone—not surprisingly given Denmark's rejection of the treaty.[71]

This brings us to the third factor that could have been at work in 1992–93: self-fulfilling attacks.[72] The mechanism is best illustrated by example.

---

[70] This process is formalized by Ozkan and Sutherland (1994).

[71] Again, this skepticism should not be overstated. A recession that raised European unemployment rates clearly lowered governments' comfort levels. There is no question that it raised public opposition to the policies of austerity required to maintain the exchange rate peg. Still, it is unclear whether policymakers became so uncomfortable that they were prepared to abandon their previous policies or that market sentiment, as measured by forward rates, attached a significant probability to this eventuality.

[72] The seminal contributions to this literature are Flood and Garber 1984 and Obstfeld 1986. The example that follows is drawn from Eichengreen 1994b. Readers will recognize the parallel with the interpretation of the 1931 sterling crisis developed in Chapter 3.

Assume that the budget is balanced and that the external accounts are in equilibrium so that no balance-of-payments crisis looms. The authorities are happy to maintain current policies indefinitely, and those policies will support the exchange rate in the absence of an attack. Now imagine that speculators attack the currency. The authorities must allow domestic interest rates to rise to ensure its defense, since speculators must be rendered indifferent between holding domestic-currency-denominated assets, on which the rate of return is the domestic interest rate, and foreign-currency-denominated assets, the return on which is the foreign interest rate plus the expected rate of depreciation. But the requisite rise in interest rates may itself alter the government's assessment of the costs and benefits of defending the rate. The higher interest rates required to defend the currency will depress absorption and aggravate unemployment, also aggravating the pain of the prevailing policies. They will increase the burden of mortgage debt, especially in countries like the United Kingdom where mortgage rates are effectively indexed to market rates. They will induce loan defaults, undermining the stability of fragile banking systems. They will increase debt-servicing costs and require the imposition of additional distortionary taxes. Enduring austerity now in return for an enhanced reputation for defending the exchange rate later may become less appealing if a speculative attack increases the cost of running the first set of policies. Even a government that would have accepted this trade-off in the absence of an attack may choose to reject it when subjected to speculative pressure.

In such circumstances, a speculative attack can succeed even if, in its absence, the currency peg could and would have been maintained indefinitely. This is in contrast to standard models of balance-of-payments crises, where speculators prompted to act by inconsistent and unsustainable policies are only anticipating the inevitable, acting in advance of a devaluation that must occur anyway.[73] In this example, devaluation will not occur anyway; the attack provokes an outcome that would not obtain otherwise. It serves as a self-fulfilling prophecy.

There are reasons to think that models of self-fulfilling crises are applicable to the ERM in the 1990s.[74] Consider the choice confronting EU member states attempting to qualify for membership in Europe's monetary union. The Maastricht Treaty makes two previous years of exchange rate stability a condition for participation. Even if a country has its domestic financial house in order and its government is willing to trade austerity now for quali-

[73] See Krugman 1979.

[74] This is argued by Eichengreen and Wyplosz (1993), Rose and Svensson (1994), and Obstfeld (1996).

fying for monetary union later, an exchange-market crisis that forces it to devalue and abandon its ERM peg may still disqualify it from participation. And if it no longer qualifies for EMU, its government has no incentive to continue pursuing the policies required to gain entry. It will be inclined therefore to switch to a more accommodating monetary and fiscal stance. Even if in the absence of a speculative attack there is no problem with fundamentals, current or future, once an attack occurs the government has an incentive to modify policy in a more accommodating direction, validating speculators' expectations. In other words, the Maastricht Treaty provided particularly fertile ground for self-fulfilling attacks.

THE EXPERIENCE OF DEVELOPING COUNTRIES

In much of the industrialized world, then, the two post–Bretton Woods decades were marked by movement toward more freely fluctuating exchange rates. This was true of the dollar/yen and dollar/deutsche mark rates; it was true of intra-European exchange rates after the EMS crisis of 1992. The trend was a response to the pressures imparted by the rise of international capital mobility.

The same pattern was evident in the developing world. Floating was unattractive for countries with underdeveloped financial markets, where disturbances could result in high levels of exchange rate volatility. It was unappealing to very small, very open developing countries, where exchange rate fluctuations could severely disrupt resource allocation. The vast majority of developing countries therefore pegged their currencies behind the shelter of capital controls.

Over time, pegging proved increasingly difficult to reconcile with the effort to liberalize financial markets. Developing countries resorted to policies of import substitution and financial repression in the wake of World War II. In Latin America, for example, where countries suffered enormously from the depression of the 1930s, the lesson drawn was the need to insulate the economy from the vagaries of international markets. Tariffs and capital controls were employed to segregate domestic and international transactions. Price controls, marketing boards, and financial restrictions were used to guide domestic development.[75] The model worked well enough in the immediate aftermath of the war, when neither international trade nor international

---

[75] The strategy was articulated in the publications of the UN's Economic Commission for Latin America; for critical analyses of this doctrine see Fishlow 1971 and Ground 1988.

lending had yet recovered and a backlog of technology afforded ample opportunity for *extensive growth*. With time, however, interventionist policy was increasingly captured by special-interest groups. Trade and lending picked up, and the exhaustion of easy growth opportunities placed a premium on the flexibility afforded by the price system. As early as the 1960s, developing countries began to shift from import substitution and financial repression to export promotion and market liberalization.

The consequences were not unlike those experienced by the industrialized countries: as domestic markets were liberalized, international financial flows became more difficult to control. Maintaining capital controls became more onerous and disruptive. And with the increase in the number of commercial banks lending to developing countries, international capital movements grew in magnitude, making their management more troublesome. It became increasingly difficult to resist the pressure to allow the currency to appreciate when capital surged in or to let the exchange rate depreciate to facilitate adjustment when capital flowed out.

Larger developing countries were most inclined to unpeg their exchange rates. Whereas 73 percent of large developing countries still pegged as late as 1982, by 1991 that proportion had fallen to 50 percent.[76] Comparable figures for small countries were 97 and 84 percent. Even there, startling transformations could take place: for example, Guatemala, whose currency was fixed to the U.S. dollar for sixty years, and Honduras, which fixed to the dollar for more than seventy years, broke those links in 1986 and 1990. Free floats remained rare; governments concerned about the volatility produced by thin markets managed their exchange rates heavily.

The diversity of developing-country experience spawned a debate about the efficacy of alternative policies. Countries that stayed with pegged-rate arrangements throughout the period enjoyed relatively low inflation rates, unlike countries that maintained flexible-rate arrangements throughout the period and those that shifted from fixed to floating rates.[77] Pegged exchange rates, it was consequently argued, imposed discipline on policymakers, forcing them to rein in inflationary tendencies. The obvious problem with the argument was that causality could run in the other direction: it was not that pegged exchange rates imposed anti-inflationary discipline but that governments able to pursue policies of price stability for independent reasons were in the best position to peg their currencies.

Sebastian Edwards considered this question in detail, analyzing the deter-

---

[76] A growing share of countries that continued to peg did so against a basket rather than to a single currency. See Kenen 1994, p. 528.

[77] See Kenen 1993 for data and further discussion.

minants of inflation in a cross section of developing countries and controlling for a wide variety of factors in addition to the exchange rate.[78] His results suggest that a pegged exchange rate provided additional anti-inflationary discipline even when other potential determinants of inflation are taken into account.

This evidence suggests that an exchange rate peg will be particularly appealing to governments seeking to bring high inflation under control. Pegging the currency can halt import-price inflation in its tracks and dramatically reduce the inflation rate. This allows order to be restored to the tax system and the adequacy of the government's fiscal and monetary measures to be evaluated. It is not surprising, then, that pegging the exchange rate has been an integral element of "heterodox" stabilization programs in Latin America, Eastern Europe, and elsewhere in the developing world.

But using a pegged exchange rate as a nominal anchor in a stabilization program is not without costs. Domestic inflation still takes time to decline, which can lead to real overvaluation. As the current-account deficit widens, the currency peg, and the stabilization program itself, can collapse in a heap. A currency peg effectively buttresses anti-inflationary credibility only if the government makes a significant commitment to its maintenance; hence, a peg that is intended only to accompany the transition to price stability may get locked in, heightening financial fragility and exposing the country to risk of a speculative crisis. Conversely, countries that announce their intention of moving away from their temporary peg may find that the latter provides little anti-inflationary credibility.

An extreme response to this dilemma, which has gained favor in recent years, is the establishment of a currency board. A country adopts a parliamentary statute or constitutional amendment requiring the central bank or government to peg the currency to that of a trading partner. This is accomplished by authorizing the monetary authority to issue currency only when it acquires foreign exchange of equal value. Since changing the law or constitution is a formidable political task, there is relatively little prospect that the peg will be abandoned. Knowledge of this fact should speed adjustment by producers and consumers to the new regime of price stability, halting inflation and minimizing the problems of overvaluation that typically afflict newly established currency pegs.

Currency boards have operated in small, open economies such as Hong Kong, Bermuda, and the Cayman Islands and in developing countries less open to trade such as Nigeria and British East Africa. They operated in

---

[78] See Edwards 1993.

Ireland from 1928 to 1943 and in Jordan from 1927 through 1964.[79] A currency-board-like arrangement was adopted by Argentina in 1991 as part of its effort to halt years of high inflation, by Estonia in 1992 to prevent the emergence of analogous problems, and by Lithuania in 1994.

The resemblance between currency boards and the gold standard is striking. Under the gold standard, statute permitted central banks to issue additional currency only upon acquiring gold or, sometimes, convertible foreign exchange; the rules are similar under a currency board except that no provision is usually made for gold. Under the gold standard, the maintenance of a fixed domestic price of gold resulted in a fixed rate of exchange; under a currency board, the domestic currency is pegged to the foreign currency directly.

The weakness of the currency-board system is also the same as under the gold standard: limited scope for lender-of-last-resort intervention. The monetary authority must stand by and watch banks fail—in the worst case scenario, watch the banking system collapse. Unless it possesses excess reserves, it is prevented from injecting liquidity into the domestic financial system. And even if it possesses excess reserves sufficient to permit lender-of-last-resort intervention, undertaking it may be counterproductive. Investors, seeing the currency board issue credit without acquiring foreign exchange, may infer that the political authorities attach a higher priority to the stability of the banking system than to the exchange rate peg. They will respond by shifting funds out of the country ahead of possible devaluation and nullification of the currency-board system, draining liquidity from the financial system faster than the authorities can replace it. In a currency-board country, as under the gold standard, there may be no effective response to financial crisis.[80]

In a sense, of course, this is the reason to have the currency board, which reflects a decision to sacrifice flexibility for credibility. But the rigidity that is the currency board's strength is also its weakness. A financial crisis that brings down the banking system can incite opposition to the currency board itself. Anticipating this, the government may abandon its currency board in fear that the banking system and economic activity are threatened.

This problem is more serious in some countries than in others. In a small country with a limited number of financial institutions and a concentrated banking system, it is possible to arrange lifeboat operations in which the stronger banks bail out their weaker counterparts. Where domestic banks are affiliated with financial institutions abroad, they can call on foreign support.

---

[79] A comprehensive list of currency board episodes appears as Appendix C in Hanke, Jonung, and Schuler 1993.

[80] This argument is elaborated by Zarazaga 1995.

It follows that currency boards have operated successfully for relatively long periods in Bermuda, the Cayman Islands, and Hong Kong. In Argentina, however, none of these conditions prevails. In 1995, when a financial crisis in Mexico interrupted capital flows to other Latin American countries, the Argentine financial system was threatened with collapse. Only an $8 billion international loan organized by the IMF, used in part to fund a deposit insurance scheme and recapitalize the banking system, helped tide it over.

Another response to the problem is for countries to peg collectively rather than unilaterally. The one notable instance of this approach is the CFA franc zone.[81] The thirteen member countries share two central banks: seven utilize the Central Bank for West African States, while six use the Bank for Central African States. The two central banks issue equivalent currencies, both known as the CFA franc, which are pegged to the French franc. That peg remained unchanged for forty-six years, before the currencies of the CFA franc zone were devalued against the French franc in 1994. Thus, not only have the members of these monetary unions enjoyed currency stability against one another, but they long maintained a stable exchange rate against the former colonial power.

The franc zone countries suffered sharp deteriorations in their terms of trade in the second half of the 1980s when the prices of cocoa and cotton declined. Yet they consistently enjoyed lower inflation than neighboring countries with independently floating currencies (the Gambia, Ghana, Nigeria, Sierra Leone, and Zaire) and nearby countries with managed floats (Guinea-Bissau and Mauritania), while output performance in the CFA franc zone was not obviously inferior.

Two special circumstances played a role in the stability of the CFA franc–French franc rate. First, all member countries maintained restrictions on payments for capital-account transactions, and several maintained limited restrictions on payments for current-account transactions. Here as elsewhere, capital controls appear to have been associated with the viability of the currency peg. Second, the CFA franc countries received extensive support from the French government. In addition to foreign aid (France being the largest bilateral donor to its former colonies), they received essentially unlimited balance-of-payments financing. France guaranteed the convertibility of the CFA franc at its fixed parity by permitting the two regional central banks unlimited overdrafts on their accounts with the French Treasury.

The contrast with the EMS is worth noting. Where intra-European cur-

---

[81] CFA stands for Communauté Financière Africaine. A basic reference to the economics of the CFA franc zone is Boughton 1993.

rency pegs have had to be changed every few years, the link between the French franc and CFA franc remained unchanged for nearly half a century. Where the unlimited support ostensibly offered under the EMS Act of Foundation has not exactly been extended, it has been provided by the French Treasury to the members of the CFA franc zone. The difference is attributable to the credibility of the franc zone countries' commitment to adjust, which assured France that its financial obligation would ultimately be limited. The two central banks were required to tighten monetary policy when making use of overdrafts. France could be confident that adjustment would take place because of the magnitude of the bilateral foreign aid it provided, which the recipient countries could not afford to jeopardize.

In the 1990s, the same factors that destabilized currency pegs elsewhere—the growing difficulty of containing international capital movements and the increasingly controversial nature of government policies—forced a devaluation of the CFA franc. Despite persistent deficits, the two African central banks hesitated to tighten monetary policies to the requisite extent. Tight credit conditions threatened to destabilize banking systems already weakened by the consequences of the collapse of commodity prices. This was too costly politically for the governments concerned, leaving them reluctant to tighten. And draconian wage cuts led to the outbreak of general strikes in Cameroon and other franc zone countries, causing the authorities to relent. In the absence of adjustment, the French government made clear that there were limits on the financial assistance it was prepared to extend. As a price for its continued support, it required adjustment, partly through a devaluation. Hence, the CFA franc was devalued by 50 percent against the French franc at the beginning of 1994.

THE ASIAN CRISIS

The region that had long seemed best insulated from this volatility was high-growth Asia. This changed in 1997, and with a vengeance. That Asia, seemingly the last bastion of stability, succumbed to the exchange rate problems that afflicted the rest of the world underscored the pervasiveness of the pressures working to transform the international monetary system.

The Asian crisis was so staggering because it occurred against the backdrop of favorable economic and financial conditions. Monetary and fiscal policies were generally well balanced. The Asian tigers exhibited neither the large budget deficits nor the persistent inflation characteristic of other crisis-prone developing countries. Their rapid growth had been fueled by impressive export growth, which minimized the balance-of-payments pressures that were so disruptive elsewhere. This admirable performance persisted into the 1990s. Between 1992 and 1995 the Chinese economy grew at double-digit rates. Indonesia, Malaysia, Singapore, South Korea, and Thailand all grew at rates in excess of 7 percent per annum. In 1994–95, the year-over-year rate of growth of exports from Malaysia, the Philippines, Singapore, and Thailand all peaked out at more than 30 percent, an astonishing figure.

Equally striking was the smooth recovery of capital inflows following the Mexican crisis. By 1996 net private capital inflows had reached 5 percent of GDP in Korea, 6 percent in Indonesia, 9 percent in Thailand, and 10 percent in the Philippines. The flip side was large current account deficits (see Figure 5.11).

Asia's admirable economic record provided obvious attractions to foreign investors, but the fact that capital flowed in large quantities even to troubled countries like the Philippines indicated that additional factors were at work. Prominent among these was the low level of interest rates in the major financial centers, which stimulated a search for yield. The costs of borrowing in yen had fallen to unprecedented low levels as a result of depressed financial conditions in Japan, and yields on U.S. equity investment had been depressed by a soaring stock market. International investors turned to emerging markets for relief. They borrowed in yen and dollars to invest in higher-yielding Asian securities. That Asian currencies were pegged to a basket in which the dollar carried the heaviest weight minimized the risk that profits on these investments would be wiped out by exchange rate movements. And that Asian governments had long used their banks as instruments of economic development, channeling funds to favored industries, obliged them to extend those banks generous public support in return. Foreign investors lent extensively to Asian banks in the belief that the latter would never be allowed to fail.

This happy situation was disturbed by a series of shocks. Japanese long rates ticked up from 2 to 2-1/2 percent in the spring of 1997, when the outlook for the Japanese economy brightened temporarily. The dollar rose against the yen, creating competitiveness problems for Asian economies whose basket pegs placed a heavy weight on the U.S. currency. Export growth stagnated, reflecting slow growth in Europe, intensifying Chinese competition, and an inventory correction in the consumer electronics industry.

Investors were not unaware of these trends. The collapse of the Bangkok Bank of Commerce in mid-1996 provided an early-warning signal of impending problems and cast a shadow over the stability of Asian banking systems. Thailand having displayed the most serious problems of overvalua-

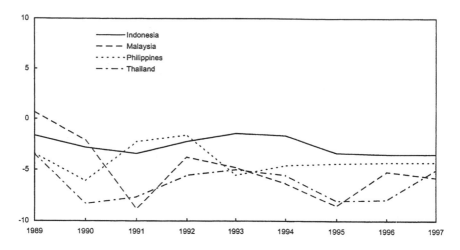

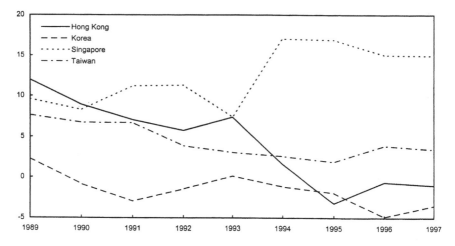

Figure 5.11. Selected Asian Economies: Current Account Balances (in percent of GDP). *Source*: International Monetary Fund.

tion, international banks and domestics began unwinding their long positions in Thai fixed-income securities. The Bangkok bourse declined steadily from the middle of 1996. Thailand's currency, the baht, came under mounting pressure.

Thailand's crisis was predictable and widely predicted. It erupted in the summer of 1997, by which time the Thai central bank had exhausted its international reserves. The country was forced to float its currency at the beginning of July. What was not foreseen was the virulence with which the crisis spread to neighboring countries. Once the Thai authorities floated the baht, speculative pressure spilled over to the Philippines, reflecting that country's substantial dependence on capital inflows and relatively rigid dollar peg. Once the Philippine authorities floated the peso (ten days after the baht), pressure was diverted to Indonesia and Malaysia, investors fearing that similar problems lurked in the financial and corporate sectors there as well. Jakarta and Kuala Lumpur responded by allowing their currencies to follow the baht down. An attack on the Hong Kong dollar was rebuffed, but the decision of the Taiwanese authorities to allow a preemptive decline of the New Taiwan dollar in October reminded investors that no peg was secure. Speculation against the Korean won and Indonesian rupiah intensified accordingly. In Korea, an impending election and uncertainty about the composition and intentions of the new government worked to further unsettle investors. The authorities in Seoul were forced to accede to the pressure by widening the currency's fluctuation band from 4-1/2 to 20 percent in November. And the won's continued fall excited worries about other currencies like the rupiah.

The crisis in the world's 11th largest economy was brought under control only when the December election brought to office a new government prepared to implement the IMF's recommendation that insolvent banks and firms be closed, and when G-7 governments convinced international banks which had extended short-term loans to Korea to exercise forbearance by renewing those credits, buying time for the new government to put reforms in place. The contrast with Indonesia, whose government failed to show similar resolve, was less than reassuring, and capital continued to hemorrhage from that country. These problems culminated in a run on the banking system—residents shifted from deposits to currency with such speed that the government found it virtually impossible to print money quickly enough to satisfy their demands, despite running its printing presses around the clock—and the declaration of an effective debt moratorium on January 27. At the time of writing, the Indonesian crisis shows no sign of abating.

Sir Walter Raleigh wrote that those who follow too close on the heels of history risk getting kicked in the teeth. Bearing in mind this stricture, three important lessons of the Asian crisis are clear. First, countries with weak banking systems are particularly prone to currency crises. At the root of the Asian crisis was governments' manipulation of their financial systems to further their national development strategies. This saddled their banks with uneconomical loans and led the authorities to extend them guarantees as a quid pro quo. Foreign investors, believing that the full faith and credit of the government stood behind their bank deposits, could not resist the high interest rates offered by the region's financial institutions. Once the crisis revealed the weak position of these institutions and the inability of even the central government to prop them up, investors scrambled for the exits.[82] In turn, this weakened the exchange rate. The banking crisis and the currency crisis thereby fed on one another in a vicious spiral. In this respect, commentators were quite right to compare the Thai and Korean crises of 1997 to the Austrian Credit Anstalt crisis of 1931.

Second, the Asian crisis provides yet another reminder of the speed and extent of contagion. Thailand's crisis may have been foreseen, but not so those of its neighbors. Competitive devaluation was one channel of transmission, but Thailand was too small for the changing competitiveness of its exports to destabilize an entire region. The fact that Korean banks had made loans to Indonesian companies provided another link, just as German banks' loans to Austria had facilitated the spread of the 1931 currency crisis. But most important, surely, was the general revision of perceptions of the Asian model. The Thai crisis reminded investors that pegged exchange rates could change and that banks could fail. If this was true of Thailand, it could also be true of other countries. If so, it might be wise to reduce one's financial exposure to the region.

Third, the Asian crisis again illustrates the pressures making for greater exchange rate flexibility. As Asian countries leave the stage of extensive growth—where the problem for policy is to mobilize savings and fund the largest possible volume of physical investment—for the stage of intensive growth—where economic development requires innovation, productivity growth, and venture capital—the countries of the region are left with no choice but to liberalize their financial systems. And with domestic financial liberalization comes an inevitable rise in international capital mobility, heightening the fragility of pegged exchange rates. With the decontrol of banking systems, the need for a domestic lender of last resort becomes more pressing, forcing governments to choose between stabilizing the banking system and stabilizing the exchange rate. And with democratization, the ability of governments to subordinate other goals of policy to stabilizing the

---

[82] Krugman 1998 provides a model of this process, which he characterizes as an alternative to models of both fundamentals-based and self-fulfilling attacks. In fact, his model is readily interpreted in terms of self-fulfilling attacks: what makes it go is the assumption that the government can bail out the banks only once. If a capital outflow occurs for any reason, forcing the government to rescue the banks, this means that the latter must stand on their own feet subsequently. The risk of investing in the country becomes correspondingly greater, and the steady-state level of foreign investment is correspondingly lower, validating the capital outflow that precipitated the crisis.

exchange rate becomes a thing of the past.[83] For all these reasons, in Asia as in other parts of the world, greater exchange rate flexibility is almost surely here to stay.

CONCLUSIONS

The quarter-century since the collapse of the Bretton Woods System has brought frustrated ambitions and uncomfortable compromises. Efforts to reconstruct a system of pegged but adjustable exchange rates have failed repeatedly. At the root of the failure has been the ineluctable rise in international capital mobility, which made currency pegs more fragile and periodic adjustments more difficult. Capital mobility increased the pressure on weak-currency countries seeking to defend their pegs. It heightened the reluctance of their strong-currency counterparts to provide support, given the unprecedented magnitude of the requisite intervention operations. Increasing numbers of governments found themselves forced to float their currencies.

Many liked these circumstances not a bit. Developing economies with thin financial markets found it difficult to endure the effects of volatile exchange rate swings. Currency fluctuations disrupted the efforts of European Community members to forge an integrated European market. Even the United States, Germany, and Japan lost faith in the ability of the markets to drive their bilateral exchange rates to appropriate levels in the absence of foreign-exchange-market intervention.

This dissatisfaction with freely floating exchange rates prompted a variety of partial measures to limit currency fluctuations. But if there was one common lesson of the Shultz-Volcker proposals to augment Bretton Woods with a system of reserve indicators, of the European Snake of the 1970s, of the European Monetary System, and of the Plaza-Louvre regime of coordinated intervention, it is that limited measures will not succeed in a world of unlimited capital mobility. Pegging the exchange rate in a world of high capital mobility requires radical reforms of a sort that governments are understandably reluctant to embrace, even in Europe, where more than forty years of progress toward political and economic integration have laid the groundwork.

---

[83] Hong Kong's defense of its currency board provides proof by counterexample. The fact that Hong Kong is hardly a normal democracy puts the authorities in an unusually strong position to pursue exchange rate stability in disregard of other goals. The fact that the banks are so internationalized means that many have their own lenders of last resort, namely, the foreign head office, relieving the government of pressure to abandon exchange-rate stability in order to undertake lender-of-last-resort operations.

Conclusion

THE QUARTER-CENTURY since the collapse of the Bretton Woods System of pegged but adjustable exchange rates has seen steady movement toward fluctuating currencies. As late as 1970 the idea of floating the exchange rate was unheard of except as a temporary expedient in extraordinary circumstances. But by 1984 nearly a quarter of IMF member countries had adopted floating rates. By the end of 1994 the proportion operating systems of managed and independent floating rates had risen to more than 50 percent (see Figure 6.1). Countries continuing to peg their exchange rates generally do so within increasingly expansive bands.

This postwar trend toward greater exchange rate flexibility is most immediately a consequence of rising international capital mobility. In the aftermath of World War II, international capital markets were becalmed. Memories of the international debt crisis of the 1930s and the fact that defaulted foreign bond issues had not yet been cleared away discouraged investors from looking abroad. Those who might have done so were constrained by controls on international capital flows. The maintenance of capital controls had been authorized in the Articles of Agreement negotiated at Bretton Woods in order to reconcile exchange rate stability with other goals: in the short run, concerted programs of postwar reconstruction; in the long run, the pursuit of full employment.

It should be no surprise, then, that controls were integral to the Bretton Woods System of pegged but adjustable rates. Controls loosened the link between domestic and foreign financial conditions; they granted governments freedom to alter domestic financial conditions in the pursuit of other goals without immediately jeopardizing the stability of the exchange rate. Controls were not so watertight as to obviate the need for exchange rate adjustments when domestic and foreign conditions diverged, but they provided the breathing space needed to organize orderly realignments and ensure the survival of the system.

Controls on capital movements were also seen as necessary for the reconstruction of international trade. If volatile capital movements destabilized currencies, governments would defend them by raising tariffs and tightening import quotas. If countries devalued, their neighbors would retaliate with tariffs and quotas of their own. The lesson gleaned from the 1930s was that

1984: 148 total countries

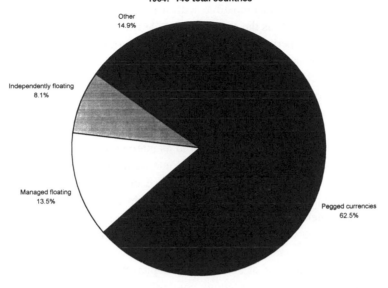

Other
14.9%

Independently floating
8.1%

Managed floating
13.5%

Pegged currencies
62.5%

1994: 178 total countries

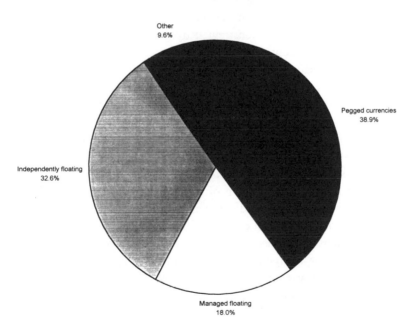

Other
9.6%

Pegged currencies
38.9%

Independently floating
32.6%

Managed floating
18.0%

Figure 6.1. Exchange Rate Arrangements, 1984 and 1994 (percent of world total). *Source*: International Monetary Fund, *International Financial Statistics*, February 1985 and May 1995.

currency instability was incompatible with a multilateral system of free international trade. Insofar as the recovery of trade was necessary for the restoration of global prosperity and growth, so were currency stability and, by implication, limits on capital flows.

But the conjunction of free trade and fettered finance was not dynamically stable. Once current-account convertibility was restored at the end of the 1950s, governments discovered how difficult it was to verify that a particular purchase of foreign exchange had been undertaken for purposes related to trade rather than currency speculation. And as international transactions were liberalized, it became impossible to keep domestic markets tightly regulated. Once financial markets joined the list of those undergoing decontrol, new channels were opened through which capital might flow, and the feasibility of controlling international capital movements diminished accordingly.

The consequence was mounting strains on the Bretton Woods System of pegged but adjustable rates. Governments could not consider devaluing without provoking a tidal wave of destabilizing capital flows. Parity adjustments during the period of current-account convertibility were few and far between. The knowledge that deficit countries would hesitate to adjust rendered surplus countries, fearing the magnitude of the cost, reluctant to provide support. And the freedom for governments to pursue independent macroeconomic policies was constrained by the rise of capital mobility. As soon as doubts arose about their willingness to sacrifice other objectives on the altar of the exchange rate, defending the currency could require interest-rate hikes and other painful policy adjustments that were politically unsupportable. Confidence in currency stability and ultimately stability itself were the casualties.

The same unstable dynamics are evident in the evolution of the European Monetary System constructed by the members of the European Community after the breakdown of Bretton Woods. Exchange rate stability was seen as necessary for the smooth operation of Europe's customs union and for the construction of a truly integrated European market. To buttress the stability of intra-European rates, capital controls were maintained when the EMS was established. Controls provided autonomy for domestic policy and breathing space for organizing realignments. But again, the conjunction of free trade and fettered finance was not dynamically stable. The liberalization of other intra-European transactions, which was after all the raison d'etre of the European Community, undermined the effectiveness of controls, which were themselves incompatible with the goal of constructing a single European market. Once they went by the board in the early 1990s, the EMS grew rigid and brittle. The 1992–93 recession then forced the issue. Currency traders knew that governments had limited political capacity in an environment of high unemployment to raise interest rates and adopt the other policies of austerity needed to defend their currency pegs. When the attacks came, governments were forced to abandon the narrow-band EMS and shift to a more accommodating system of wide bands and fluctuating rates.

The obvious conclusion is that the trend toward greater exchange rate flexibility is an inevitable consequence of rising international capital mobility. It is important, therefore, to recollect earlier historical periods, like that of the classical gold standard, when high international capital mobility did not preclude the maintenance of stable rates. Before World War I there was no question in most countries of the priority attached to the gold standard peg. There was only limited awareness that central bank policy might be directed at targets such as unemployment. And any such awareness had little impact on policy, given the limited extent of the franchise, the weakness of trade unions, and the absence of parliamentary labor parties. There being no question about the willingness and ability of governments to defend the currency peg, capital flowed in stabilizing directions in response to shocks. Workers and firms allowed wages to adjust because they knew that there was little prospect of an exchange rate change to erase the consequences of disequilibrium costs. Together these factors operated as a virtuous circle that lent credibility to the commitment to pegged rates.

The credibility of this commitment obviated the need for capital controls to insulate governments from market pressures that might produce a crisis. The authorities could take the steps needed to defend the currency without suffering dire political consequences. Because the markets were aware of this fact, they were less inclined to attack the currency in the first place. In a sense, limits on the extent of democracy substituted for limits on the extent of capital mobility as a source of insulation. With the extension of the electoral franchise and the declining effectiveness of controls, that insulation disappeared, rendering pegged exchange rates more costly and difficult to maintain.

To say that this trend was entirely unanticipated would not be correct. As mentioned in the introduction, Karl Polanyi for one, writing more than half a century ago, described how the operation of pegged exchange rates had been complicated by the politicization of the policy environment.[1] Polanyi saw the spread of universal suffrage and democratic associationalism as a reaction

---

[1] Polanyi 1944, pp. 133–34, 227–29, and passim.

against the tyranny of the market forces that the gold standard had helped to set loose. The consequent politicization of the policy environment, he recognized, had destroyed the viability of the gold standard itself.

Thus, the construction after World War II of a system of managed flexibility in which capital controls reconciled the desire for exchange rate stability with the pursuit of other goals would not have surprised Polanyi. Nor would the politicization of the policy environment. What would have surprised him, presumably, was the extent to which resurgent market forces undermined the effectiveness of capital controls and how these forces overwhelmed the efforts of governments to manage their currencies. It is understandable that neither he nor John Maynard Keynes, Harry Dexter White, and the other architects of the postwar international monetary system, working in the aftermath of the Great Depression, appreciated fully the resilience of the market or anticipated the extent to which markets would frustrate efforts to tightly regulate economic activity and, in the case of exchange rates, to use capital controls as a basis for management.

A consequence of the market's unanticipated resilience was therefore the post-1971 shift toward more flexible exchange rates. For large economies like the United States and Japan, this is a bearable condition. Relatively large, relatively closed economies are able to pursue the domestic objectives required in a Polanyian world without suffering intolerable pain from currency swings. There is good reason, therefore, to think that their currencies will continue to float against one another. For the majority of smaller, more open economies, however, the costs of floating are difficult to bear. While domestic political constraints preclude the successful maintenance of unilateral currency pegs except in the most exceptional circumstances, volatile exchange rate swings impose almost unbearable costs and are disruptive to the pursuit of domestic economic goals. As their economies are buffeted by exchange-market turbulence, these countries are likely to seek cooperative agreements that tie their currencies securely to that of a larger neighbor. This desire is already evident in Europe in the effort to form a monetary union centered on the Federal Republic of Germany. One can imagine that, with sufficient time, similar tendencies will surface in the Western Hemisphere and Asia, and that the United States and Japan will be at the center of their respective monetary blocs. But a happy conclusion to this story remains at best a distant prospect.

* Glossary *

adjustment mechanism — The changes in prices and quantities by which market forces eliminate balance-of-payments deficits and surpluses.

balance of trade — The difference between merchandise exports and imports. A positive (negative) difference indicates a trade surplus (deficit).

Balassa-Samuelson effect — The tendency for prices to rise rapidly in fast-growing economies where the rapid increase of productivity in the tradable-goods sector induces increases in the demand for the products of the service sector.

Bank rate — See central bank discount rate.

beggar-thy-neighbor devaluation — An exchange rate devaluation by one country that, by compressing its demand for imports, leaves its trading partners worse off.

bimetallic standard or *bimetallism* — A commodity-money standard under which the authorities grant legal-tender status to coins minted with two metals (say, gold and silver). See also *monometallic standard.*

brassage — The fee paid for coining precious metal under a commodity money standard. It covered the expenses of the mint master and allowed him a modest profit.

capital account — The component of the balance of payments that reflects foreign investment. A capital-account deficit signifies that outward investment exceeds inward investment.

capital controls — Regulations limiting the ability of firms or households to convert domestic currency into foreign exchange. Controls on capital-account transactions prevent residents from converting domestic currency into foreign exchange for purposes of foreign investment. Controls on current-account transactions limit the ability of residents to convert domestic currency into foreign exchange in order to import merchandise.

capital flight — The withdrawal of funds from assets denominated in a particular currency, motivated typically by expectations of its subsequent devaluation.

capital levy — An exceptional tax on capital or wealth.

central bank — Banker to the government. The bank vested with responsibility for the operation of the monetary standard.

central bank discount rate — The rate at which the central bank stands ready to lend by discounting (purchasing bills or promissory notes at a discount).

Committee of Central Bank Governors — Committee consisting of governors of central banks participating in the European Monetary System.

Common Agricultural Policy — A system of agricultural price supports that has traditionally absorbed more than half of the European Community's budget. Its principles were set out in Article 38 of the Treaty of Rome that established the EEC.

consols — British Treasury bonds of infinite maturity, which paid a given amount of interest each year.

convertibility — The ability of a currency to be freely converted into foreign exchange. Under the gold standard, a convertible currency could be freely exchanged for gold at a fixed price.

currency board — A substitute for central banking and a monetary arrangement under which a country ties its monetary policy to that of another country by statute or constitution.

currency reform — When a new currency is issued, generally to replace an existing currency debased by rapid inflation.

current account — The component of the international balance of payments that reflects transactions in goods and services. A current-account deficit signifies that purchases of goods and services from foreigners exceed sales of goods and services to foreigners.

Delors Report — 1989 report of a committee chaired by European Commission president Jacques Delors that recommended a three-step transition to European monetary union.

discount house — Financial intermediary found in Great Britain that discounts promisory notes and resells them or holds them to maturity.

ecu — The European currency unit, a composite of European currencies. It serves as the accounting unit of the European Monetary System.

escape clause — A provision allowing for temporary abrogation of a rule governing economic policy.

European Central Bank — Central bank to come into existence upon the inauguration of Stage III of the process of European monetary unification.

European Commission — The European Union's independent executive with power of proposal, consisting of individuals appointed by member states to serve four-year terms. Responsible for executing policies set by the European Council.

European Council — A European Union decision-making body consisting of ministers drawn from member states, which represents national rather than EU interests.

European Economic Community — Created by the Treaty of Rome in 1958 and consisting initially of six countries (France, Germany, Belgium, the Netherlands, Luxembourg, and Italy). Enlarged on three subsequent occasions.

European Monetary Cooperation Fund — The component of the European Snake designed to finance payments imbalances between the participating countries.

European Monetary Institute — The temporary entity created in 1994 under the provisions of the Maastrict Treaty to coordinate the policies of EU member states and plan the move to monetary union.

European Monetary System — System of pegged but adjustable currencies established by members of the European Community in 1979.

European Parliament — Legislative body consisting of members directly elected by member state electorates for five-year terms. Consulted on a wide range of legislative proposals, it forms one part of the EU's budgetary authority.

European Snake — A collective arrangement of European countries in the 1970s to peg their exchange rates within 2-1/4 percent bands.

exchange control — See capital controls.

Exchange Equalization Accounts — Government agencies responsible for carrying out intervention in the foreign-exchange market.

exchange rate — The domestic price of a unit of foreign currency.

Exchange Rate Mechanism — The component of the European Monetary System under which participating countries peg their exchange rates.

expenditure-switching policies — Policies, including but not limited to exchange rate changes, designed to correct an external imbalance by altering relative prices and switching expenditure between domestic and foreign goods.

Export-Import Bank — Bank headquartered in Washington, D.C., established in 1934 as an agency of the federal government with responsibility for providing loans and credit guarantees to promote U.S. exports.

extensive growth — Growth based on the use of additional resources in established modes of production. Intensive growth, in contrast, entails the use of new technologies and organizational forms.

fiat money — Paper currency not backed by gold, convertible foreign exchange, or even, in some cases, government bonds.

fiduciary system — A system of backing domestic monetary liabilities with gold, under which a fixed quantity of such liabilities (the fiduciary issue) is uncollateralized.

fineness — The purity of the gold or silver minted into coin.

floating exchange rate — An exchange rate that is allowed to vary. A "clean float" occurs in the absence of government intervention; under a "dirty float" the authorities intervene to limit currency fluctuations.

fractional reserve banking — Banking in which loans are financed with deposits and with capital subscribed by shareholders; the alternative to "narrow" banking, in which the capital subscribed by shareholders is the only source of funds for loans.

free gold — Under the gold standard statute in force in the 1930s, the Federal Reserve System was required to hold gold or eligible securities (essentially commercial paper) as collateral against its monetary liabilities; free gold was that amount left over after this obligation was discharged.

General Arrangements to Borrow — Credit lines established in 1962 by the industrial countries to lend their currencies to one another through the IMF.

gold bloc — Currency bloc consisting of countries that remained on the gold standard after Britain and some two dozen others departed in 1931.

gold devices — Interest-free loans to gold arbitragers and other devices designed to widen or narrow the gold points (see below), thereby increasing or reducing the degree of exchange rate variability consistent with the maintenance of convertibility.

gold-exchange standard — A gold-standard-like system under which countries' international reserves can take the form of convertible foreign currencies as well as gold.

gold points — Points at which it became profitable to engage in arbitrage because of deviations between the market and mint prices of gold.

Gold Pool — An arrangement in which the principal industrial countries cooperated in supporting the official price of gold at $35 in the 1960s.

Gresham's Law — The idea that when two currencies circulate, individuals will want to dispose of the one that is losing value more quickly. That currency will therefore dominate transactions, driving the "good money" out of circulation.

Group of Ten (G-10) — An informal grouping of industrial nations established after World War II, including Belgium, Canada, France, Germany, Italy, Japan, the Netherlands, Sweden, the United Kingdom, and the United States.

hyperinflation — Rapid inflation, commonly defined as at least 50 percent a month.

imperial preference — A policy of extending preferential treatment (in the form of tariff concessions, for example) to members of an empire.

inconvertibility — A situation in which a currency cannot be freely exchanged for gold (under a gold standard) or foreign exchange (under a fiat money standard).

Interest Equalization Tax — Tax levied by the United States starting in 1964 on interest earned on foreign securities.

international liquidity — The international reserves required in order for central banks to issue domestic monetary liabilities and finance a given volume of international trade.

international reserves — A monetary system's convertible financial assets (e.g., gold, convertible currencies such as the U.S. dollar, special drawing rights), with which it backs paper currency and token coin and effects international settlements.

invisibles account — Component of current account associated with interest and dividends paid on prior foreign investments and international transactions in shipping, insurance, and financial services.

Lombard rate — The rate of interest charged by a central bank when acting as lender of last resort.

Maastricht Treaty on European Union — Treaty committing the signatories to a three-stage transition to monetary union.

managed floating — A regime under which exchange rates are allowed to float but governments intervene in the foreign-exchange market. Known also as "dirty floating."

misaligned currency — A currency whose market value bears little relationship to economic fundamentals.

monetary base — The money supply narrowly defined, generally comprising cash, bankers' deposits with the central bank, and short-term monetary assets.

monometallic standard — A monetary regime in which domestic currency is convertible at a fixed price into one precious metal (in contrast to a bimetallic standard, under which the currency is convertible into two metals at fixed prices).

network externalities — External effects in which the practices of an agent depend on the practices adopted by other agents with whom he interacts.

open-market operations — Purchases or sales of government bills or bonds by the central bank.

overvaluation — The condition of a currency that, at the prevailing exchange rate, purchases too many units of foreign exchange. Overvaluation tends to be associated with competitive difficulties for producers and balance-of-payments deficits.

path dependence — A characteristic of a system whose equilibrium, or resting point, is not independent of its initial condition.

price-specie flow model — Model of international adjustment under the gold standard proposed in the eighteenth century by David Hume.

proportional system — A system of backing domestic monetary liabilities with gold, in which the value of gold reseves must equal or exceed some minimum share (usually 35 or 40 percent) of the value of liabilities.

realignment — Term used by participants in the Exchange Rate Mechanism of the European Monetary System to denote changes in ERM central rates.

Reconstruction Finance Corporation — Created in December 1931 by the Hoover administration to provide financing for banks and firms in need of liquidity.

scarce-currency clause — Provision of IMF Articles of Agreement authorizing the application of exceptional exchange and trade restrictions against a country whose currency became scarce within the Fund.

Short-Term and *Very-Short-Term Financing Facilities* — Foreign-currency financing or credits available to weak-currency central banks within the Exchange Rate Mechanism of the European Monetary System.

Single European Act — An act negotiated at the intergovernmental conference in 1986 committing the members of the European Community to remove barriers to movements of merchandise and factors of production within the Community.

special drawing rights — An increase in IMF quotas authorized in 1967 that allowed the IMF to provide member countries with credit that exceeded their subscriptions of gold and currency.

stand-by arrangement — An IMF procedure adopted in 1952 that allows a country to negotiate in advance its access to Fund resources up to specific limits without being subject to review of its position at the time of drawing.

sterilization — Central bank policy of eliminating the impact of international reserve movements on domestic credit conditions.

sterilized intervention — Foreign-exchange-market intervention whose impact on the domestic money supply is eliminated through domestic purchases or sales of bonds.

sterling area — Area comprising countries that, starting in the 1930s, pegged their currencies to the pound sterling and held their international reserves in London.

swap arrangements — Agreements among central banks under which stongcurrency countries provide foreign assets to their weak-currency counterparts.

target zone — A zone beyond which the exchange rate is prevented from moving because the authorities intervene in the foreign-exchange market and/or otherwise alter policy when the rate reaches the edge of the band.

terms of trade — The ratio of export to import prices.

* References *

Aliber, Robert Z. 1978. "The Integration of National Financial Markets: A Review of Theory and Findings." *Weltwirtschaftliches Archiv* 114: 448–79.

Arndt, H. W. 1944. *The Economic Lessons of the 1930s*. London: Oxford University Press.

Bagehot, Walter. 1874. *Lombard Street*. London: Kegan Paul, Trench.

Balogh, Thomas. 1946. "The United States and the World Economy." *Bulletin of the Oxford Institute of Statistics* 8: 309–23.

———. 1949. *The Dollar Crisis: Causes and Cure*. Oxford, Eng.: Blackwell.

Bank for International Settlements. 1993. *63rd Annual Report*, Basel: BIS.

Barsky, Robert, and J. Bradford DeLong. 1991. "Forecasting Pre–World War I Inflation: The Fisher Effect and the Gold Standard." *Quarterly Journal of Economics* 106: 815–36.

Bayoumi, Tamim, and Barry Eichengreen. 1996 "The Stability of the Gold Standard and the Evolution of the International Monetary System." In Tamim Bayoumi, Barry Eichengreen, and Mark Taylor, eds., *Modern Perspectives on the Classical Gold Standard*, 165–88. Cambridge: Cambridge University Press.

Berger, Helge, and Albrecht Ritschl. 1995. "Germany and the Political Economy of the Marshall Plan: A Re-revisionist View." In Barry Eichengreen, ed., *Europe's Postwar Recovery*, 199–245. Cambridge, Eng.: Cambridge University Press.

Bergsten, C. Fred. 1993. "The Rationale for a Rosy View: What a Global Economy Will Look Like." *Economist* 328 (September), 57–59.

Bini-Smaghi, Lorenzo, Tommaso Padoa-Schioppa, and Francesco Papadia. 1994. "The Transition to EMU in the Maastricht Treaty." Princeton Essays in International Finance 194. International Finance Section, Department of Economics, Princeton University, Princeton, N.J.

Blanchard, Olivier, and Pierre-Alain Muet. 1993. "Competitiveness through Disinflation: An Assessment of the French Macroeconomic Strategy." *Economic Policy* 16: 11–56.

Block, Fred L. 1977. *The Origins of International Economic Disorder*. Berkeley: University of California Press.

Bloomfield, Arthur. 1959. *Monetary Policy under the International Gold Standard, 1880–1914*. New York: Federal Reserve Bank of New York.

———. 1963. "Short-Term Capital Movements under the Pre-1914 Gold Standard." Princeton Studies in International Finance 11. International Finance Section, Department of Economics, Princeton University, Princeton, N.J.

Borchardt, Knut. 1991. *Perspectives on Modern German History and Policy*. Cambridge, Eng.: Cambridge University Press.

Bordo, Michael D. 1993. "The Bretton Woods International Monetary System: An Historical Overview." In Michael D. Bordo and Barry Eichengreen, eds., *A Retro-*

spective on the Bretton Woods System, 3–98. Chicago: University of Chicago Press.

Bordo Michael D., and Finn E. Kydland. 1995. "The Gold Standard as a Rule: An Essay in Exploration." *Explorations in Economic History* 32: 423–65.

———, Dominique Simard, and Eugene White. 1994. "France and the Bretton Woods International Monetary System." NBER Working Paper 4642. National Bureau of Economic Research, Cambridge, Mass.

Boughton, James M. 1993. "The Economics of the CFA Franc Zone." In Paul R. Masson and Mark P. Taylor, eds., *Policy Issues in the Operation of Currency Unions*, 95–129. Cambridge, Eng.: Cambridge University Press.

Branson, William. 1994. "German Reunification, the Breakdown of the EMS, and the Path to Stage Three." In David Cobham, ed., *European Monetary Upheavals*, 16–29. Manchester, Eng.: Manchester University Press.

Bretton Woods Commission. 1994. *Bretton Woods: Looking to the Future*. Washington, D.C.: Bretton Woods Commission.

Broadberry, S. N. 1986. *The British Economy between the Wars: A Macroeconomic Survey*. Oxford, Eng.: Blackwell.

Brown, William Adams, Jr. 1929. *England and the New Gold Standard, 1919–1926*. New Haven, Conn.: Yale University Press.

———. 1940. *The International Gold Standard Reinterpreted, 1914–1934*. New York: National Bureau of Economic Research.

Buiter, Willem H. 1987. "Borrowing to Defend the Exchange Rate and the Timing and Magnitude of Speculative Attacks." *Journal of International Economics* 23: 221–40.

Cairncross, A. K. 1953. *Home and Foreign Investment, 1870–1913*. Cambridge, Eng.: Cambridge University Press.

Cairncross, Alec, and Barry Eichengreen. 1983. *Sterling in Decline: The Devaluations of 1931, 1949 and 1967*. Oxford, Eng.: Blackwell.

Cairnes, John Elliot. 1874. *Some Leading Principles of Political Economy Newly Expounded*. New York: Harper and Brothers.

Calomiris, Charles. 1993. "Greenback Resumption and Silver Risk: The Economics and Politics of Monetary Regime Change in the United States, 1862–1900." In Michael D. Bordo and Forrest Capie, eds., *Monetary Regimes in Transition*, 86–134. Cambridge, Eng.: Cambridge University Press.

Campa, José M. 1990. "Exchange Rates and Economic Recovery in the 1930s: An Extension to Latin America." *Journal of Economic History* 50: 677–82.

Canzoneri, Matthew. 1985. "Monetary Policy Games and the Role of Private Information." *American Economic Review* 75: 1056–70.

Capie, Forrest, Terence Mills, and Geoffrey Wood. 1986. "What Happened in 1931?" in Forrest Capie and Geoffrey Wood, eds., *Financial Crises and the World Banking System*, 120–48. London: Macmillan.

Cernuschi, Henri. 1887. *Le pair bimétallique*. Paris: Guillaumin.

Clapham, John. 1945. *The Bank of England: A History*. Cambridge, Eng.: Cambridge University Press.

Clarke, Stephen V. O. 1967. *Central Bank Cooperation, 1924–1931.* New York: Federal Reserve Bank of New York.

Cleveland, Harold van Buren, and Thomas F. Huertas. 1985. *Citibank, 1812–1970.* Cambridge, Mass.: Harvard University Press.

Commission of the European Communities, Directorate-General for Economic and Financial Affairs. 1993. "The ERM in 1992." *European Economy* 54: 141–57.

Commmittee for the Study of Economic and Monetary Union (Delors Committee). 1989. *Report on Economic and Monetary Union in the European Community.* Luxembourg: Office for Official Publications of the European Communities.

Committee of Governors of the Central Banks of the Member States of the European Economic Community. 1993a. *Annual Report 1992.* Basel: Committee of Governors.

———. 1993b. "The Implications and Lessons to be Drawn from the Recent Exchange Rate Crisis—Report of the Committee of Governors." Basel, 21 April. Duplicated.

Committee on Currency and Foreign Exchanges after the War (Cunliffe Committee). 1919. *First Interim Report.* Cmd. 9182. London: HMSO.

Committee on Finance and Industry (Macmillan Committee). 1931. *Report.* Cmd. 3897. London: HMSO.

Condliffe, J. B. 1950. *The Commerce of Nations.* New York: Norton.

Cooper, Richard N. 1971. "Currency Devaluation in Developing Countries." Princeton Essays in International Finance 86. International Finance Section, Department of Economics, Princeton University, Princeton, N.J.

———. 1990. "What Future for the International Monetary System?" In Yoshio Suzuki, Junichi Miyake and Mitsuake Okabe, eds., *The Evolution of the International Monetary System,* 277–300. Tokyo: University of Tokyo Press.

———. 1992. "Whither Europe?" *Yale Review* 80: 10–17.

———. 1993. "Comment." In Michael D. Bordo and Barry Eichengreen, eds., *A Retrospective on the Bretton Woods System,* 104–7. Chicago: University of Chicago Press.

Coquelin, Charles. 1851. "De la dépréciation de l'or et du système monétaire français," *Journal des économistes* 28 (January): 55–67.

Cottrell, P. L. 1992. "Silver, Gold and the International Monetary Order." In S. N. Broadberry and N. F. R. Crafts, eds., *Britain in the International Economy,* 221–43. Cambridge, Eng.: Cambridge University Press.

Cunliffe Committee (Committee on Currency and Foreign Exchange after the War). 1919. *First Interim Report.* Cmd. 9182, London: HMSO.

Darby, Michael R., Arthur E. Gandolfi, James R. Lothian, Anna J. Schwartz, and Alan C. Stockman. 1983. *The International Transmission of Inflation.* Chicago: University of Chicago Press.

David, Paul. 1994. "Why Are Institutions the Carriers of History? Path Dependence and the Evolution of Conventions, Organizations and Institutions." *Structural Change and Economic Dynamics* 5: 205–20.

de Cecco, Marcello. 1974. *Money and Empire: The International Gold Standard*. London: Blackwell.

de Grauwe, Paul. 1989. *International Money: Post-war Trends and Theories*. Oxford, Eng.: Clarendon Press.

Del Mar, Alexander. 1895. *History of Monetary Systems*. London: Effingham Wilson.

Deprés, Emile. 1973. *International Economic Reform: Collected Papers of Emile Deprés*, ed. Gerald M. Meier. New York: Oxford University Press.

Dick, Trevor J. O., and John Floyd. 1992. *Canada and the Gold Standard: Balance of Payments Adjustment, 1871–1913*. Cambridge, Eng.: Cambridge University Press.

Diebold, William, Jr. 1952. "The End of the ITO." Princeton Essays in International Finance 16. International Finance Section, Department of Economics, Princeton University, Princeton, N.J.

––––––. 1972. *The United States and the Industrial World: American Foreign Economic Policy in the 1970s*. New York: Praeger.

Dominguez, Kathryn. 1993. "The Role of International Organizations in the Bretton Woods System." In Michael D. Bordo and Barry Eichengreen, eds., *A Retrospective on the Bretton Woods System*, 357–97. Chicago: University of Chicago Press.

Dooley, Michael, and Peter Isard. 1980. "Capital Controls, Political Risk, and Deviations from Interest-Rate Parity." *Journal of Political Economy* 88: 370–84.

Dornbusch, Rudiger. 1976. "Expectations and Exchange Rate Dynamics." *Journal of Political Economy* 84: 1161–76.

Drake, Louis S. 1985. "Reconstruction of a Bimetallic Price Level." *Explorations in Economic History* 22: 194–219.

Dulles, Eleanor Lansing. 1929. *The French Franc*. New York: Macmillan.

Edwards, Sebastian. 1993. "Exchange Rates as Nominal Anchors." *Weltwirtschaftliches Archiv* 129: 1–32.

Edwards, Sebastian, and Fernando Losada. 1994. "Fixed Exchange Rates, Inflation and Macroeconomic Discipline," NBER Working Paper 4661. National Bureau of Economic Research, Cambridge, Mass.

Edwards, Sebastian, and Julio Santaella. 1993. "Devaluation Controversies in the Developing Countries: Lessons from the Bretton Woods Era." In Michael Bordo and Barry Eichengreen, eds., *A Retrospective on the Bretton Woods System*, 405–55. Chicago: University of Chicago Press.

Eichengreen, Barry. 1986. "The Bank of France and the Sterilization of Gold, 1926–1932." *Explorations in Economic History* 23: 56–84.

––––––. 1987. "Conducting the International Orchestra: Bank of England Leadership under the Classical Gold Standard, 1880–1913." *Journal of International Money and Finance* 6: 5–29.

––––––. 1988. "The Australian Recovery of the 1930s in International Comparative Perspective." In R. G. Gregory and N. G. Butlin, eds., *Recovery from the Depression: Australia and the World Economy in the 1930s*, 33–60. Sydney: Cambridge University Press.

———. 1992a. "The Gold Standard since Alec Ford." In S. N. Broadberry and N. F. R. Crafts, eds., *Britain in the International Economy 1870–1939*, 49–79. Cambridge, Eng.: Cambridge University Press.

———. 1992b. *Golden Fetters: The Gold Standard and the Great Depression, 1919–1939*. New York: Oxford University Press.

———. 1992c. "More Speculation on Destabilizing Speculation." *Explorations in Economic History* 29: 93–98.

———. 1993. *Reconstructing Europe's Trade and Payments*. Manchester and Ann Arbor: Manchester and University of Michigan Presses.

———. 1994a. *International Monetary Arrangements for the 21st Century*. Washington, D.C.: Brookings Institution.

———. 1994b. "The Crisis in the EMS and the Prospects for EMU: An Interim Assessment." In Seppo Honkapohja, ed., *Economic Policy Issues in Financial Integration*, 15–72. Helsinki: Institute of International Economic Law, University of Helsinki.

Eichengreen, Barry, and Marc Flandreau. 1996. "The Geography of the Gold Standard." In Jorge Braga de Macedo, Barry Eichengreen and Jaime Reis, ed., *Currency Convertibility: The Gold Standard and Beyond*, 113–43. London: Routledge.

Eichengreen, Barry, and Peter B. Kenen. 1994. "Managing the World Economy under the Bretton Woods System: An Overview." In Peter B. Kenen, ed., *Managing the World Economy Fifty Years after Bretton Woods*, 3–57. Washington, D.C.: Institute for International Economics.

Eichengreen, Barry, and Ian McLean. 1994. "The Supply of Gold under the Pre-1914 Gold Standard." *Economic History Review* new ser. 47: 288–309.

Eichengreen, Barry, Andrew Rose, and Charles Wyplosz. 1994. "Speculative Attacks on Pegged Exchange Rates: An Empirical Exploration with Special Reference to the European Monetary System." University of California, Berkeley. Unpublished manuscript.

Eichengreen, Barry, and Jeffrey Sachs. 1985. "Exchange Rates and Economic Recovery in the 1930s." *Journal of Economic History* XLV: 925–46.

Eichengreen, Barry, and Charles Wyplosz. 1993. "The Unstable EMS." *Brookings Papers on Economic Activity* 1: 51–124.

Einzig, Paul. 1937. *The Theory of Forward Exchange*. London: Macmillan.

Ellis, Howard S. 1941. *Exchange Control in Central Europe*. Cambridge, Mass.: Harvard University Press.

Emminger, Otmar. 1986. *D-Mark, Dollar, Wahrungskrisen*. Stuttgart: Deutsche Verlags-Anstalt.

Epstein, Gerald, and Thomas Ferguson. 1984. "Monetary Policy, Loan Liquidation and Industrial Conflict: The Federal Reserve and the Open Market Operations of 1932." *Journal of Economic History* 44: 957–84.

Esposito, Chiarella. 1994. *America's Feeble Weapon: Funding the Marshall Plan in France and Italy, 1948–1950*. Westport, Conn.: Greenwood Press.

Feavearyear, A. E. 1931. *The Pound Sterling*. Oxford, Eng.: Clarendon Press.

Federal Reserve Board. 1943. *Banking and Monetary Statistics, 1914–1941*. Washington, D.C.: Board of Governors of the Federal Reserve System.

Feis, Herbert. 1930. *Europe: The World's Banker*, New Haven, Conn.: Yale University Press.

Feldstein, Martin. 1986. "New Evidence on the Effects of Exchange Rate Intervention," NBER Working Paper 2052. National Bureau of Economic Research, Cambridge, Mass.

Fetter, Frank. 1965. *The Development of British Monetary Orthodoxy*. Cambridge, Mass.: Harvard University Press.

Field, Alexander J. 1984. "A New Interpretation of the Onset of the Great Depression." *Journal of Economic History* 44: 489–98.

Fink, Carole. 1984. *The Genoa Conference: European Diplomacy, 1921–1922*. Chapel Hill: University of North Carolina Press.

Fisher, Irving. 1933. "The Debt-Deflation Theory of Great Depressions." *Econometrica* 1: 337-57.

Fishlow, Albert. 1971. "Origins and Consequences of Import Substitution in Brazil." In Luis Di Marco, ed., *International Economics and Development*, 311–62. New York: Academic Press.

———. 1985. "Lessons from the Past: Capital Markets during the 19th Century and the Interwar Period." *International Organization* 39: 383–439.

Flandreau, Marc. 1993a. "As Good As Gold: Bimetallism in Equilibrium, 1848–1870." University of California, Berkeley. Unpublished manuscript.

———. 1993b. "An Essay on the Emergence of the International Gold Standard." Stanford University, Stanford, Calif. Unpublished manuscript.

———. 1995. *La France et la stabilité du système monétaire international, 1848–1873*. Paris: l'Harmattan.

Flood, Robert P., and Peter Garber. 1984. "Gold Monetization and Gold Discipline." *Journal of Political Economy* 92: 90–107.

Ford, A. G. 1962. *The Gold Standard, 1880–1913: Britain and Argentina*. London: Oxford University Press.

Frankel, Jeffrey A. 1994. "Exchange Rate Policy." In Martin Feldstein, ed., *American Economic Policy in the 1980s*, 293–341. Chicago: University of Chicago Press.

Fratianni, Michele, and Jürgen von Hagen. 1992. *The European Monetary System and European Monetary Union*. Boulder, Colo.: Westview.

Frieden, Jeffry. 1988. "Sectoral Conflict and U.S. Foreign Economic Policy, 1914–1940." *International Organization* 42: 59–90.

———. 1994. "Greenback, Gold, and Silver: The Politics of American Exchange Rate Policy, 1870–1913." CIBER Working Paper 91–04. Anderson School of Management, UCLA.

Friedman, Milton. 1953. *Essays in Positive Economics*. Chicago: University of Chicago Press.

————. 1968. "The Role of Monetary Policy." *American Economic Review* 58: 1–17.

————. 1990. "Bimetallism Revisited." *Journal of Economic Perspectives* 4: 85–104.

Friedman, Milton, and Anna J. Schwartz. 1963. *A Monetary History of the United States, 1867–1960*, Princeton, N.J.: Princeton University Press.

Funabashi, Yoichi. 1988. *Managing the Dollar: From the Plaza to the Louvre.* Washington, D.C.: Institute for International Economics.

Galenson, Walter, and Arnold Zellner. 1957. "International Comparisons of Unemployment Rates." In National Bureau of Economic Research, *The Measurement and Behavior of Unemployment*, 439–500. Princeton, N.J.: Princeton University Press.

Gallarotti, Giulio. 1993. "The Scramble for Gold: Monetary Regime Transformation in the 1870s." In Michael D. Bordo and Forrest Capie, eds., *Monetary Regimes in Transition*, 15–67. New York: Cambridge University Press.

————. 1995. *The Anatomy of an International Monetary Regime: The Classical Gold Standard, 1880–1914.* New York: Oxford University Press.

Garber, Peter. 1993. "The Collapse of the Bretton Woods Fixed Exchange Rate System." In Michael D. Bordo and Barry Eichengreen, eds., *A Retrospective on the Bretton Woods System*, 461–95. Chicago: University of Chicago Press.

Gardner, Richard. 1969. *Sterling-Dollar Diplomacy.* 2d ed. New York: McGraw-Hill.

Giavazzi, Francesco, and Alberto Giovannini. 1989. *Limiting Exchange Rate Flexibility: The European Monetary System.* Cambridge, Mass.: MIT Press.

Giovannini, Alberto. 1989. "How Fixed Exchange Rate Regimes Work: The Gold Standard, Bretton Woods and the EMS." In Marcus Miller, Barry Eichengreen, and Richard Portes, eds., *Blueprints for Exchange Rate Management*, 13–42. New York: Academic Press.

Goldenweiser, E. A. 1925. *The Federal Reserve System in Operation.* New York: McGraw-Hill.

Gordon, Robert J. 1982. "Why U.S. Wage and Employment Behavior Differs from That in Britain and Japan." *Economic Journal* 92: 13–44.

Greenfield, Robert L., and Hugh Rockoff. 1992. "Gresham's Law Regained." NBER Working Paper on Historical Factors in Long Run Growth 35. National Bureau of Economic Research, Cambridge, Mass.

Grigg, James. 1948. *Prejudice and Judgment.* London: Jonathan Cape.

Gros, Daniel, and Niels Thygesen. 1991. *European Monetary Integration from the European Monetary System to the European Monetary Union.* London: Macmillan.

Grossman, Richard. 1988. "The Role of Bank Failures in Financial Crisis: Three Historical Perspectives." Ph.D. diss., Harvard University.

————. 1994. "The Shoe That Didn't Drop: Explaining Banking Stability during the Great Depression." *Journal of Economic History* 54: 654–82.

Ground, Richard L. 1988. "The Genesis of Import Substitution in Latin America." *CEPAL Review* 36: 179–203.

Gyohten, Toyoo. 1994. "Comment." In Barry Eichengreen, *International Monetary Arrangements for the 21st Century*, 142–49. Washington, D.C.: Brookings Institution.

Hamilton, James. 1987. "Monetary Factors in the Great Depression." *Journal of Monetary Economics* 13: 145–69.

Hanke, Steve H., Lars Jonung, and Kurt Schuler. 1993. *Russian Currency and Finance: A Currency Board Approach to Reform*. London: Routledge.

Hardy, Charles O. 1936. *Is There Enough Gold?* Washington, D.C.: Brookings Institution.

Harrod, Roy F. 1952. "The Pound Sterling." Princeton Essays in International Finance 13. International Finance Section, Department of Economics, Princeton University, Princeton, N.J.

Hawtrey, Ralph. 1938. *A Century of Bank Rate*. London: Longmans, Green.

Heckscher, Eli F. 1954. *An Economic History of Sweden*. Cambridge, Mass.: Harvard University Press.

Henning, Randall. 1994. *Currencies and Politics in the United States, Germany and Japan*. Washington, D.C.: Institute for International Economics.

Hirsch, Fred. 1966. *Money International*. New York: Doubleday.

Holtfrerich, Carl-Ludwig. 1988. "Relations between Monetary Authorities and Governmental Institutions: The Case of Germany from the 19th Century to the Present." In Gianni Toniolo, ed., *Central Banks' Independence in Historical Perspective*, 105–59. Berlin: Walter de Gruyter.

Horiuchi, Akiyoshi. 1993. "Monetary Policies: Japan." In Haruhiro Fukui, Peter H. Merkl, Hubertus Müller-Groeling, and Akio Watanabe, eds., *The Politics of Economic Change in Postwar Japan and West Germany*, 101–15. New York: St. Martin's Press.

Horn, Hendrik, and Torsten Persson. 1988. "Exchange Rate Policy, Wage Formation and Credibility." *European Economic Review* 32: 1621–36.

Horsefield, J. Keith. 1969. *The International Monetary Fund, 1945–1965*. Washington, D.C.: International Monetary Fund.

Howson, Susan. 1975. *Domestic Monetary Management in Britain, 1919–38*. Cambridge, Eng.: Cambridge University Press.

———. 1980. "Sterling's Managed Float: The Operations of the Exchange Equalisation Account, 1932–1939." Princeton Studies in International Finance 46. International Finance Section, Department of Economics, Princeton University, Princeton, N.J.

Hume, David. 1752. "On the Balance of Trade." In *Essays, Moral, Political and Literary*, vol. 1, 330–45. 1898 ed. London: Longmans, Green.

International Conference of Economic Services. 1938. *International Abstract of Economic Statistics, 1931–1936*. The Hague: International Conference of Economic Services.

Irwin, Douglas. 1995. "The GATT's Contribution to Economic Recovery in Post-War Western Europe." In Barry Eichengreen, ed., *Europe's Postwar Recovery*, 127–50. Cambridge, Eng.: Cambridge University Press.

Jacoby, Sanford. 1985. *Employing Bureaucracy: Managers, Unions, and the Transformation of Work in American Industry, 1900–1945*. New York: Columbia University Press.

James, Harold. 1984. *The German Slump: Politics and Economics, 1924–1936*. Oxford, Eng.: Clarendon Press.

———. 1992. "Financial Flows across Frontiers during the Interwar Depression." *Economic History Review* 45: 594–613.

———. 1995. *International Monetary Cooperation since Bretton Woods*. New York: Oxford University Press.

Jeanne, Olivier. 1995. "Monetary Policy in England, 1893–1914: A Structural VAR Analysis." *Explorations in Economic History* 32: 302–26.

Johnson, Harry G. 1973. "The Exchange-Rate Question for a United Europe." In Melvyn Krauss, ed., *The Economics of Integration*, 201–15. London: George Allen and Unwin.

Kaplan, Jacob, and Günther Schleiminger. 1989. *The European Payments Union: Financial Diplomacy in the 1950s*. Oxford, Eng.: Clarendon Press.

Kenen, Peter B. 1960. *British Monetary Policy and the Balance of Payments, 1951–1957*. Cambridge, Mass.: Harvard University Press.

———. 1969. "The Theory of Optimum Currency Areas: An Eclectic View." In Robert A. Mundell and Alexander K. Swoboda, eds., *Monetary Problems of the International Economy*, 41–60. Chicago: University of Chicago Press.

———. 1988. *Managing Exchange Rates*. London: Royal Institute of International Affairs.

———. 1993. "Financial Opening and the Exchange Rate Regime." In Helmut Reisen and Bernhard Fischer, eds., *Financial Opening*, 237–62. Paris: OECD.

———. 1994. *The International Economy*. 3d ed. New York: Cambridge University Press.

———. 1995. *Economic and Monetary Union in Europe: Moving Beyond Maastricht*. Cambridge, Eng.: Cambridge University Press.

Kennedy, Ellen. 1991. *The Bundesbank: Germany's Central Bank in the International Monetary System*. London: Royal Institute of International Affairs.

Kennedy, Susan Eastabrook. 1973. *The Banking Crisis of 1933*. Lexington: University Press of Kentucky.

Keynes, John Maynard. 1925. *The Economic Consequences of Mr. Churchill*. London: Hogarth Press.

———. 1930. *A Treatise on Money*. London: Macmillan.

———. 1932. *Essays in Persuasion*. London: Macmillan.

———. 1980. *The Collected Writings of John Maynard Keynes*. Vol. 25, *Activities 1940–1944: Shaping the Postwar World: The Clearing Union*, ed. Donald Moggridge. London: Macmillan and Cambridge University Press.

Kindleberger, Charles P. 1973. *The World in Depression, 1929–1939*, Berkeley: University of California Press.

King, Wilfred T. C. 1936. *History of the London Discount Market*. London: G. Routledge.

Kouri, Pentti J. K., and Michael G. Porter. 1974. "International Capital Flows and Portfolio Equilibrium." *Journal of Political Economy* 82: 443–67.

Krugman, Paul. 1979. "A Model of Balance-of-Payments Crises." *Journal of Money, Credit and Banking* 11: 311–25.

———. 1985. "Is the Strong Dollar Sustainable?" In *The U.S. Dollar: Recent Developments, Outlook, and Policy Options*, 103–32. Kansas City, Mo.: Federal Reserve Bank of Kansas City.

———. 1991. "Target Zones and Exchange Rate Dynamics." *Quarterly Journal of Economics* 106: 669–82.

———. 1998. "The Asian Crisis." MIT, Cambridge, Mass. Unpublished manuscript.

Kunz, Diane. 1987. *The Battle for Britain's Gold Standard in 1931*. London: Croom Helm.

Laughlin, J. Lawrence. 1885. *The History of Bimetallism in the United States*. New York: Appleton.

League of Nations. 1930. *Interim Report of the Gold Delegation of the Financial Committee*. Economic and Financial Series II.26. Geneva: League of Nations.

Lewis, Cleona. 1938. *America's Stake in International Investments*. Washington, D.C.: Brookings Institution.

Lindert, Peter. 1969. "Key Currencies and Gold, 1900–1913." Princeton Studies in International Finance 24. International Finance Section, Department of Economics, Princeton University, Princeton, N.J.

Little, I. M. D., Richard N. Cooper, W. Max Corden, and Sarath Rajapatirana. 1993. *Boom, Crisis, and Adjustment: The Macroeconomic Experience of Developing Countries*. New York: Oxford University Press.

Lucas, Robert. 1973. "Some International Evidence on Output-Inflation Tradeoffs." *American Economic Review* 63: 326–34.

Ludlow, Peter. 1982. *The Making of the European Monetary System*. London: Butterworth.

Lüke, R. E. 1958. *Von der Stabilisierung zur Krise*. Zurich: Polygrashisher Verlag.

MacDougall, Donald. 1957. *The World Dollar Problem*. New York: St. Martin's Press.

Machlup, Fritz. 1964. *International Payments, Debts and Gold*. New York: Charles Scribner's Sons.

McKinnon, Ronald. 1964. "Optimum Currency Areas." *American Economic Review* 53: 717–25.

———. 1994. "A Fiscally Consistent Proposal for International Monetary Reform." Stanford University, Stanford, Calif. Unpublished manuscript.

Maier, Charles. 1987. "The Two Post-War Eras and the Conditions for Stability in Twentieth Century Western Europe." In *In Search of Stability*, 153–84. Cambridge, Eng.: Cambridge University Press.

Marris, Stephen. 1985. *Deficits and the Dollar: The World Economy at Risk.* Washington, D.C.: Institute for International Economics.

Marshall, Alfred. 1925. *Memorials of Alfred Marshall*, Arthur C. Pigou, ed., London: Macmillan.

Marston, Richard. 1993. "Interest Differentials under Bretton Woods and the Post–Bretton Woods Float: The Effects of Capital Controls and Exchange Risk." In Michael Bordo and Barry Eichengreen, eds., *A Retrospective on the Bretton Woods System*, 515–46. Chicago: University of Chicago Press.

Meltzer, Allan H. 1991. "U.S. Policy in the Bretton Woods Era." *Federal Reserve Bank of St. Louis Review* 73 (May/June): 54–83.

Metzler, Lloyd. 1947. "Exchange Rates and the I.M.F." *Postwar Economic Studies* 7: 1–45.

Mikesell, Raymond F. 1954. *Foreign Exchange in the Postwar World.* New York: Twentieth Century Fund.

———. 1994. "The Bretton Woods Debates: A Memoir." Princeton Essays in International Finance 192. International Finance Section, Department of Economics, Princeton University, Princeton, N.J.

Miller, Marcus, and Alan Sutherland. 1994. "Speculative Anticipations of Sterling's Return to Gold: Was Keynes Wrong?" *Economic Journal* 104: 804–12.

Miller, Victoria. 1995. "Exchange Rate Crises with Domestic Bank Runs: Evidence from the 1890s." University of Quebec at Montreal. Unpublished manuscript.

Milward, Alan. 1984. *The Reconstruction of Western Europe, 1945–1951.* London: Methuen.

Mitchell, B. R. 1978. *European Historical Statistics.* New York: Columbia University Press.

Moggridge, Donald E. 1969. *The Return to Gold, 1925.* Cambridge, Eng.: Cambridge University Press.

———. 1970. "The 1931 Financial Crisis—A New View." *The Banker* 120: 832–39.

Morgan-Webb, Charles. 1934. *The Rise and Fall of the Gold Standard.* New York: Macmillan.

Morgenstern, Oskar. 1959. *International Financial Transactions and Business Cycles.* Princeton, N.J.: Princeton University Press.

Mundell, Robert A. 1961. "A Theory of Optimum Currency Areas." *American Economic Review* 51: 657–65.

———. 1992. "The Global Adjustment System." In Mario Baldassarri, John McCallum, and Robert A. Mundell, eds., *Global Disequilibrium in the World Economy*, 351–456. London: Macmillan.

Neme, Colette. 1986. "Les possibilités d'abolition du contrôle des changes français." *Revue d'économie politique* 2: 177–94.

Nurkse, Ragnar. 1944. *International Currency Experience.* Geneva: League of Nations.

Obstfeld, Maurice. 1986. "Rational and Self-Fulfilling Balance-of-Payments Crises." *American Economic Review* 76: 72–81.

———. 1993a. "Destabilizing Effects of Exchange Rate Escape Clauses." NBER Working Paper 3603. National Bureau of Economic Research, Cambridge, Mass.

———. 1993b. "The Adjustment Mechanism." In Michael D. Bordo and Barry Eichengreen, eds., *A Retrospective on the Bretton Woods System*, 201–68. Chicago: University of Chicago Press.

———. 1994. "The Logic of Currency Crises." *Cahiers Economiques et Monétaires* 43: 189–213.

———. 1996. "Models of Currency Crises with Self-Fulfilling Features." *European Economic Review* (forthcoming).

Office of Business Economics. 1954. *The Balance of Payments of the United States, 1919–1953*. Washington, D.C.: U.S. Government Printing Office.

Officer, Lawrence. 1993. "Gold-Point Arbitrage and Uncovered Interest Parity under the 1925–31 Dollar-Sterling Gold Standard." *Explorations in Economic History* 30: 98–127.

Ohlin, Bertil. 1936. *International Economic Reconstruction*. Paris: International Chamber of Commerce.

Oppers, Stefan. 1992. "A Model of the Bimetallic System." University of Michigan, Ann Arbor. Unpublished manuscript.

———. 1994. "Was the Worldwide Shift to Gold Inevitable? An Analysis of the End of Bimetallism." University of Michigan, Ann Arbor. Unpublished manuscript.

Organisation for European Economic Cooperation. 1950. *First Annual Report*. Paris: OEEC.

———. 1954. *Fifth Annual Report*. Paris: OEEC.

Ozkan, F. Gulcin, and Alan Sutherland. 1994. "A Model of the ERM Crisis." CEPR Discussion Paper 879. Centre for Economic Policy Research, London.

Palyi, Melchior. 1972. *The Twilight of Gold, 1914–1936*. Chicago: Regnery.

Phelps, Edmund. 1967. "Phillips Curves, Expectations of Inflation, and Optimal Unemployment." *Economica* second ser. 34: 254–81.

Pippinger, John. 1984. "Bank of England Operations, 1893–1913." In Michael D. Bordo and Anna Schwartz, eds., *A Retrospective on the Classical Gold Standard, 1821–1931*, 203–33. Chicago: University of Chicago Press.

Plessis, Alain. 1985. *La politique de la Banque de France de 1851 à 1870*. Geneva: Droz.

Pöhl, Karl Otto. 1995. "International Monetary Policy: A Personal View." In Yegor Gaidar and Karl Otto Pöhl, *Russian Reform/International Money*, 55–140. Cambridge, Mass.: MIT Press.

Polak, Jacques J. 1980. "The EMF: External Relations." *Banca Nazionale del Lavoro Quarterly Review* 134: 359–72.

Pollard, Sidney. 1969. *The Development of the British Economy, 1919–1967*, 2d ed. London: Edward Arnold.

Polyani, Karl. 1944. *The Great Transformation*. New York: Rinehart.

Prati, Alessandro. 1991. "Poincaré's Stabilization: Stopping a Run on Government Debt." *Journal of Monetary Economics* 27: 213–39.

Pressnell, L. S. 1968. "Gold Reserves, Banking Reserves and the Baring Crisis of 1890." In C. R. Whittlesey and J. S. G. Wilson, eds., *Essays in Honour of R.S. Sayers*, 167–228. Oxford, Eng.: Clarendon Press.

Putnam, Robert, and Nicholas Bayne. 1987. *Hanging Together: The Seven Power Summits*. 2d ed. Cambridge, Mass.: Harvard University Press.

Putnam, Robert, and C. Randall Henning. 1989. "The Bonn Summit of 1978: A Case of Cooperation." In Richard N. Cooper, Barry Eichengreen, Gerald Holtham, Robert D. Putnam, and C. Randall Henning, *Can Nations Agree? Issues in International Economic Cooperation*, 12–140. Washington, D.C.: Brookings Institution.

Rastel, Georges. 1935. *Les controverses doctrinales sur le bimétallisme au XIXème siècle*. Paris: Presses Modernes.

Redish, Angela. 1990. "The Evolution of the Gold Standard in England." *Journal of Economic History* 50: 789–805.

———. 1992. "The Evolution of the Classical Gold Standard: The Case of France." University of British Columbia, Vancouver. Unpublished manuscript.

Redmond, John. 1984. "The Sterling Overvaluation in 1925: A Multilateral Approach." *Economic History Review* 37: 520–32.

Ricardo, David. [1810] 1951. "Three Letters on the Bullion Report." In *Pamphlets and Papers 1809–1811*. Vol. 3., 136–37. Cambridge, Eng.: Cambridge University Press.

———. [1819] 1952, "Minutes of Evidence Taken before the Secret Committee on the Expediency of the Bank Resuming Cash Payments." Reprinted in Piero Sraffa, ed., *The Works and Correspondence of David Ricardo*. Vol. 5, *Speeches and Evidence*, 371–400. Cambridge, Eng.: Cambridge University Press.

Rich, Georg. 1989. "Canadian Banks, Gold, and the Crisis of 1907." *Explorations in Economic History* 26: 135–60.

Rolnick, Arthur, and Warren Weber. 1986. "Gresham's Law or Gresham's Fallacy?" *Journal of Political Economy* 94: 185–99.

Roosa, Robert. 1965. *Monetary Reform for the World Economy*. New York: Harper and Row.

Rose, Andrew. 1994. "Are Exchange Rates Macroeconomic Phenomema?" *Federal Reserve Bank of San Francisco Economic Review* 19: 20–30.

Rose, Andrew, and Lars Svensson. 1994. "European Exchange Rate Credibility before the Fall." *European Economic Review* 38: 1185–1216.

Rueff, Jacques. 1972. *The Monetary Sin of the West*. Trans. Roger Glemet. New York: Macmillan.

Ruggie, John Gerald. 1983. "International Regimes, Transactions, and Change: Embedded Liberalism in the Postwar Economic Order." In Stephen D. Krasner, ed., *International Regimes*, 195–223. Ithaca, N.Y.: Cornell University Press.

Russell, Henry B. 1898. *International Monetary Conferences*. New York: Harper and Brothers.

Sachs, Jeffrey D., and Charles Wyplosz. 1986. "The Economic Consequences of President Mitterrand." *Economic Policy* 2: 261–321.

Sala-i-Martin, Xavier, and Jeffrey D. Sachs. 1992. "Fiscal Federalism and Optimum Currency Areas: Evidence for Europe from the United States." In Matthew B. Canzoneri, Vittorio Grilli, and Paul R. Masson, eds., *Establishing a Central Bank: Issues in Europe and Lessons from the United States*, 195–220. Cambridge, Eng.: Cambridge University Press.

Sargent, Thomas J. 1983. "Stopping Moderate Inflation: The Methods of Poincaré and Thatcher." In Rudiger Dornbusch and M. H. Simonsen, eds., *Inflation, Debt and Indexation*, 54–96. Cambridge, Mass.: MIT Press.

Sayers, Richard S. 1976. *The Bank of England, 1891–1944*. 3 vols. Cambridge, Eng.: Cambridge University Press.

Scammell, W. M. 1975. *International Monetary Policy: Bretton Woods and After*. London: Macmillan.

Schacht, Hjalmar. 1927. *The Stabilization of the Mark*. New York: Adelphi.

Schelling, Thomas. 1978. *Micromotives and Macrobehavior*. New York: Norton.

Schenk, Catherine. 1994. *Britain and the Sterling Area: From Devaluation to Convertibility in the 1950s*. London: Routledge.

Schoorl, Evert. 1995. "Working Party Three and the Dollar, 1961–1964." University of Groningen, the Netherlands. Unpublished manuscript.

Schubert, Aurel. 1991. *The Credit-Anstalt Crisis of 1931*. Cambridge. Eng.: Cambridge University Press.

Schumpeter, Joseph. 1954. *History of Economic Analysis*. New York: Oxford University Press.

Shelton, Judy. 1994. *Money Meltdown*. New York: Free Press.

Shirer, William L. 1969. *The Collapse of the Third Republic*. New York: Simon and Schuster.

Sicsic, Pierre. 1992. "Was the Franc Poincaré Deliberately Undervalued?" *Explorations in Economic History* 29: 69–92.

Sorensen, Theodore. 1965. *Kennedy*. New York: Harper and Row.

Spooner, Frank. 1972. *The International Economy and Monetary Movements in France, 1493–1725*. Cambridge, Mass.: Harvard University Press.

Stoddard, Lothrop. 1932. *Europe and Our Money*. New York: Macmillan.

Summers, Robert, and Alan Heston. 1991. "The Penn World Tables (Mark 5): An Expanded Set of International Comparisons, 1950–1988." *Quarterly Journal of Economics* 106: 327–68.

Taus, Esther Rogoff. 1943. *Central Banking Functions of the United States Treasury, 1789–1941*. New York: Columbia University Press.

Taussig, Frank. 1927. *International Trade*. New York: Macmillan.

Temin, Peter. 1989. *Lessons from the Great Depression*. Cambridge, Mass.: MIT Press.

———. 1994. "Universal Banks and Financial Instability in the 1920s and 1930s." MIT, Cambridge, Mass. Unpublished manuscript.

———. 1995. "The 'Koreaboom' in West Germany: Fact or Fiction?" *Economic History Review* XLVIII: 737–53

Tew, Brian. 1988. *The Evolution of the International Monetary System, 1945–1988.* 4th ed. London: Hutchinson.

Thuillier, Guy. 1983. *La monnaie en France au début du XIXème siècle.* Geneva: Librairie Droz.

Triffin, Robert. 1947. "National Central Banking and the International Economy." *Postwar Economic Studies* 7: 46–81.

———. 1960. *Gold and the Dollar Crisis: The Future of Convertibility.* New Haven, Conn.: Yale University Press.

———. 1964. "The Evolution of the International Monetary System: Historical Reappraisal and Future Perspectives." Princeton Studies in International Finance 12. International Finance Section, Department of Economics, Princeton University, Princeton, N.J.

———. 1966. *The World Money Maze.* New Haven, Conn.: Yale University Press.

United Nations. 1949. *International Capital Movements during the Inter-War Period.* Lake Success, N.Y.: United Nations.

van der Wee, Herman. 1986. *Prosperity and Upheaval.* Trans. Robin Hogg and Max R. Hall. New York: Viking.

Viner, Jacob. 1951. *International Economics: Studies.* Glencoe, Ill.: Free Press.

Viren, Matti. 1994. "A Note on Interest Rate Policy during the Great Depression." *Journal of European Economic History* 23: 115–29.

Volcker, Paul, and Toyoo Gyohten. 1992. *Changing Fortunes: The World's Money and the Threat to American Leadership.* New York: Times Books.

von Hagen, Jürgen. 1994. "Credible Roads to EMU." University of Mannheim, Germany. Unpublished manuscript.

Warren, George F., and Frank A. Pearson. 1933. *Prices.* New York: John Wiley and Sons.

———. 1935. *Gold and Prices.* New York: John Wiley and Sons.

Werner, Pierre, Baron Hubert Ansiaux, Georg Brouwers, Bernard Clappier, Ugo Moscq, Jean-Baptiste Schöllhorn, and Giorgio Stammati. 1970. *Report to the Council and the Commission on the Realisation by Stages of Economic and Monetary Union in the Community.* Supplement to Bulletin II-1970 of the European Communities. Brussels: European Communities.

Whale, P. Barrett. 1939. "Central Banks and the State." *Manchester School* 10: 38–49.

Wheelock, David C. 1991. *The Strategy and Consistency of Federal Reserve Monetary Policy, 1924–1933.* Cambridge, Eng.: Cambridge University Press.

White, Harry D. 1933. *The French International Accounts, 1880–1913.* Cambridge, Mass.: Harvard University Press.

Wicker, Elmus. 1966. *Federal Reserve Monetary Policy, 1917–1933.* New York: Random House.

Wigmore, Barrie. 1984. "Was the Bank Holiday of 1933 Caused by a Run on the Dollar?" *Journal of Economic History* 47: 739–55.

Williams, David. 1968. "The Evolution of the Sterling System." In C. R. Whittesley and J. S. G. Wilson, eds., *Essays in Money and Banking in Honour of R.S. Sayers*, 266–97. Oxford, Eng.: Clarendon Press.

Williams, John H. 1952. *Economic Stability in the Modern World*. London: Athlone Press.

Williamson, John. 1977. *The Failure of World Monetary Reform, 1971–74*. New York: New York University Press.

———. 1993. "Exchange Rate Management." *Economic Journal* 103: 188–97.

Williamson, John, and C. Randall Henning. 1994. "Managing the Monetary System." In Peter B. Kenen, ed., *Managing the World Economy Fifty Years after Bretton Woods*, 83–117. Washington, D.C.: Institute for International Economics.

Willis, Henry Parker. 1901. *A History of the Latin Monetary Union*. Chicago: University of Chicago Press.

Wilson, Harold. 1971. *The Labour Government, 1964–1970: A Personal Record*. London: Weidenfeld and Nicolson and Michael Joseph.

Working Group on Exchange Market Intervention. 1983. *Report*. Washington, D.C.: U.S. Treasury.

Yeager, Leland. 1966. *International Monetary Relations*. New York: Harper and Row.

———. 1968. *The International Monetary Mechanism*. New York: Holt, Rinehart and Winston.

Zaragaza, Carlos E. 1995. "Can Currency Boards Prevent Devaluations and Financial Meltdowns?" *Southwest Economy* 4: 6–9.

* Index *